Jasse -
Well RCF
brought us together
but the Cavs made
it happen.

TO A Feeling
Too Special
TO Forget

CHRIS PARKER
Perg

KING JAMES

BRINGS THE LAND
A CROWN

The Definitive Tale of the Cavaliers' 2016 Title Run

BY

CHRIS PARKER

Cover design by Preston Pisellini
Color insert design by Ron Kretsch
Interior design by Damonza
Edited by David Aretha

Inquiries should be addressed to
Mountain Loins Press
mountainloinspress@gmail.com

Library of Congress Cataloging-in-Publication Data
Parker, Chris, 1967-
King James Brings The Land a Crown / By Chris Parker

ISBN: 978-0-9981624-0-9 (hardcover: alk. Paper)
Ebook ISBN: 978-0-9981624-1-6

Library of Congress Control Number: 2016916076

First Edition: October 2016

For Mom, Dad, Michele and, well, LeBron, without whom none of this would be possible

CONTENTS

PRESEASON

PROLOGUE
LEBRON, LARRY, AND ME

THOUGH THERE ARE but a few remaining kings and just one LeBron James, there can be an untold number of witnesses. All possess their own tale of how they were present when Cleveland made history. Their stories will vary—like any eyewitness testimony or Hollywood book adaptation—but at their core is a uniting truth: Something special happened.

The Cavaliers' 2016 NBA championship is arguably the most triumphant sports tale this side of Hollywood and certainly the greatest Finals comeback in NBA history. They did what 32 teams before them couldn't, rallying from a 3-1 deficit in the Finals while also becoming only the fourth team in NBA history to win a Finals Game 7 on the road. It ended Cleveland's 52-year sports championship drought that extended back to the Cleveland Browns' (pre-Super Bowl) 1964 NFL championship, led by Hall of Fame running back Jim Brown.

In LeBron James, Cleveland had a larger-than-life hero like Brown, but even the four-time MVP couldn't end Cleveland's Curse during his first go-round with the Cavaliers. Like many promising talents in Northeast Ohio (*see* the Black Keys), James left the city, bolting in 2010 for better weather (check!) and a better chance of realizing his championship dreams (check and check!) after seven failed years in Cleveland.

It set in motion the greatest "the prodigal returns" narrative in sports history. Only a handful of stars in any professional sport have ever led their hometown team to a championship (Kent Hrbek, Pete Rose, Dick Butkus), and none have ever returned home with such fanfare and promise. It was part biblical—he is the chosen one!—part fairy tale. That's what attracted me: I'd already witnessed something like this.

As a kid growing up in Oxford, Ohio, in the 1970s, I had already begun to cultivate a contrarian inclination when the Big Red Machine became a force in baseball. It would've been easy to fall into fandom for the Cincinnati Reds, but I already wasn't much for the crowd, and besides, I hated Pete Rose.

It had nothing to do with gambling. It was the 1970 All-Star Game when Rose plowed into Cleveland Indians phenom Ray Fosse. The 23-year-old catcher had 16 homers and was hitting .313 during the first half of 1970, earning a spot on the American League squad.

Rose, whose true nature would emerge in the ensuing years, bull-rushed Fosse, bowling him over in the 12th inning of a meaningless game to score the winning run. The play broke Fosse's shoulder, which wasn't X-rayed and healed wrong, and needless to say he was never the same. I may have been only eight, but I knew enough biology to know an asshole when I saw one.

It was 1975, and the Reds were going to the World Series against the Boston Red Sox. I became a fan of the Red Sox that year, particularly a sweet-swinging kid from Southern California named Freddy Lynn, who not only played with great abandon but incredible skill. He became the first person in baseball history to win a league MVP Award during his rookie year.

Of course, the Red Sox lost that year to the Reds in one of the most exciting World Series ever, inaugurating a personal 29-year vigil. I was a latecomer—Red Sox fans had been hankering for that vindication since 1919—but that painful, heartbreaking (Bucky Dent! Aaron Boone!) journey impressed upon me the strange joy of such a bittersweet fascination.

When I moved to Cleveland in 2006, I became acquainted with the town's ne'er-do-well sports history, and immediately commiserated. I became a Browns fan, because if you're going to start loving Cleveland sports, you should start at the bottom. I joined the region in demonizing James when he left, and got swept up in the exultation when he returned. I realized there might be an opportunity to be something more than a bystander to sports history. I could be a witness.

As a journalist, I'd wound my way through a couple beats already. I spent 15 years covering music and arts, where I acquired the belief that journalism was about more than simple reporting; it was also about entertaining and trying to communicate an essential mood that might help you understand the art. If writing about music is like dancing about architecture, as the old saying goes, then by all means make it as funky as possible.

Coming to Cleveland brought me in contact with Pete Kotz, editor of the local alt-weekly *Cleveland Scene*, then an arm of *New Times* (soon to be Village Voice Media). After bringing me here to be the music editor, Pete fired me, befriended me, and helped me get a foothold in longform journalism. I spent several years writing about larcenous for-profit colleges, tax-evading corporations, the hacker collective Anonymous, healthcare, the fracking oil crash, and the microbiome, among other serious subjects.

I'd been a sports fan all along, but shied away from pursuing sports journalism. If I'd long harbored the time-honored, self-hating feeling that journalism amounted to little more than fish-and-chip paper—back when it was useful like that—I couldn't stop to consider how disposable sports beat reporting was. Especially given that the style seemed stuck in the 1960s when boxscores weren't math labs.

Most stories amounted to little more than a confabulation of some petty drama, a brief vignette from the early part of the game when they first started writing the piece, and a passel of stats I could get from the boxscore, which is right here on my phone. And the trumped-up emotions that sought to elevate each contest of an 82-game season into Aristotelian theatre produced enough eye rolls to prepare me for the Olympic trials.

Somewhat impulsively in retrospect—the only way anyone ever engages in something that will swallow their life for more than two years—I contacted the *Cleveland Scene* in 2014 and offered to write columns for them about the basketball team if they helped me get credentialed. More of a lifestyle magazine than the type to run a lot of sports coverage, they trusted me enough to give it a shot, and I brought them something they never expected.

Since no one was paying me, and I was investing so much time, I decided to go about it my way. I didn't ask how it felt to win, if something got them extra fired up, or to describe another player's performance. I wanted to know why the ball movement stopped and how that caused the offense to stagnate. I wanted to understand how defensive rotations affected rebounding. And at my most frivolous I wondered about their routines growing up shooting baskets alone all those years, not about their headband or who they followed on Twitter.

I won't lie, many didn't like me, wondering who I was to come in here with judgment. (Someone that's been writing a lot longer than you, Sonny.) They didn't appreciate my calling bullshit on anonymous sourcing, which allows them to float just about anything and face fewer repercussions than a lousy weatherman. And they didn't like my rapport with coach David Blatt, who was as openly contemptuous of their querying disability as Gregg Popovich.

I went to all but a couple home games during the 2014-15 regular season, and followed the Cavaliers on the road to the Finals (other than the first round in Boston). I did write-ups of every game, home or away, replete with video and stills, trying to replicate the rigor Zach Lowe brings to his coverage of the sport. If they can show you how a defense "ices" the pick-and-roll on TV, why can't sportswriters bring the same level of sophistication? (The answer apparently is that their editors want to keep the content at a *Married with Children* level of lowest common denominator.)

It was as painful to watch the Cavaliers run out of gas in the fourth quarters of Games 4, 5, and 6 of the 2015 NBA Finals as it was to watch Lynn collapsed on the center field track, Schiraldi sweating buckets, or Wakefield craning his neck to the right. To go through the entire season, to get so close and yet fall short…well, I understood a little bit of how they felt.

But LeBron is such an extraordinary creation—sort of Alexander the Great, Magic Johnson, and The Terminator rolled into one—that I couldn't resist and reupped. Surely a healthy Cavaliers team would be a lock to win the 2016 Finals, I reasoned. But I also wanted another front-row seat to James' immense gravitational force, which allows him to bend time and space to his own ends. Like any superpower, he can't do it all the time but just enough to frequently leave your jaw agape as you struggle to express what you just witnessed.

It wasn't a straight line but neither are roller coasters, because the ups and downs are where the fun is. There were moments of doubt, concentrated in the middle of the season when coach Tyronn Lue took over. I was skeptical at first, but Lue won me over as the right man for the job, and in the playoffs he proved that just because he was green it didn't mean he would shrink from the moment. Indeed, he stood large.

For some this is a neat story. But for those Cavaliers and Cleveland sports fans that invested heart and soul in the teams' succession of soul-sucking, heart-crushing failures, it was nothing less than validation that God doesn't hate Cleveland, that there is respite from grim, gray skies and an assurance that Mudville need not remain perpetually mirthless.

The yoke is off Cleveland. Let someone else wear the "L" on their forehead. For the next 12 months they're the champs. Nothing can take that away. Like the memories of those committed fans who followed their run, the Cavaliers' 2016 championship was indelible, and the Larry O'Brien NBA Championship Trophy is theirs.

.

1

UNFINISHED BUSINESS

I'T WASN'T SUPPOSED to end this way. But there sat LeBron James, head bowed beneath a towel before his locker stall, while down the hall cheap champagne varnished the visiting locker room walls. The prodigal King's return had failed to produce Cleveland's first major sports championship in over a half century, yet again Believeland had become Mudville.

Despite perhaps the single greatest performance in NBA Finals history—35.8 points/game, 13.3 rebounds, 8.8 assists—James wasn't able to carry the Cavaliers across the finish line. They'd gone farther than anyone expected, sparks spinning off battered rims after losing two of their Big Three, Kyrie Irving and Kevin Love, to playoff injuries.

Against all odds they took a 2-1 advantage in the 2015 best-of-seven series against the Western Conference winners, the Golden State Warriors, only to run out of gas in sight of their goal. The ragged batch of role players Cleveland had increasingly relied on to augment LeBron's outsized contributions withered beneath the klieg lights, leaving most of the offense on James' shoulders.

As broad and willing as those shoulders are, they couldn't carry the day. Emblazoned with the script-tat "CHOSEN1" in a pique of pride (after his teenage *Sports Illustrated* cover story), they slumped beneath the weight. Heavy were the personal expectations and those of a hollowed-out industrial city desperate for sports sunshine after decades of acid rain.

During the last 18 minutes of Games Four and Five, the Warriors outscored the Cavaliers by 30 points. They lost those games by 34 points.

The Cavs lacked enough bullets or guns. Sitting there, knees wrapped in ice and feet in an ice bath, James was Job doing whatever was asked, but somehow not nearly enough.

"If I could have gave more, I would have done it, but I gave everything I had," James said from the 2015 Finals postgame podium. "You've got to be healthy. You've got to be playing great at the right time, and you've got to have a little luck. We were playing great, but we had no luck and we weren't healthy. It just wasn't our time."

It hadn't been their time since the late 1950s. Even when the mighty Jim Brown carried the Browns to their final NFL championship in 1964, the manufacturing that built the city into a major metropolis had already begun to decline. Cleveland tumbled from the sixth largest city in the country in 1950, with just short of a million people, to a city three-fifths that size— 573,000—in just three decades.

There may be no such thing as bad publicity, but Cleveland wasn't even aware there was another kind. Its river caught fire (again), the city nearly went bankrupt, its school system failed, county executives were convicted of corruption, and Cleveland's police department generated enough settlements to start their own colony.

If there were ever a region in America in need of a win, it was Northeast Ohio. Nobody seemed better suited to deliver it than the world's best basketball player and hometown hero, LeBron James.

That 6-foot-8 and 240 pounds Adonis of chiseled athleticism, power, and keen basketball knowledge had overcome great personal odds while being raised by his single mom, Gloria James (who gave birth to him at age 16), in a troubled area of Tire City, Akron, Ohio.

He became the most hyped high school player in basketball history, leading small parochial school St. Vincent-St. Mary to three Ohio state championships. During his junior year of high school he appeared on that *Sports Illustrated* cover, and by his senior year ESPN was broadcasting their games. St. Vincent crisscrossed the country challenging the nation's best basketball prep schools on its way to *USA Today*'s season-ending top prep ranking.

Basketball legend Bill Walton went to check out the hype and still came away awed. "I'm leaving more impressed than I could have ever believed," he told the Associated Press. "This guy has the complete package. What I saw tonight was a special basketball player. It was an eye-opening experience."

James jumped to the pros after the 2002-03 season, bypassing college. As luck would have it, the Cleveland Cavaliers received the number one pick in the NBA lottery, allowing LeBron to play just over a half hour from home. He was a real Horatio Alger-style "overnight success" story, who joked to *GQ*, "I go from $10 in my pocket to $100 million. In high school."

James had talent to rival Michael Jordan, but from the beginning his coaches stressed the value of sharing, teamwork, and trust. The lessons took. He found some of the family he had lacked as a child on the court. It's no surprise that his closest teenage friends were teammates or that they became his close confidants and business associates when his career took off.

James played for seven years in Cleveland. During his fourth year, he took them to the 2007 Finals with one of the weakest rosters in history, where they were swept by the 58-win San Antonio Spurs. Even in his early 20s, though, James was the best player in the league, twice winning the Most Valuable Player Award (four times total). Two years later he led his team to 66 victories, which was then the tenth-best regular season mark in NBA history.

But it wasn't enough. The Cavaliers never assembled the right talent and/or coaching to get over the hump and beat the best of the best, setting this story in motion.

For the prodigal to return, he first must leave. Cleveland couldn't give James the championship he craved, so he found someone that could. On July 8, 2010, he told the world in an ill-conceived hour-long televised announcement show, dubbed *The Decision*, which was rivaled in its emptiness only by Al Capone's vault.

For Northeast Ohio, the move was a mouth-kick as painfully predictable as Lucy yanking the football away from Charlie Brown. The Decision joined The Drive, The Fumble, The Shot, and Red Right 88 in the long annals of Cleveland sports disappointments.

Nobody brought more passion, if not quite eloquence, to the region's bewilderment, anger and sense of betrayal than Cavaliers majority owner Dan Gilbert. He penned the type of angry letter (in **Comic Sans** typeface) you hope you sober up before sending, crystallizing the feelings of a spurned sports nation.

"You simply don't deserve this kind of cowardly betrayal. You have given so much and deserve so much more," Gilbert told the region's beleaguered fans. "This shocking act of disloyalty from our home grown 'chosen one' sends the exact opposite lesson of what we would want our children to learn. And 'who' we would want them to grow-up to become."

James convened in Miami with his chums Dwyane Wade and Chris Bosh, dubbed the "Big 3," helping James win his first two crowns. Upon failing to win the third straight in 2014, he felt the only mountain left to climb was the Pikes Peak of sports failure, back home in Cleveland.

But this time James didn't reveal his plans in a glitzy TV spectacle, instead opting for the decidedly old-media manner of a letter run in *Sports Illustrated*, cowritten by Lee Jenkins. For LeBron, leaving home only made him realize how much he missed it, and how much it was a part of his identity.

"It's where I walked. It's where I ran. It's where I cried. It's where I bled. It holds a special place in my heart. People there have seen me grow up. I sometimes feel like I'm their son," he wrote. "Their passion can be overwhelming. But it drives me. I want to give them hope when I can. I want to inspire them when I can. My relationship with Northeast Ohio is bigger than basketball. I didn't realize that four years ago. I do now."

The response from Cleveland was incredible. People honked their horns downtown, cheered, and screamed. It was as if an entire region had just hit the Lotto. Some cried tears of joy. People hugged in the streets. It was Northeast Ohio's version of V-J Day.

Cleveland Cavaliers and Quicken Loans Arena CEO Len Komoroski was walking back from a meeting downtown when the news hit. "Someone ran up to me and hugged me," he said. "People were slapping high-fives and giving thumbs up. It was like we won the Super Bowl."

Not only was it a chance to make amends for leaving, it was a public relations coup. What could be better than the prodigal son returning to the home he'd spurned four years earlier, wiping away the wrongs by bringing home the long-sought golden cup? He could go from Judas to Galahad.

But it was easier said than done.

No one was more aware of that than LeBron James. "I'm not promising a championship. I know how hard that is to deliver," he wrote in the letter announcing his return home. "We're not ready right now. No way. Of course, I want to win next year, but I'm realistic. It will be a long process, much longer than it was in 2010. My patience will get tested."

For James to even be in a position to return, the Cavaliers had to get lucky. And that they did—to say the least. Twice they secured the number one choice in the NBA Draft despite sub-3 percent chances of winning each pick. (The NBA assigns odds to the pick held by every team that didn't make the playoffs, weighted to favor those with the very worst records.)

Three times in all (2011, '13, and '14) they'd received the top pick, not counting the 2003 pick that landed LeBron. The pick they used to select Kyrie Irving wasn't the pick Cleveland received for having the second-worst record in 2010-11, but one they received from the Clippers in a trade deadline deal involving Mo Williams. It possessed a 2.8 percent chance of being the top pick. And yet, the lucky ping-pong ball fell to them.

In 2014 Irving won the All-Star Game Most Valuable Player Award and caught James' eye as a keen potential protégé. Those other two first overall picks—2013's Anthony Bennett and the top choice in 2014 (which boasted only a 1.7 percent chance), Andrew Wiggins—secured, at James' suggestion, former Olympic teammate Kevin Love. He came over in a trade with the Minnesota Timberwolves to create a new Big Three in Cleveland.

None of the national press had expected James to bolt Miami after going to the NBA Finals each of his four years in a Heat uniform. Surely Pat Riley would make the necessary maneuvers to entice James back. The Cavaliers were oblivious enough to James' potential change of heart that they didn't consider his desires when they chose their new head coach.

Cleveland fired James' one-time coach Mike Brown in May 2014, ending a one-year reconciliation after the Lakers unceremoniously dumped him five games into his second season. The Cavaliers' brain trust spent 39 days in an exhaustive search before settling on an out-of-the-box choice: David Blatt.

An esteemed European coach for two decades, Blatt never played or coached in the NBA, and hadn't lived in America since leaving Princeton to play and eventually coach abroad. Blatt had pulled off two of the more extraordinary upsets in European basketball history.

In 2007 he led an undermanned Russian team to the Eurobasket Championships. He had one NBA-caliber star, Andrei Kirilenko, but bested the favored host, Spain, which fielded six NBA players including current pros the Gasol brothers (Marc and Pau) and Knicks point guard Jose Calderon. Several years later he led the Russian national team to a bronze medal at the 2012 Olympics.

While James and Miami were losing to the Spurs in 2014, Blatt was pulling off his greatest magic, with Israeli team Maccabi Tel Aviv. Despite a middling roster and regular season results, they responded in the postseason. They upset Russian powerhouse CSKA Moscow after trailing the entire game, then topped the Spaniards again, beating FC Barcelona with a dramatic burst in overtime to take the Euroleague Championship.

Before the Cavaliers could even offer the job, Blatt had an assistant offer from Golden State that he'd already accepted. The Warriors let him out of the deal, just as the Knicks had let new Warriors head coach Steve Kerr out of his deal a month earlier.

From the season's start, James continually emphasized "the process" and patience, but like the team, struggled to maintain it in the face of great expectations. LeBron knew it wasn't easy to get a new coach and new players on the same page, but the frustration boiled over in bad body language as the Cavaliers lost seven of their first 12 games to start the 2014-2015 season.

This included a four-game mid-November losing streak, in which three jitterbug point guards (Ty Lawson, John Wall, Lou Williams) abused the Cavs, exploiting Irving's acknowledged defensive deficiencies. The last was a two-point loss to the Spurs when LeBron lost a behind-the-back dribble out of bounds in the final seconds.

The Cavaliers refocused during a six-game homestand after losing to Toronto. They won their next eight, including a rematch with the Raptors in Toronto, where the Wine and Gold rallied from 10 down with eight minutes to go, behind LeBron's 35 points. They'd won 11 of 14 for a 16-10 record when the first of three devastating injuries struck.

It was two days before Christmas. Midway through the third quarter, energetic Brazilian starting center Anderson Varejao, the lone holdover from James' first run in Cleveland, went down with a season-ending Achilles injury. Cleveland beat the Timberwolves 125-104, but the loss of the beloved floppy-haired Brazilian left the team reeling and their interior defense exposed.

With the Cavs already short up front, his loss revealed the roster's haphazard construction, forcing undersized power forward Tristan Thompson to play center. It was a taller task than he was up to. Following Varejao's injury, James, Love, and Irving also missed games with maladies.

At the end of December James took two weeks off to rest his sore back and tired body.

Over the next two and a half weeks the Cavaliers lost six of eight, including a loss to Philadelphia, the league's perennial bottom-feeder. The 76ers rallied from a 17-point deficit to beat Cleveland 95-92, securing their first home win in 15 tries. Irving didn't play, while shooting guard Dion Waiters and a couple deep reserves discovered they'd been traded moments before tip-off.

Waiters was shipped to Oklahoma City while Lou Amundson and Alex Kirk went to the New York Knicks, bringing Knicks wings J. R. Smith and Iman Shumpert to the Cavaliers along with a conditional first-round pick from the Thunder. Cleveland sent that pick and another first they'd acquired from Memphis to Denver for 7-foot center Timofey Mozgov.

Mozgov had played for Blatt's medal-winning Russian Olympic team and provided much needed rim protection. Shumpert and Smith offered a skilled perimeter defender and streaky-but-deadly long-range shooter, respectively. They helped lengthen the team's thin bench, until Love and Irving's playoff injuries exposed it again.

The league considered Smith, 29, an incorrigible recidivist with less possibility of rehabilitation than Chucky. In four years he'd been suspended or fined 38 times, costing him over half a million dollars, including incidents for untying opponents shoes, flopping, throwing elbows, low blows, and inappropriate tweeting.

A former Sixth Man of the Year with a hair-trigger hot stroke, Smith was the undesirable contract attached to younger, perennially injured defensive whiz Shumpert. Indeed, at the time Shumpert was out for another two weeks recovering from a separated shoulder. By season's end he'd have a torn muscle in his groin as well.

When the trade occurred, the Wine and Gold were 19-17 and bound for a five-game West Coast road trip. James returned for the third game in Phoenix, which they also lost, bringing the team's record to 19-20.

Rumors circulated about David Blatt's job, tempered by the fact that Cavs owner Dan Gilbert was still paying two previous head coaches. Drama-hungry scribes, caught up in the media circus that's always surrounded James, played up any perceived disconnects between the star and his "rookie" coach, thereby perpetuating the narrative.

While in Los Angeles, rather than practice, Blatt took the team to a bowling alley instead so they might relax and bond. Some later credited this moment as the one that turned the season around. Another target might have been a conversation between the Big Three while visiting the UCLA courts, when James pulled Love and Irving aside and challenged them to make this work.

Mostly, James was concerned about defensive effort. During the two-week break he approached his former high school coach, Keith Dambrot, for advice. Dambrot's success coaching LeBron had led to a position on University of Akron's staff and ultimately the Zips' head coaching job.

"One of the things I talked to LeBron about was that he had to be the impetus behind their defensive effort—if he doesn't play great defense, which he's capable of, he can't expect the rest of them to play great defense," Dambrot said.

The discussion also turned to Blatt. "The other part of it is trusting in the coach," Dambrot told him. "There are a lot of great coaches at all levels. Obviously David Blatt has won game after game after game at a high level. He's capable of being a very good coach. But sometimes guys don't get that opportunity because they don't have that pedigree people are looking for. That's where LeBron was smart enough to put trust in David Blatt."

Whether it was the new trade additions, Love and Irving's better defensive effort, a rejuvenated and more trusting James, or the simpler, pick-and-roll heavy offense Blatt instituted in the second half of the season to ease Shumpert, Mozgov, and Smith's transitions, the Cavaliers turned it around dramatically.

Beginning with the road trip's final two games in Los Angeles, Cleveland won their next dozen games and 18 of the next 20. They closed the season 34-9, with a 30-3 record in games featuring each of the Big Three—James, Irving, and Love.

Suddenly the Cavaliers seemed worthy of the preseason hype. Whatever rancor and dysfunction existed maybe didn't disappear but was overshadowed by their second half success. If it were possible, winning would solve world peace.

The Cavs took second seed in the Eastern Conference with a 53-29 record. They were on their way to sweeping the Celtics when Boston center Kelly Olynyk caught Kevin Love's right arm under his while both chased a loose ball. Olynyk wrenched Love's arm, dislocating his shoulder and sidelining Love for the rest of his first-ever playoffs.

J. R. Smith promptly retaliated, popping Jae Crowder in the mouth with the back of his hand during a rebound tussle. The Cavs won but the NBA suspended Smith for the first two games of their second-round series with Chicago. Smith's absence contributed to the Cavs' lackluster Game 1 home loss to the Bulls. The Cavs also lost Game 3 on a last-second three-point bank shot/prayer by Derrick Rose from several feet beyond the arc.

The team nearly lost Game 4 when Blatt almost called a timeout he didn't have. The team had burned three timeouts at the 21-second mark, advancing the ball and trying to inbound it. After Rose scored with nine seconds left, Blatt attempted to signal a timeout, but assistant coach Tyronn Lue quickly stopped him though a ref did appear to see him. It prevented a violation that would've given the Bulls a technical foul shot and the ball.

James took the ball to the hole but Nikola Mirotic blocked it out of bounds. There was just over a second left with the score tied. In the Cavaliers huddle Blatt drew up a play for James to inbound the ball. He protested.

"The play that was drawn up, I scratched it," LeBron said at the postgame presser. "I told coach, 'Just give me the ball. We're either going to go into overtime or I'm going to win it for us.'" James, who was 9-for-29 with as many turnovers (eight) as assists, wanted redemption. He got it by hitting a 21-foot fallaway jumper over Jimmy Butler as time expired for the road win to even the series.

The press, who were not fond of Blatt, initially reported J. R. Smith as saying the play call was "dumb," before correcting it to "doubt." It wasn't enough that James had heroically seized victory despite an off game; Blatt got hung with a near-loss for the near-timeout and what the press, at least, felt was a questionable play call.

Never mind that the Cavs had successfully used LeBron on multiple occasions as an inbounder during the regular season and prior series. He *was* the team's best passer. Or that James is only 9-for-60 when attempting a tying or go-ahead shot in the final five seconds of the fourth quarter or overtime over the last decade, according to ESPN. The league rate is just over 20 percent. Don't confuse them with facts; they just didn't like the guy.

That win changed the series' momentum. The Cavs won the next two, including Game 6 in Chicago by more than 20. Irving was struggling through a bad ankle that kept him out of two games versus the next opponent, the top-seeded Atlanta Hawks. No matter, James took the team on his back.

After shocking the Hawks by winning the first two in Atlanta, James put up a performance for the ages at home for Game 3, scoring 37 points on 37 shots after missing his first 10. He added 18 rebounds and 13 assists in a 114-111 overtime win.

The Cavs were Kings of the East, but heavy underdogs going into the Finals. All anyone could talk about was how the Warriors had fairly rolled through the first three rounds, losing but three times. Most reporters had the undermanned crew from Middle America quivering before an epic beatdown.

That's not what happened. Irving (23 points, six assists, four steals) nearly matched Steph Curry's totals (26 points, eight assists, two steals) in Game 1 and blocked Curry's layup in the final minute of regulation. James scored 44, but couldn't hit his last shot in regulation, or find a witness amongst the referees. They lost in overtime 108-100. To make matters worse, Irving left injured in the extra session with a fractured left kneecap that ended his postseason.

Despite losing Varejao, Irving, and Love, the Cavaliers soldiered on, winning two straight against the Warriors. In Game 4, the Warriors started their small lineup with Draymond Green at center and Andre Iguodala on LeBron James. It wore down the already battered Cavs, who didn't have the personnel to match up—and especially when their guards couldn't buy a bucket.

When Irving went down, Shumpert, Smith, or Aussie fan fave Matthew Dellavedova needed to step up, but fell short repeatedly. During the NBA Finals the backcourt trio shot 50-for-173 (29 percent). The frontcourt of Tristan Thompson and Timofey Mozgov earned additional possessions on the offensive boards, but they're only so useful if you can't find the bucket.

As the Warriors celebrated on the Cavaliers' logo during their Game 6 win, LeBron James was storing this moment away as motivation. When training would burn and muscles ache in the off-season, he could reflect back on this moment and push harder.

Sitting beneath that towel surveying the wreckage of his fairytale ending, James knew it would take more than him. That such an extraordinary Finals performance could fall short, not just of the title but the MVP, served notice that more was required. James knew winning on the court would always be larger than himself and take a team.

2

TEEN JAMES BRINGS HOME HIS FIRST TITLE

SPEAKING TO ESPN reporter Rachel Nichols for an *Unguarded* segment in the months following his return to Cleveland, James said, "I didn't just make the choice for myself, but also I had in the back of my mind of how so many people are going to benefit from me making this decision. We all are defined by where we come from and where we're going in life, and I think Akron, Ohio was meant for me."

Home has special meaning to everyone. It's why we find ourselves returning to the places and things that remind us of our first budding connections to this world, from the music playing in the house as a child to dinner smells and the peculiar regional course of the seasons. For someone growing up as James did, without the stability of a place to call his own, home is something even more sacred.

Living on the couches of relatives and family friends, he learned to make home portable, something he could pile into a backpack on his way to their next stop. "I just grabbed my little backpack, which held all the possessions I needed, and said to myself what I always said to myself: It's time to roll," James wrote in his 2009 memoir *Shooting Stars*, written with Buzz Bissinger.

It didn't start that way. Early on, there was a real home. Even though LeBron was born to 16-year-old Gloria James on December 30, 1984, her mother, Freda, took an active role in his upbringing. No one knows for sure who James' biological father was, and his lifelong absence made that question essentially moot.

Gloria and LeBron lived at 439 Hickory Street, on a dirt road in a house framed by oak trees and railroad tracks. It was an old, rambling Victorian that had been in the James family for four generations, and as such, was seemingly in endless need of repair.

They lived with Freda, a hairdresser, and Gloria's brothers: Terry, three years her senior, and Curt, seven years her junior. When LeBron was eight months old, Gloria began dating Eddie Jackson, who would live with them and at times be a surrogate father in James' life.

On Christmas, just before LeBron's third birthday, Jackson and Gloria gave LeBron a toy basketball hoop and ball. Early that morning, after returning from a Christmas Eve party, Gloria and Eddie heard a loud thump and found Freda dead on the kitchen floor. She'd suffered a massive heart attack at the age of 42.

Rather than rob James of Christmas morning, they waited to tell him of his grandmother's death so he could have some joy first. When he finally was told, he later would describe it as the angriest moment in his life. In the ensuing months the family struggled to keep up with repairs and the bills. Soon, the gas company shut off the heat and eviction notices collected like dust.

Eventually their neighbor, Wanda Reaves, insisted Gloria and LeBron stay with her, which they did for several months. James played basketball on the street outside with Reaves' sons, shooting into a milk crate nailed to an electrical pole.

When that old house was condemned and then bulldozed, the security of James' earliest years disappeared with it. It inaugurated a five-year odyssey in which Gloria and LeBron moved no less than 10 times, shuffling between apartments, relying on the kindness and goodwill of friends and relatives.

As a toddler, shuffling from couch to couch, backpack in tow, LeBron faced bewildering chaos that could've crippled him emotionally. The devoted love of his mother and the early dose of close family in Freda's house forestalled that fate until his fourth grade year, when the foundation began to crack.

"That kind of life builds up a lack of trust, a feeling that what you care about and the friends you have made will disappear," he wrote in his memoir. "At the same time, it made me realize that wherever we were going, I would have to assume responsibility for myself."

When LeBron James discusses the year that changed his life, he talks about what happened between his fourth and fifth grade school years. It's when LeBron James discovered team sports, which quenched his need for fellowship and purpose. It was his first step in a journey from long, lean, shy youth to international sports icon. It's a story about how some kids require a village, and the potential that's unlocked when that happens.

During fourth grade, James missed more than half of the 160-day school year. A December 2002 article by *ESPN Magazine*'s Tom Friend cited the shame James felt over his mother's petty misdemeanors (trespassing, disorderly conduct, contempt of court) as the reason he stopped going to elementary school.

There's no quote, and it's not something that gets discussed in his memoir. James is as fiercely protective of his mother as she was of him, so it's not surprising that this potential slip in one of the first interviews James ever offered has not been repeated.

Instead of school that fourth grade year, James satisfied himself playing video games and walking down to the corner store to buy snacks with their food stamps. Though he'd never gotten into drugs or gangs, James was heading in a bad direction. "I was on the edge of falling into an abyss from which I could never escape," he wrote.

Into the midst of that mounting dysfunction stepped little eight-year-old LeBron James' first ticket to something better, and he grabbed it. In late summer 1993, Bruce Kelker pulled into the faded red-brick Elizabeth Park housing project where Gloria and LeBron James were staying just north of downtown Akron. Kelker was seeking eight- and nine-year-olds for his rec football team.

Kelker was a former star high school cornerback who had frittered away his talent on alcohol and drugs. Now sober, he was seeking redemption coaching pee wee football, which had been a positive influence early in his own life. It was his first year coaching, and in his enthusiasm, he'd assembled a 30-page playbook.

He had been tipped off about LeBron and discovered a kid that at 5-foot-5 was even then big for his age. Kelker challenged James to race 100 yards against his friends. He won by 15 yards, and Kelker had his new tailback. On his first play from scrimmage of their first game, James ran 80 yards for a touchdown. James loved football, and it offered the structure he craved.

Kelker was the first reliable man in James' life. He picked his star up for practice each day at 3:45 from wherever the lad might be staying, and kept his equipment safe in the trunk. Gloria couldn't afford the participation fee, so Kelker covered it, remembering how as a kid his own mother had offered him a choice between new Chuck Taylors or rec league football.

Gloria became den mother to the team and LeBron's biggest cheerleader. She raced the length of the field along the sidelines for each of his 18 touchdowns, screaming encouragement. The East Dragons won all six of their games.

Kelker could tell LeBron's life was on edge. After witnessing enough of their precarious living situation, Kelker felt he had to do something. He told Gloria and LeBron they could move in with him and his girlfriend of 14 years. Still, James continued to miss school, unsure which one to attend or where to catch the bus.

Frankie Walker worked for the Akron Metropolitan Housing Authority (AMHA), and his wife, Pam, was an aide to a local congressman. They lived in a nice suburban home on the West Side with two daughters and a son, Frankie Jr., who played on James' football team. The senior Walker knew something of James' circumstances and grew worried when LeBron didn't return to school after Christmas break.

The Walkers became more active in LeBron's life. They had James over to the house, and Frankie Sr. took him out on the playground blacktops for one-on-one with Frankie Jr. LeBron lost the game 21-7 and didn't take it well. He could shoot some, but there was much more to the game than that. Walker consoled the dejected nine-year-old and promised to teach him.

James absorbed everything quickly, proving adept at left-handed layups just a month after Walker taught him. He coached LeBron on his son's Summit Lake summer rec basketball team, and made LeBron assistant coach of the eight-year-olds, giving the young boy his first chance to lead. It was something he took pride in.

Before the beginning of his fifth grade year, Pam and Frankie Sr. approached Gloria with their concerns about James' school attendance, offering a solution. They suggested an arrangement where the Walkers cared for LeBron during the week and Gloria saw him on weekends, until she could get her life and finances in better order. That arrangement would continue for more than a year until Gloria finally qualified for rent-subsidized housing.

In the Walker household LeBron discovered discipline he'd never known. For the first time in his life he had chores, a bedtime, and most importantly, a whole family watching him and watching out for him. He was up at 6:30 every morning and finished his homework before he could play outside. Given firm, reliable boundaries for the first time in his life, James thrived.

He took so well to his newly scheduled life that he received an award for perfect fifth grade attendance. Beyond rules and responsibilities, LeBron learned family. He learned to share—which even as an only child was relatively easy after having practically nothing—and he discovered how to be part of a team.

"I adapted to it easily, maybe because having already moved around so much in my life, I was good at dealing with new situations," James wrote. "I saw how life was meant to be lived, as a part of something essential and valuable and permanent."

Dru Joyce II spotted James playing basketball against his own son in the summer rec league, and remembered him that winter while assembling an AAU team from the area. James didn't have many skills besides his height. He barely could dribble.

"He'd turn his back to the defender, and back his way up the court. He only used his right hand," Joyce told the *Plain Dealer*. However, his speed, like his size, was already special. "Even back then, no one got up and down the court quicker."

Joyce recalled that when James first joined his team, the nine-year-old would shoot every time he touched the ball. He mentioned to the impressionable future superstar how great players make others better by setting them up with passes and putting them in a better position to score. James took that lesson to heart and began passing the very next day.

The team, known as the Shooting Stars, featured fifth and sixth graders, until the older boys left to form their own team. Still, the team, which also featured coach Joyce's boy (Little Dru) and beefy Sian Cotton, qualified for the national AAU tournament in Cocoa Beach, Florida, for kids 11 and under. During this time, the trio would develop a bond to last their lives.

It was the first time many of them ever had seen the ocean, James included. The opposition's size and their snazzy corporate-sponsored uniforms awed them. Nonetheless, they finished ninth out of 64 teams.

If they did that well having barely played together, they thought, how far could they go? James' first journey to answer that question would inform later chases, with a an accent on focus, discipline, family, and finding that missing piece.

The next year, Gloria got a rent-assisted home in Spring Hill Apartments. LeBron moved back in with his mother, and for the first time in his life, the 11-year-old James had his own room. His grades were good, and he was beginning to scratch the surface of his basketball talent.

That year, the Shootings Stars won the 12-and-under division of Youth Basketball of America's national tournament in Orlando. James, now 5-foot-10, was named MVP. But they did no better than tenth at the AAU nationals in Salt Lake City that year.

They felt they needed something else to get over the hump, and recruited another talented player from a different AAU team whose team lost in the quarterfinal qualifier.

Willie McGee lived in the West Side Chicago projects until fifth grade, when he moved in with his older brother Illya, who had just graduated from the University of Akron. He was initially aloof but they pulled him in, and soon this band of brothers—LeBron, Sian, Willie, and Lil Dru—began dubbing themselves the "Fab Four."

They grew steadfast in their camaraderie. "We shared everything with each other, and it became an unspoken rule," James wrote. "Pizza, Starbursts, the thin sticks of Twizzlers, it didn't matter. All for one and one for all."

They played well together and qualified for the 13-and-under AAU nationals in Memphis that Fourth of July weekend. However, they underperformed and were bounced from the tournament early.

The boys had been playing in the pool and flirting with girls before the game. Coach Joyce questioned their focus. Rather than stick around for the holiday, he packed the van up after the loss and drove them straight back to Akron, over even his wife's objections.

The four returned for their eighth grade year determined to redeem their mistake and take advantage of their one last chance to win a national championship. They lost but a single game all year, during an early-season tournament game against a Houston AAU team featuring Kendrick Perkins.

James had grown to 6-foot-2 and dunked for the first time in a teachers-students game at Reidinger Middle School. The Shooting Stars advanced to the AAU nationals in Orlando, and this time remained focused, ignoring the amusement parks and attractions to stay honed in on basketball.

In the finals, they met the Southern California All-Stars, who had won the AAU national championship in their age group three years running. Down all game, the Shooting Stars battled back to within two. As time expired, James launched a shot from 10 feet beyond the three-point line that went halfway down, then popped back out.

The loss was heartbreaking. They had grown so close, offering the family that the nomadic only child James had barely experienced. That kinship had been driven in part by their competition for a national AAU title. Now that it was beyond reach, they turned their attention to high school.

The boys were pulled in many directions by friends and the community. Akron public school powerhouse Buchtel was just a few blocks from Lil Dru's, so his friends were probably surprised when he expressed interest in predominantly white parochial high school St. Vincent-St. Mary.

The pint-sized Lil Dru, who was a generous 5-foot-6, got the impression Buchtel's coach didn't see him as varsity material his freshman year. The junior Joyce had a chip on his shoulder about his height, and compensated with drill-like discipline, perfectionism, and a no-quit attitude.

Lil Dru had grown attached to St. Vincent-St. Mary coach Keith Dambrot at his local basketball clinics. Dambrot, too, had been a scrappy undersized player whose understanding of the game and fierce determination made up for his athletic deficiencies.

After he finished playing, Dambrot shot through the coaching ranks. At the tender age of 32 he became the head coach of Central Michigan, a Division I program. Dambrot's rise came to an abrupt end two years later, when during a halftime speech he used a racial epithet (after asking his players permission). The controversy cost him his college coaching career, or so he thought.

Dambrot became a stockbroker but held Sunday night coaching clinics at his local Jewish Community Center, because he couldn't quite give it up. Soon the entire "Fab Four" was attending his clinics.

In 1998, Dambrot took a job at a small Catholic school just beyond downtown Akron on the West Side (in addition to his stockbroker's job).

That very first year, he took St. Vincent-St. Mary to the Division III regional finals.

In Dambrot, Lil Dru saw a way to play on the varsity as a freshman, something he couldn't see happening at Buchtel no matter how hard he played. He remembered Dambrot saying that if a freshman was close to even with a senior, he'd play the freshman because he'd have him for three more years.

Midway through their eighth grade year, Lil Dru told his friends he was going to go to St. Vincent-St. Mary, challenging the other three to follow him. James loved his basketball family and wanted them to share in a national championship. Winning it with anyone else wouldn't have been as sweet.

Indeed, James' memoir is as much about his teammates on those AAU and high school teams as it is about him, emblematic of the equanimity that makes him such an extraordinary ballplayer. So he chose St. Vincent-St. Mary over 97 percent-minority Buchtel, choosing his family over what the world outside expected of him.

When coach Dambrot gave Dru Joyce a job on his staff, some whispered it was payment for delivering the boys when he was really grooming his heir apparent.

Coach Dambrot was a disciplinarian and drove them hard. From the type of drills to the level of practice intensity, he ran his team like a Division I college program. He screamed and cussed at the kids, and if parents came in, he'd cuss even more, just to show he didn't care. He was so much tougher and meaner than at those Sunday clinics; the four questioned whether they'd made a huge mistake. James particularly felt targeted by Dambrot's withering criticism. He broke down James' weaknesses, belittled his effort, called him a ball-hogging showboat.

"He cracked my game open as if it were worthless," James wrote. "I play no defense. I was selfish. I knew fundamentals but snubbed them. I figured at the time he hated me…. I now realize what he was doing, and I'm lucky he was doing it."

Dambrot knew James had the potential to be one of the best ever if he kept working at it, and he felt some of that responsibility, especially as he noted how quickly James digested his lessons. "I was very difficult on LeBron," Dambrot said. "But in the long run, it was good for him. The pressure I felt was that he had a chance to make something great out of his life."

The team's senior leader, Maverick Carter, developed a close friendship with James on the court and the football field. Football remained James' favorite sport, and he played three years in high school. Carter was the team's go-to receiver, but James played alongside him and later won All-State honors at the position.

Carter and James also started on the hardwood for St. Vincent-St. Mary, with LeBron's three buddies coming off the bench. Dambrot wasn't giving anyone something they didn't earn. That team went undefeated and won the state Division III basketball championship. In the finals game, Lil Dru got in for his customary 10 minutes, and took full advantage, draining seven three-pointers without missing.

They'd repeat the feat again James' sophomore year, winning the state championship en route to a 27-1 record. Dambrot realized what he had, and reduced the number of local teams on his schedule to accommodate games against out-of-state powerhouses, none bigger than Oak Hill Academy.

The perennially top-ranked Virginia prep school had produced numerous NBA players including Josh Smith, Rajon Rondo, Jerry Stackhouse, Rod Strickland, Ty Lawson, and Brandon Jennings. That year, Oak Hill had mammoth 7-footer DeSagana Diop, who'd go number eight to Cleveland in the next year's draft.

Dambrot had scouted them and believed Oak Hill wasn't fundamentally sound defensively. With the St. Vincent-St. Mary Irish leading by seven and three minutes left in the game, LeBron's legs started cramping up, a problem that would recur in his pro career.

Dambrot pulled James for a minute, but he came back flat and never got his rhythm. He missed a midrange jumper and a couple free throws (another recurrent trope). With time running out, his jumper just inside the three-point line rolled in and out. It was the only blemish on an otherwise perfect season.

The play of this gangly, 6-foot-6, 180-pound sophomore caught the eye of NBA talent evaluators there to scout Diop. Word started circulating among scouts and general managers of this sophomore basketball prodigy in Akron. One of Dambrot's colleagues, a head coach in the Pac-10, watched James in practice and predicted the 16-year-old would never need to play a game of college.

After that season, University of Akron offered Dambrot a job on their staff, ending his eight-year exile from Division I college basketball. It was a bittersweet departure, but a great homecoming as well. The Akron Zips made him an assistant, and three years later he was named head coach. Since then he has won over 250 games.

Dambrot knew the door could swing closed as quickly as it opened, and worried about all the attention surrounding his young star. Shoe companies and agents, scouts and reporters all wanted to siphon off a piece of this incipient supernova. He worried about his ability to weather the coming storm and any potential scandal—real or imagined—that might scotch his chance to return to the college ranks.

Dru Joyce took the reins, completing his own odyssey from the fledgling AAU coach hungry to learn into the head of a winning high school program. Dambrot told school leaders the truth: Joyce had been there every step of the way alongside the boys and his stewardship was responsible for their growth.

Joyce called it "a dream come true" in the *Akron Beacon Journal*, but took the position with some trepidation. He knew the challenge would be great, if only because the school was moving up a level from Division III to II, meaning a higher caliber of competition.

He also worried about his ability to control rebellious 17-year-olds intoxicated with their success. The "Fab Four" had grown to a five-some with the addition of skilled but sullen 6-foot-6 big man Romeo Travis. He gave the new "Fab Five" a needed post-presence alongside Cotton as well as the ability to step out and hit the three.

Travis' tough background had made him hard and standoffish. He initially chafed at his teammates' sharing ways, and thawed slowly. His inconsistent fit with the other four would be a continuing source of tension, as they started calling themselves the "Fab Four Plus One." Yet they needed Travis' skills for a daunting schedule thick with out-of-state tourneys. There would be no dodging the spotlight.

That spring James was Ohio's first sophomore to be named Mr. Basketball, and that summer he attended several prestigious basketball camps, competing against ballplayers such as Deron Williams, Raymond Felton, and J. J. Redick and rooming with Carmelo Anthony. The season started promisingly enough, but the transition to the more fatherly Joyce was not easy. The players did not respect and fear him the way they had Dambrot.

Joyce had trouble disciplining the kids, and practices devolved into petty disagreements. Still, they won, even if by smaller margins than they should have. The continued success reinforced that bad behavior, and Joyce was powerless to stop them. They saw him as the fatherly figure who had driven a bunch of rambunctious 10-year-olds to Florida for a basketball tournament, not the stern taskmaster Dambrot.

They treated Joyce's instructions as suggestions and it cost them. Up by one with seconds left on the clock against Long Island's Amityville High early in the season, they ignored coach Joyce's call to pressure the inbounds play. Future NBA guard A. J. Price got loose from Lil Dru's coverage, forcing James to foul him. He hit the free throws, and James' last-second shot failed to go down, for their first loss.

That hardly changed their tune; indeed, it grew worse. They were old enough to drive and just the right age to think they knew better than everyone else. In the past, they stayed after practice and worked on their skills, but now they couldn't wait to leave.

As they pulled away from their coach, they grew testier with each other, losing the fundamental fun-loving camaraderie that had characterized them. Travis grew so moody and withdrawn that he had to be kicked out of practice several times. Another practice ended when the team flat-out refused to run the laps Joyce had demanded.

When the Irish reprised the previous year's matchup against Oak Hill, they were 15-1 and ranked fifth in the nation by *USA Today*. Oak Hill was 25-1 and ranked fourth. James' old roommate, Anthony, had transferred after the summer and now was a senior on Oak Hill. They had six other future Division I college players as well. LeBron scored 36 and Anthony 34 in an epic display as LeBron won the MVP of the tourney, but they lost 72-66.

The second loss of the season didn't change their tune, and the deluge of press to follow only made it worse. If teen rebellion and Dambrot's absence were the oily box of rags, then James' appearance on *Sports Illustrated*'s cover was the lit cigar.

The article, entitled "The Chosen One," compared the 17-year-old to Michael Jordan. In a fit of youthful hubris, he had it tattooed across his shoulders, where it later would symbolize the burden he put on himself. Early on, it served as notice of James' callow immaturity.

"I was arrogant, dubbing myself King James; my head did swell," he wrote. "We had become bigheaded jerks, I in particular, and we are to blame for that."

They'd lose three times that season, costing them any chance of a national championship. They felt invincible as teenagers often do, drunk on their new liberty. They had a hotel room donated by a sponsor where they would hang out and meet girls, Joyce discovered after the season when the team expressed its collective contrition.

On the night before the big state title game the team partied with the cheerleaders, who somehow were housed on the same floor. No one went to bed before the early morning hours, even after coach Joyce came out of his room and reprimanded them.

The crowd of 18,375 in Columbus was a state tournament record. Though they had beaten their opponent, Cincinnati's Roger Bacon High, earlier in the season, it had been a close game. The title game seesawed back and forth, but the Irish fell short.

The team was devastated. It recalled their next-to-last AAU season when they lost focus in Memphis. They knew it was their own fault, and like that last AAU year, they came back fully focused. LeBron, who had played football until his junior season, gave it up as an unnecessary risk and distraction, even though some had him ranked as the best prep receiver in the country.

During LeBron's junior season, Travis was fully embraced among their ranks and they finally dubbed themselves the "Fab Five." Their fellowship continued without pause from school to practice to James' house. They'd play video games, such as Shaq Fu and Madden, and eat pizzas bought by team boosters. His friends complained about James' eidetic memory, which allowed him to recall their favorite Madden plays from the last time they played or quickly memorize the series of button mashes that activated brutal fighting game finishing moves.

James loved hosting the brothers he'd never had. "I always wanted companionship, I tried to basically kidnap them for days," he wrote. "The bond between us only grew stronger."

Though there were controversies over a tricked-out Hummer and gratis throwback jerseys, the team negotiated the scrutiny and the challenges, turning inward and toward each other. Nothing outside them mattered; they were on a mission.

They marched through the season, losing but once to old rival Akron Buchtel. It didn't stand in their way of securing the top spot in *USA Today's* final prep poll. They won the state title in a tight 40-36 game against Kettering Alter, who took the air out of the ball to slow LeBron and company down. It didn't work. James scored 25 points and grabbed 11 rebounds to give St. Vincent-St. Mary its third state title and the Shooting Stars their coveted national championship.

It took eight years to accomplish, and it wasn't easy, but LeBron had taken his friends to the summit. The media microscope would only grow more invasive over the years, but the script was written years ago. Tussle with the coach, lose focus and discipline, reach the summit and fall short, come back rededicated, pull the family even closer, and triumph against the odds.

It didn't work during his first tour in Cleveland, or his first year back either. Then again it took eight years for him to succeed with the Shooting Stars. In the fall of 2015, James entered his ninth season playing for the Cavaliers.

3
ALSO GUEST STARRING...

THERE'S NO LEADER without followers, no general without foot soldiers. As great as LeBron James' individual skills are, he could not deliver a crown on his own. The 2015 Finals demonstrated that. Not that James didn't know, having taken a similarly undermanned Cavs team to the 2007 Finals, only for the San Antonio Spurs to sweep them.

One of the reasons LeBron returned to Cleveland was the youth and talent of Kyrie Irving, who had the potential, James said, to be the league MVP. Irving was the first pick of the 2011 NBA Draft and that season's Rookie of the Year. Two years later he was the MVP of the 2014 All-Star Game, after scoring 31 points and dishing out 14 assists.

James certainly wasn't the first to see greatness in Irving. New Jersey AAU coach Sandy Pyonin has coached 35 future NBA players, and saw in Irving the potential to be better than any of them. Indeed, Pyonin believes Irving is already better than Stephen Curry.

Kyrie's father, Drederick Irving, played collegiately at Boston University and professionally around the world, including Melbourne, Australia, where Kyrie was born. His mother, Elizabeth, died when he was just four, leaving Drederick to raise Kyrie and his older sister, Asia, alone.

Drederick remembers Kyrie dribbling a basketball at 13 months, and in fourth grade making a goal of becoming an NBA player. After seventh grade, Drederick enlisted Pyonin to train the young Irving in basketball's finer points.

"Sandy gave me an opportunity to work on my game, and basically being a kid in the gym [that] he picked up every day, was like a second father to me. When I was 15 years old until 18, he gave me a lot of advice, and instilled a confidence that I've carried on since then," Irving said. "I can't give all the credit to him, but some of the credit for my development goes to Sandy."

Drederick eventually took a job at a Wall Street brokerage firm. He was walking through the World Trade Center on 9/11 when American Airlines Flight 11 hit the North Tower. He ran out of the building to see it flaming above and people falling from the sky.

Unable to reach his children by phone, he walked nine miles to his old neighborhood in the Bronx, where he contacted a friend to drive over and let his kids and the babysitter in Newark know he was okay. (The bridges were closed; phone lines jammed.) The experience shook him profoundly. He became more hands-on with his children's education and athletics. It played a role in Kyrie working with Pyonin.

By Irving's sophomore year of high school, the results of his tutelage began to bloom as Kyrie took Montclair Kimberley Academy to a state prep championship. Realizing Kyrie needed better competition to grow, Drederick enrolled him at storied basketball powerhouse St. Patrick's in Elizabeth, New Jersey.

Kyrie won another state title his junior year under St. Patrick's coach Kevin Boyle, their third in four years. At the time, Boyle said Irving had the potential to be the best guard ever to come out of New Jersey. They might've won a second title but St. Patrick's was under sanctions for violating off-season training rules over the summer.

Irving played in the McDonald's All-American Game and enrolled at Duke University, but suffered a severe ligament injury to his right toe eight games into the season. He played in three more games. They came during the NCAA Tournament, where Arizona eliminated Duke in the Sweet 16 despite Irving's team-high 28 points and three assists.

If Irving lacked in big-time collegiate exposure, he compensated with pure offensive firepower. There were quicker, more athletic guards but none equally gifted in finishing around the basket and pulling up for a jumper. His shooting form was picturesque and his range reached the parking lot.

His handle was unbreakable, elastic, and extraordinary like Flubber, allowing him to get wherever he wanted on the court. He also possessed an uncanny ability to spin the ball off the backboard amidst the tall limbs with the mathematical precision of a pool shark working the rails. He developed the skill doing the Mikan drill (named after '50s Hall of Famer George Mikan); while standing under the basket, the player alternates shooting layups from the left and right side with the correct corresponding hand repeatedly.

"I'm not finishing over top of anybody so I have to be good with the angles on the backboard," Irving explained. "When I was seven or eight years old we started doing it; first overhand regular Mikan drill, then he made me do the underhand reverse. I remember my nose started bleeding in the backyard. I just got so dizzy that I passed out."

Kyrie was the first pick of the draft, landing in Cleveland thanks to a trade deadline deal four months earlier that sent Mo Williams and Jamario Moon to the playoff-contending Los Angeles Clippers for their first round pick and an aging Baron Davis. The deal wound up being a heist for the Cavs even though Davis played just 15 games for the Cavaliers. (He played 29 more the next year for the Knicks before calling it quits.)

The Clippers failed to make the playoffs despite the deal, placing the pick in the NBA Lottery. The Clippers pick boasted a 2.8 percent chance of landing the top choice, while Cleveland, which possessed the league's second-worst record, had a hair under 20 percent chance of choosing number one.

In the end, the Clippers pick won, giving the Cavaliers the opportunity to select Irving, while their own pick landed fourth overall. They used it to select Texas power forward Tristan Thompson, a Canadian known for his physical play and rebounding.

That draft has proven to be one of the richest in recent memory, producing additional stars such as Kawhi Leonard, Klay Thompson, Jimmy Butler, Reggie Jackson, Kemba Walker, Brandon Knight, Chandler Parsons, Nikola Vucevic, Marcus and Markieff Morris, Tobias Harris, Jonas Valanciunas, and almost a dozen more borderline starters.

Kyrie accumulated many accolades in the three years before LeBron James' return, including two All-Star appearances and the 2013 NBA Three-Point Contest title, but there remained two fundamental knocks on his game. He didn't play enough defense and, unlike a traditional point guard, looked to score too much to the exclusion of teammates.

Neither tag disappeared after Irving's first year with James. While he showed the ability to play good defense, particularly after the addition of Timofey Mozgov gave him better support at the rim, his effort or focus were at times wanting. Other guards would go by him with their first step or he'd die like a fly on a screen.

To compensate, the Cavaliers often needed the defender of the man setting the screen to jump out and force the ballhandler around him (also known as "hedging" or "showing hard"), giving Irving time to recover, though that gave the screener an unimpeded opportunity to roll toward the basket, requiring defensive help to rotate over from other players.

Irving adapted well offensively to James' arrival, due in part to the fact that he'd never been a traditional point guard. Though used to creating his own shot, sharing ballhandling duties didn't significantly impact his scoring.

Irving took one less shot per game (16.5 vs. 17.4) in 2014-15 than the year before James' arrival, but made more of them (7.7 vs. 7.5), thanks to Irving's highest shooting percentage (46.8 percent) since his rookie year (46.9 percent). His assists fell (6.1 to 5.2), but his turnovers also dropped slightly (2.7 to 2.5).

It's to Irving's credit that he is as effective playing off the ball as dribbling it. It wasn't for nothing that he won that three-point championship in 2013. Irving has become a deadly catch-and-shoot sniper from beyond the arc. Only Curry, Eric Gordon, Paul George, and Kyle Korver shot a higher percentage (46.6 percent) with at least one three-point field goal per game during the 2014-15 season.

On July 1, 2014, Irving announced that he had agreed to re-sign with the Cavaliers after meeting with General Manager David Griffin and new head coach David Blatt. The deal was for five years and worth over $90 million. It also assured James of a fellow young star to play off of and vice-versa.

If Kyrie provided the scoring backcourt foil LeBron had in Miami with Dwyane Wade, then Kevin Love was destined to be the much-maligned third wheel like the Heat's Chris Bosh, responsible for rebounding, spacing the floor with his shooting, and, on occasion, low-post scoring.

After spending his entire basketball life as "the man" with the ball always in his hands, first at UCLA and then professionally with the Timberwolves, Love had to adjust to life on the edge of the spotlight with fewer opportunities to make a difference.

"It's going to be very difficult for him," Bosh told the *Sporting News* after

Love's trade to the Cavaliers. "Even if I was in his corner and I was able to tell him what to expect and what to do, it still doesn't make any difference. You still have to go through things, you still have to figure out things on your own. It's extremely difficult and extremely frustrating. He's going to have to deal with that."

Like Bosh, Love found himself pushed to the perimeter by the need to keep the low-post clear as a driving lane to the basket for both James and Irving. Unlike Bosh, Love doesn't have the length, quickness, or instincts to make up for lost offensive opportunities at the defensive end. However, Love is a much better rebounder than the taller Bosh.

Love's rebounding tenacity, especially on the offensive boards, was his first calling card in the NBA. During his third season, 2010-11, Love averaged 15.2 rebounds a game to lead the league, and he never averaged less than 12.5 in his six seasons with Minnesota. Though he lacked the prototypical big man body and wasn't overly athletic, Kevin understood the game. His father, Stan Love, had played four seasons in the NBA, including two seasons with the Lakers from 1973 to 1975, and a handful of games in the ABA.

Stan instilled in Kevin a passion for the game. Like Kyrie, there are pictures of toddler Kevin with a ball in his hands, though at one point Stan had to chase him off the baseball mound. Kevin was a pretty good pitcher with a fastball clocked at ninety miles per hour his freshman year of high school. "I still wonder about it sometimes," Love said.

Already six feet tall in the sixth grade, Kevin played with agile fifth grade shortstop (and future NBA star) Klay Thompson on an Oregon team that won the state title and narrowly missed a berth in the 2001 Little League World Series. But when Kevin entered high school, Stan let his son know basketball would be his sole focus.

From the beginning, Kevin was a student of basketball. As a child, he demanded his own VCR, from which he watched videos of such greats as Bill Walton, Pistol Pete Maravich, Larry Bird, and Kareem Abdul-Jabbar. His father remembers him watching the tapes and then going out and practicing the moves.

One of the signature moves Kevin adopted was the two-handed overhead outlet pass, which initially developed out of a childhood desire to shoot from far beyond his range. "I used to shoot like that when I was young, because

I wasn't strong enough," Love said. "I used to throw that from three-point range, and then one summer I sat there and got my arm in right."

Yet the outlet pass remained a part of his arsenal going forward. "I was always a big fan of that pass and it leading into a fastbreak," he said. "You saw guys like Bill Walton throwing that pass; Pete Maravich would throw it underhand."

His coach at Lake Oswego High, Bob Shoff, saw Kevin play in sixth grade and could already tell he was going to be a superstar. He had sophisticated post moves and was a willing passer who appreciated setting up his teammates as much as scoring.

Playing his father one-on-one certainly helped Kevin hone his inside game. Stan knew how to clutch and grab to upset a shooter, initiating Kevin from an early age to the physicality of the post. Stan must've known the lesson had registered during their final father/son one-on-one game.

"I belted him hard in the chest one time and went around him. It was my freshman year in high school," Love said. "He was still pretty good until I was about 15 years old and he could really shoot the ball—but that's when he stopped playing me."

That year Love led an unranked Lake Oswego team to the state tournament and made second-team all-state. He took it to another level his sophomore year. He won Oregon Player of the Year honors and played for the state title for the first of three consecutive years, winning only during his junior year when he beat his local nemesis, future NBA player Kyle Singler.

The summer before that junior year, Love played with Singler on Nike's Portland Elite team, but was "fired" for attending a rival shoe company's event. Love had played in a Reebok invitational camp in New Jersey during the same dates as the rival Nike camp in Indianapolis. Shoe companies can be vindictive like that.

"I'm a 16-year-old kid," Love told *The Oregonian* at the time. "Why should I have to make a decision to play in one tournament or another? I just wanted to play where the best players were."

It was at the Reebok camp where Kevin Love met LeBron James for the first time (as well as hip-hop mogul Jay-Z), finishing as the third-ranked player in camp behind Greg Oden and O. J. Mayo.

The experience invigorated Love, according to coach Shoff. Where once

Love gave enough effort to get by, he was now the hardest-working player on the team. He had the NBA in his sights.

That summer before his senior year Love played for the Southern California All-Stars, a Reebok AAU team featuring guard Brandon Jennings, and considered one of the greatest AAU teams ever. They won all 47 of their games, including wins over O. J. Mayo's well-regarded D-1 Greyhounds and Derrick Rose's Meanstreets teams.

During his senior year, Love won every major player of the year award including Wooden, Naismith, *Parade*, McDonald's, and *USA Today*. He scored 37 in the state championship against South Medford, including 24 straight, but lost 58-54 to Singler's team in a rematch. Despite all those accolades, Lake Oswego didn't name him Male Athlete of the Year as a senior, an honor that went to golfer Kevin Gay, a snub Love still notes publicly years later.

UCLA won Love's collegiate favor when they introduced him to the "Wizard of Westwood," retired Bruins coaching legend John Wooden. During his year there, Love called Wooden on several occasions, asking advice and picking his brain.

"That was one of the main reasons I came here," Love told ESPN in 2007, explaining he wanted to learn what it took to win from one of the greatest. "I just want to know what it takes to hang one of those banners up."

Love stayed for only one year but was named Pac-10 Player of the Year, leading the Bruins to the Final Four alongside future NBA players Russell Westbrook, Darren Collison, and Luc Mbah a Moute. He was the fifth pick in the 2008 NBA Draft, taken by the Memphis Grizzlies and traded to the Minnesota Timberwolves for the number three pick—old nemesis O.J. Mayo, as it turned out—in an eight-player deal.

Love suffered through six years of dysfunction as a member of the Timberwolves. When Kevin McHale was his coach, he told Love not to shoot outside the lane, effectively eliminating Love's ability to stretch defenses. Kurt Rambis took over the coaching duties for the next two years, and Love's scoring jumped from 11 his rookie season to 14 and then 20 points a game while averaging 15 boards. He won the NBA's Most Improved Player Award.

Minnesota fired Rambis, who won 32 games in two years. New coach Rick Adelman worked to cut Love loose. From 2010-11 to the following year, his three-point attempts jumped from 2.9 to 5.1 per game, and his scoring improved from 20.2 to 26.0 points per game. His free throw attempts also jumped, from 6.8 to 8.4 a game, as Adelman cleverly utilized Love in the elbow and low-post regions.

But tense contract negotiations with Timberwolves General Manager David Kahn overshadowed Love's breakout season. A former *Oregonian* reporter-turned-lawyer-turned-sports executive, Kahn would not give Love Minnesota's "cornerstone" five-year contract, instead offering a four-year contract with a player opt-out after three years. It was inarguably the dumbest of Kahn's many boneheaded moves.

That summer Love would play for the U.S. Olympic team alongside LeBron James, where they bonded. The next season was a loss as Love twice fractured his shooting hand and played in only 18 games. He returned to form in 2013-14 with 26.1 points and 12.5 rebounds a game, but the Wolves again fell short of the playoffs with a 40-42 record.

Kahn was fired prior to the season and replacement GM, ex-coach Flip Saunders, worked hard (and unsuccessfully) to rebuild the bridges Kahn had burned. The Timberwolves were no closer to contention and they had no choice but to trade Love, lest he become a free agent and leave them with nothing in return.

Saunders tried to hang tough, but finally took the only reasonable deal, accepting Anthony Bennett and Andrew Wiggins from the Cavaliers and Thaddeus Young from the Philadelphia 76ers in a three-team trade that sent Love's old UCLA teammate, Luc Mbah a Moute, and Russian guard Alexey Shved to the 76ers.

Despite some questions about his defensive ability and/or effort his first year in Cleveland, and some struggles to find the proper role, Love adapted pretty well as third wheel in the Cavaliers' offense.

Under coach David Blatt, he did complain a bit about being consigned to simply spacing the floor—standing out at the three-point line like a heat-sink for defenders, pulling them away from the basket to open up space for James and Irving to operate.

"I'm trying to find my way," he said after a February game. "It's one of the toughest situations I've had to deal with, but at the end of the day we're winning basketball games. I know tonight was different, but at the same time, there's no blueprint for what I should be doing."

Blatt would also sit Love during the fourth quarters at times, going instead with big man Tristan Thompson, whose quicker feet allowed him to stay in front of guards after a pick-and-roll switch.

The fact that Love's contract was up at the end of the season complicated matters, though mostly in the eyes of the press. Love always talked about winning above all and reiterated time and again that he planned to re-sign with the Cavaliers in the off-season, and was committed to the organization and the process.

The loss of Love in the opening round of the 2015 playoffs elevated Tristan Thompson's role. Until then, Thompson had been mostly an energy big who brought his quick feet and relentless jumping ability to bear on the game's outcome like no one since rebounding machine Dennis Rodman. Though not as agile or effective defensively as Rodman, Thompson's effort on the offensive boards is comparable—as are his apparent offensive limitations.

Since the time he started playing, Thompson has possessed the same characteristic: doggedness. The Toronto native had to be dogged in order to make it in the NBA from a place better known for its hockey players. Thompson gives a lot of credit to his AAU coach, Ro Russell of Grassroots Elite, who saw his talent in eighth grade and recruited him to the team.

"Being from Toronto and not being exposed to the AAU scene or American competition, it helped me develop a lot," Thompson said. "If it wasn't for [coach Russell] I don't know where I'd be right now."

After the experience with coach Russell, Thompson knew he wanted to go to the U.S. to face the best competition possible. So beginning his sophomore year of high school in 2007, Thompson began a three-year basketball "internship" at two of America's biggest prep basketball factories, St. Benedict's in New Jersey and Findlay Prep in Las Vegas.

"I knew the competition at the time in Toronto wasn't that good and my goal was to play in the NBA," said Thompson. "I knew to accomplish that I'd need to make sacrifices and I knew one of them was that I'd have to leave home."

Thompson turned enough heads his sophomore year to be one of the top two prep power forwards in the country, and a top five collegiate recruit overall. Russell reported that Thompson came away from his visits to Duke and North Carolina unimpressed, feeling that while both were good teams, those teams weren't a good fit. Thompson demonstrated his self-awareness and maturity in this determination to find a home, not simply the nicest house.

That's why it was a surprise when Thompson clashed with St. Benedict's coach Danny Hurley (brother of Duke legend Bobby Hurley) on the court during a game his junior year. Hurley dismissed him from the court and ultimately the team for insubordination. St. Benedict's was 20-2 at the time, and Thompson has since explained it as a youthful mistake whose lesson he's digested. He and Hurley patched their differences and still stay in touch.

Thompson spent his senior year at Findlay Prep, a private basketball program that operates outside state scholastic regulation and outsources the kids' education to a private school. They can do that because they don't compete for state high school basketball titles, instead barnstorming the country for over 30,000 miles a year playing the nation's best prep teams. West Virginia's Huntington Prep and Arizona's Westwind Prep Academy have replicated this model.

After Findlay Prep, Thompson spent a year at the University of Texas, where he was the Big 12 Freshman of the Year. He averaged 13.1 points, 7.8 rebounds, and 2.4 blocks a game. Texas lost in the Big 12 Championship Game to Kansas, but received an at-large bid and lost to Arizona, 70-69, in their bid for the Sweet Sixteen. Thompson decided to jump to the NBA afterward, and was picked fourth overall, which some thought a reach considering his still-rough offensive skills.

While perhaps the league's most tenacious rebounder, Thompson had trouble his first few years getting his shot off around the basket. Despite great leaping ability and decent size, during his first two years in the league Thompson had 15 percent of his shots rejected, one of the highest rates in the league. The year before James returned, he dropped it to 13 percent, then reduced it to 10 percent in 2014-15.

Initially a lefty, he's probably the only NBA player to switch his shooting hand since arriving, which neither helped nor hurt him. Until LeBron's return, Tristan never shot above 50 percent (a low percentage for most big men), but his on-court work ethic and infectious energy had proven invaluable to the Cavs.

His overwhelming energy is apparent not just on defense, but the offensive glass as well. In 2014-15 Thompson was fifth in offensive rebounds a game while playing less than 27 minutes a night. That energy could demoralize opponents who held the Cavaliers scoreless for an entire possession late in the game, only to have Thompson recover the rebound to defibrillate the clock.

Thompson's been unable to replicate his collegiate shot-blocking skills in the NBA, where he's averaged less than a block a game since his rookie year. But what he lacks above the rim he's been able to replace on the floor with his speed and agility. His quick feet have made him a fine perimeter defender, and most guards have difficulty going by him. Plus he's long enough to contest their three-point shots.

The challenge is that Thompson's limited shooting range lets defenders hang in the lane without guarding him, confident they can recover before Thompson gets a shot off. Thompson wasn't the only player Cleveland counted on for their energy. The team boasted two other foreign-born sparkplugs: Australian point guard Matthew Dellavedova and Brazilian center Anderson Varejao.

Varejao played his entire 11-year career in Cleveland, including almost all of James' first tour. Nicknamed "Wild Thing" for his unbridled on-court energy and wild mane of dark curly hair, Varejao was a member of the Brazilian Olympic team and frequently demonstrated his veteran savvy with keenly timed cuts to the hoop or crafty foul-drawing flops on opponents' offensive moves.

During his tenure, Varejao developed good chemistry with James, showcased especially during the second go-around with deadly pick-and-roll action. James knew just when Varejao was about to roll, and Andy knew LeBron would get him the ball. It was heartbreaking when Varejao tore his Achilles tendon in late December 2014, the kind of injury that was often a career-ender. Indeed, it had ended coach Blatt's European playing career. Successful rehab was not a given.

The other foreign-born player, Matthew Dellavedova, signed with Cleveland as a rookie free agent the year before LeBron's return. Born in Maryborough, Victoria, a small Australian town of 7,500, Dellavedova was the son of an Australian rules football player, and his sisters also all played basketball.

By high school, Dellavedova was a top prep player in Australia. He received a scholarship to play for St. Mary's College of California, where he led the Gaels to the NCAA Tournament three of his four years. He was also on the bubble for the Australian Olympic team. Brett Brown, Philadelphia 76ers coach and one-time Australian Olympic coach, twice had to cut "Delly." Each time Delly fought his way back onto the team.

"It hurt him so much. I have cut many players—none compares to the difficulty of telling Dellavedova," Brown said of the gritty guard. "He mirrors the attitude of the people in that country. Again, they are street fighters. Their mentality is one of tremendous pride. That camaraderie is the pulse of the nation."

Dellavedova was the kind of player whose speed, shot, and athleticism everyone doubted until he proved them wrong with his no-surrender attitude. Blatt in particular saw some of himself in Dellavedova and relied on him heavily throughout the year, even before the results began to show.

That faith was repaid in the playoffs when Delly replaced the injured Irving. He worked so hard stopping Steph Curry in the Cavs' Game 3 victory that he had to be taken to the hospital afterward for intravenous fluids. It was typical Delly—he gave absolutely everything he had (and wasn't quite the same the rest of series).

The final pieces of the puzzle came midway through the 2014-15 season, when GM David Griffin added three crucial parts in center Timofey Mozgov and wings J. R. Smith and Iman Shumpert, essentially for Dion Waiters and two potential future first round draft picks. ("Potential future" because the picks involve various conditions that continue to delay their conveyance.)

Inarguably the biggest piece of the trade—if not the most important— was 7-footer Timofey Mozgov. Blatt gave the late-blooming Mozgov his first real opportunity to shine in 2009 while coaching the Russian team. It raised his profile enough that the Knicks drafted him and gave him a three-year deal.

With a good motor and the ability to run the floor, protect the rim, and step out for the midrange jumper, Mozgov was what you'd want from a prototypical center at a time when such a center was going out of style. While a great shot-blocker and surprisingly agile, he wasn't the floor-stretching, three-point shooting big that had come into vogue. Mozgov's struggles covering players outside the paint sometimes kept him off the court.

Mozgov's biggest issues were his hands and confidence, which were related. He had a tendency to fumble perfect passes while wide open.

Timo would get frustrated and it could sometimes snowball into a series of mistakes on the court. In the off-season he had his knee scoped after several years of discomfort, in hopes of putting up big numbers in his contract year.

J. R. Smith, though, might have been an even more valuable piece of the trade than Mozgov, though nobody would've expected it initially. Smith bypassed college like LeBron, who's a year older. They developed a friendship during the summer AAU circuit and during Smith's time playing for St. Benedict's High School. Smith even trained with James the summer before his jump to the pros.

An impulsive, emotional player, Smith goes on hot streaks capable of bankrupting Vegas. His fallaway jumper rides atop a series of dribble moves that unbalance the defender and provide Smith an opening, but when he's got it going nothing short of a bullet will stop him. He's even better just with the catch-and-shoot, making over 40 percent of such threes over the past three years.

Smith won the 2013 NBA Sixth Man of the Year Award, but when the Knicks slid into mediocrity the next year, his playful side spun into dysfunction. With the Cavaliers and James, though, Smith found a second life. Having turned 30 just before the trade, he admitted that Cleveland's slower nightlife offered a pleasant respite, and the trust Blatt and James showed in him made him want to repay it.

That said, Smith remained a mercurial player. While a surprisingly good on-ball defender, he could sometimes lose track of his man when without it. Similarly, his first (and second and third) impulse is to shoot, which leads to some terrible "heat-check" shots showcasing a snuffed pilot light. Nor did it help that when it came to fouls of the common and flagrant varieties, Smith was magnetic north and the refs were compasses.

That's why with Smith, it's often a case of taking the good with the bad. When he has it going, as he did against the Atlanta Hawks in the playoffs, he can almost single-handedly take out a team. When he wasn't able to move beyond third/fourth option against Golden State, the Cavaliers found themselves outgunned.

Smith's former Knicks running partner, Iman Shumpert, offered a different set of skills. Shumpert's ability to play hardnosed defense, handle the ball, and make three-pointers (hence, spacing the floor) had made him the centerpiece of the trade. But injuries and ineffectiveness soon rendered him almost an afterthought.

Shumpert came to the Cavaliers still rehabbing a shoulder injury, which gave Smith a chance to steal the shooting guard position initially ticketed for him. Shumpert continued to provide a spark off the bench and has the athleticism and demeanor to guard the opponent's best player. Whether it was turnovers dribbling into traffic, bad shots early in the clock, or an inability to avoid the trainer's table, Shump proved more tease than performer his first year with the Cavs, echoing his Knicks history.

Filling out the rest of the roster were players who may have logged less court time, but proved essential to the Cavs' run. James Jones returned for his sixth straight season alongside James. Aside from being a great three-point shooter, Jones was a pro's pro, the veteran voice in the locker room, the player's representative to the union and the go-to guy for a sober, even-handed quote.

At 34, Jones played more in 2014-15 than his prior two seasons in Miami combined. Though typically a small forward, Blatt played him as a stretch 4 to provide floor spacing the team otherwise lacked. However, Jones' skinny frame couldn't offer much resistance defensively against bigs, nor was he truly a threat off the dribble. He was a one-way street at this point, but could drain a three in his sleep, and talk to anyone and everyone in the locker room.

Richard Jefferson is just a few months younger than Jones, but retains a surprising amount of the athleticism that made him a lottery pick in the 2001 draft. Jefferson was a high-flier who developed into a 20-point-a-game scorer, yet gave that up in his prime to be a role player on San Antonio and then Golden State. He still had game left in him, especially in 15- to 20-minute doses.

The son of missionaries, Jefferson was an open-minded, engaging fellow who brought a professional demeanor to the court, disguising his playful behind-the-scenes personality. He joined the team during the early off-season after promising to re-sign with the Dallas Mavericks. When Dallas' disastrous-comic pursuit of DeAndre Jordan went West (back to Los Angeles), owner Mark Cuban gave Jefferson the opportunity to escape his commitment and subsequently sign with the Cavaliers.

These role and bit players gave the performances of their lives to make something special bloom in Cleveland. No one would've been surprised if the effort failed to take root in such cold, hard-bitten ground, but like a fan, a ballplayer is nowhere without his unwavering belief. Sometimes it's not misplaced.

REGULAR SEASON

4

IF FIRST YOU
DON'T SUCCEED...

DESPITE THE LOSS to Golden State in the 2015 Finals, Cleveland's summer off-season emanated an air of possibility. The Cavaliers had pushed the Warriors to six games without Love and minus Irving for all but one game of the series. A favorable call on one of LeBron James' fourth quarter Game 1 drives or a bucket on his last shot in regulation and the Cavs maight have been up 3-0 and on the verge of an enormous upset.

GM David Griffin's actions echoed this sentiment, as he decided to retain the core pieces and work around the fringes. The first move was re-signing Kevin Love. After a year during which journalists incessantly hounded Love about whether he might pull a runaway bride, Love did just what he had said all along. On July 1, 2015, he signed a five-year contract worth around $110 million.

It's not that Love didn't consider his options. In a video on the athlete-run website The Players' Tribune, he said it weighed heavily on him. Before signing, Love met with James at a poolside cabana in Los Angeles where the King holds his annual skills camp for high school and college players.

"We talked everything out. A lot of stuff was very honest and we came to a really good place," Love said. "I expressed this to LeBron and he had been through it a couple times now. I can actually go wherever I want to play for, but every time I went through the different scenarios I always came out at the same place—that was to be in Cleveland and to try to win championships."

In signing a contract without an opt-out or player option, Love missed out on an opportunity to sign a shorter contract and take advantage of the rising salary cap max, a yearly rite recently for James. Love seemed relieved simply to put the questions to rest.

"I always say chase what you love and everything you love will chase you right back—that's happiness," said Love. "So now I just get to focus on the game I grew up watching. I grew up watching the Finals, watching the superstar tapes, getting my ass beat by my dad in the driveway.... The truth is that after we lost [in the Finals] there was a sense of unfinished business. So that's where everything is left."

Love wasn't the only one cashing in on Griffin's generosity. The Cavaliers' other free agent, Tristan Thompson, engaged in a protracted stalemate that lasted through training camp. Some thought that because James' agent, Rich Paul, represented Thompson, LeBron's contract might be leverage that Paul could use to open up the bank for Tristan.

Yet on July 10 James signed another two-year deal (with the second-year a player option) for $47 million. Thompson had turned down a four-year, $52 million offer during the season, and was looking for a max contract. NBA maximums are based on years of service and the size of the cap. For Thompson, this meant he wanted a contract for either three years/$53 million or five years/$94 million.

That's an unprecedented contract for a player who had been a sixth man/energy big off the bench. Yet Thompson was only 24 years old with room to improve and the cap would explode in a year, making yearly salaries in the mid-teens the province of merely above average/good starters. By the end of his contract—so the argument went—Thompson might be a bargain.

After plenty of posturing by both sides, Thompson signed for less than the max, accepting a five-year, $82 million contract on October 21, two days after the last preseason game. "It's been a long summer of grinding and hard work," Tristan tweeted, "but now it's back to The Land to take care of some unfinished business."

Several days before training camp, Iman Shumpert—who had signed a four-year, $40 million contract on July 1—injured his hand during informal workouts. Ironically, Shumpert hurt his wrist on the rim attempting an alley-oop. He'd had less serious mishaps at the rim the year before, missing a third of his 30 dunk attempts.

The injury—a ruptured extensor carpi ulnaris sheath—required surgery and 10 to 12 weeks of rest, postponing his return until December. Meanwhile, Kevin Love was still rehabbing his injured right shoulder at the start of camp, and only played in the final two preseason games. He would lift after games much of the season to compensate for his inability to lift in the off-season and better prepare his body for the grueling season without sacrificing recovery time.

Even LeBron James was not immune, battling back issues. Throughout the preseason and early regular season, James performed balance ball exercises for his back in the locker room before the game. LeBron sat on his knees on a huge inflatable ball, and trainers tossed balls to him as he strove to stay balanced.

The team blamed James' intense off-season regimen, which he had taken to another level following the loss to Golden State. He did three workouts a day five days a week in Miami beginning in September to prepare for the season. The sore back seemed to suggest he overdid it, but Griffin criticized the staff, not James.

"I'm really, really disappointed that we didn't do a better job as an organization of keeping him from doing three-a-days this off-season," Griffin said.

The injury was serious enough to elicit a facet injection on October 13, after two games, to ease inflammation in his lumbar region. He sat the rest of the preseason. The shot was similar to the one he'd received covertly in December the year before, which also required two weeks of rest, though the team didn't reveal the true reason for James' 2014-15 holiday break until much later.

"I will take all the pain that comes with competing for a championship at the end of the day," said James. "I'll take all the bumps and bruises that I get when I'm playing because I know that I left it all out on the floor."

Opening Night. Tuesday, October 27, 2015, Chicago. (0-0)

Due to the injuries, the Cavaliers couldn't accomplish much in training camp. New faces Mo Williams and Richard Jefferson saw serious minutes, as did returning players Timofey Mozgov, Matthew Dellavedova, Anderson Varejao, and J. R. Smith. Yet the number of unfamiliar players produced poor or uneven play, as the Cavs lost every preseason game before winning the finale, 103-97 over Dallas.

The Cavaliers opened the season 10 days later in Chicago, and the President of the United States was on hand for the game. This Bulls team would prove but a pale shadow of the team that had battled the Cavaliers the year before under coach Tom Thibodeau, winning eight fewer games.

Former NBA player and Iowa State coach Fred Hoiberg had taken over the Bulls in June on a five-year, $25 million contract with the expectation that he might invigorate the offense. (Strong defense and muddled offense long characterized Thibodeau's teams.) They came out sharp enough, jumping out to a 26-17 lead that the Cavaliers spent the next two quarters chipping away at.

Mo Williams, replacing the injured Kyrie Irving for the first month or two, hit his third three of the evening to tie the score at 71 early in the fourth quarter. He finished with 19. The Cavaliers took the lead 83-82 on a James hoop, but Bulls forward Nikola Mirotic scored five points in an 11-2 run as the Bulls retook the lead, 93-85.

The Cavaliers didn't surrender. Kevin Love hit a couple threes and two free throws in a 60-second stretch to close the lead to two with 33 seconds left. When Derrick Rose missed a jumper, the Cavaliers had a chance to inbound with 10 seconds left.

Thompson screened for James, forcing Pau Gasol to switch onto him as he drove to the rim. But LeBron didn't get enough extension or the foul call—Gasol was holding James' left arm before takeoff—and Gasol blocked it out of bounds with three seconds left. The Bulls stole Williams' subsequent inbounds attempt to end the game.

The opening day loss echoed the preseason's discontinuity and lack of focus with bursts of inspired play. Cleveland would need time to round into shape. It took less than 24 hours.

The Cavaliers played in Memphis the next night and mauled the Grizzlies 106-76, fueled by a 26-10 first quarter. More bench players (Dellavedova, Jefferson, Jared Cunningham) hit double figures than starters (James and leading scorer Love with 17), as the Cavs won every quarter. After the Memphis win, James sounded like Love's biggest cheerleader, suggesting that the bearded Banana Republic model would be the straw stirring the drink—chocolate milk presumably.

"Kevin is going to be our main focus. He's going to have a hell of a season. He's going to get back to that All-Star status. He's the focal point of us offensively," James said. "I can go out and get mine when I need it. But I need Kev to be as aggressive as he was tonight."

Blatt made it an off-season goal to incorporate sets into the offense what would take full advantage of Love's skills. In his first season, the Cavs often posted him up early in the first quarter, but he'd often gradually disappear, becoming little more than a corner catch-and-shoot weapon for long stretches.

That year Love shot 45 percent from the field, 40 percent from three, and took 7.7 shots in the first half. In the second half he shot 40 percent and 33 percent while taking 5.1 shots a game. It's just hard to stay in rhythm without touches.

The plan was to make Love a more organic part of the offense all game long. Kevin began screening for LeBron, popping out to the three-point line or "slipping the screen" (pretending to screen and then cutting toward the basket) and establishing himself in the post with his back to the basket.

"[It's] our desire to put him in positions to carry the offense a little more," GM David Griffin said told the *Portland Tribune* in December. "When we work through him, it's easier for [teammates] to take a bit of a break on the offensive end."

With Irving injured there was more room on the floor for Love and increased call for his skills. When starting guards Williams and Smith shot a collective 3-for-18 from the field in Miami, Love picked it up with 24 points, 14 boards, and five assists in a 102-92 win over the Heat.

The Cavaliers won eight in a row after the loss to the Bulls, but the wins grew progressively less impressive despite wide disparities in talent. It was the season's first indication that the Cavaliers might grow bored with success and play down to their competition.

The sixth game of the season, against the lowly 76ers, offered a hint of things to come. Cleveland fell behind the 76ers 50-49 at halftime, requiring an 18-point third quarter from James (31 points) to retake the lead and hold on for a 108-102 victory. Love finished with just 12 points on 5-of-16 shooting.

James Jones, who called out the team's play and LeBron in particular during halftime of the 76ers game, lit into Love at the half of their next game as well. "He wanted to get me going," said Love. "It's no secret. We've had a lot of conversations over the past, not only last year, but leading up into this season. He's a guy that's a leader. When he speaks up, we listen."

It was a tough half against the Pacers for Love, as he missed a layup and committed a couple of turnovers. He was 1-of-6 with three points and seven boards in 18 minutes. It wasn't a terrible half. He did a decent job defending Jordan Hill, though, c'mon, Jordan Hill?

LeBron told Love, "If he would just get his motor going offensively the ball would start to go in for him." Kevin turned up his effort and James followed through, finding him on a backdoor cut for a layup with 27 seconds left and then a dunk with eight seconds left for the winning margin in the 101-97 victory.

"LeBron talked to me at halftime—just got me going, that's all it was," said Love. "I mentioned to him I kind of wanted to just free-flow and get myself near the basket and that's what I did. I got myself into a good rhythm rebounding the ball."

It would take a 17-3 burst midway through the fourth quarter to overcome the Jazz at home 118-114, giving fans reason to worry their longest road trip so far of the season would bring disappointment. The first night in New York it almost did, as again Love struggled to be a scoring threat in Kyrie's absence, managing just 11 points on 13 shots.

"We didn't have it going offensively," Blatt said afterward. "Defensively in the first half we weren't where we needed to be and where we normally are. Some games you have to win without your fastball and this was another of those games."

That meant James. With the scored tied at 82, he tied Carmelo Anthony up in the post and forced him into a traveling violation. Then with 75 seconds left, James backed Anthony down by the right elbow and, after a head and shoulder fake, nailed a fallaway jumper for the 84-82 lead. Arron Afflalo would tie the game again at 84, but Williams' 17-foot jumper the following possession sealed a 90-84 win.

"We've been playing against each other since I was a sophomore and he was a junior," said James of his late-game showdown with Anthony. "Every single year we've been playing against each other from Colorado Springs at the Junior Olympics through high school all the way to the NBA. Obviously we know each other personally and we know each other's games, but it's hard to stop each other."

The Knicks game was the front end of the dreaded back-to-back, both on the road. In recent years the league had reduced the number of back-to-backs and the even worse four-games-in-five-nights because of player fatigue and the increased threat of injury.

As recently as 2010 the league had an outer limit of 23 back-to-backs and four "four-in-fives." This season the league culled those limits to 20 and two, with Cleveland enduring 19 back-to-backs and a single four-in-five-nights, occurring over the Christmas holiday.

James usually picks up his performance on the road to help carry his mates (role players typically perform better at home). He scored 37 against the Bucks including five threes, and Love chipped in 24, but the Cavs struggled to score outside that pair while the Bucks put seven players in double figures.

The effort was sloppy and unfocused for the first 36 minutes as the Bucks took an 80-71 lead into the fourth. The Cavs outscored the Bucks 17-6 over the final six minutes, but Love and James each missed free throws in the stretch that could've prevented overtime.

Cleveland missed 10 free throws and shot 63 percent from the line. Play declined from there, as James seemed to run out of juice. He committed four turnovers in the two overtimes, including two offensive fouls, had a shot blocked, missed a layup and two free throws, and finished 6-of-12 from the line.

James ripped the team's intensity afterward, saying, "We have to play with a lot more sustainable effort throughout the 48 minutes. And we don't do that. We give a half-assed effort sometimes and expect that we can just make a run at the end. We're not good enough to do that right now."

Wasted Charity. Tuesday, November 17, Detroit. (8-2)

The team had two days off before the final road game three hours north in Detroit. The rest didn't do any good as they again failed to sustain their focus. After falling behind early, the Cavaliers tightened up in the middle quarters, outscoring the Pistons by 10 and taking a six-point lead into the last stanza. Detroit roasted Cleveland 25-12 over the final seven and a half minutes, with Pistons center Andre Drummond scoring 11 of his team-high 25 points down the stretch. James finished with 30 points and Love had 19.

The Cavaliers settled for the three too much, going 11-of-33 from beyond the arc but 27-of-47 (57 percent) within it. They also missed too many free throws (12-of-20, 60 percent) as Timofey Mozgov, J. R. Smith, and James Jones all missed two free throws. James and Mo Williams missed one apiece. Cleveland was 29th in the league in free throw percentage at the time. (They finished the season 21st.)

"We've got to practice it a little bit more," said James afterward. "We're just out of rhythm as a team as far as shooting free throws and it's key. Tonight we didn't shoot well again. I think we missed eight or even more than that. At one point when we had a lead in the third we missed five in a row. We can't put ourselves in that position."

One of the great things about LeBron James is that he holds himself to a higher standard than anyone. When James called out teammates on their free throw shooting, he was shooting 62 percent. From that point in mid-November until Christmas Eve he shot 84 percent.

It didn't persist. He shot 70 percent from Christmas until the All-Star break, then shot 77 percent from the break until the season's end, finishing the season at 73 percent. It's interesting LeBron shot better in playoff losses and away (mostly one in the same) than at home, perhaps marshalling keener focus. However, the most salient variable in any circumstance appears to be how many days of rest he had enjoyed.

James' FT Percentage	Wins	Losses	Home	Away	Days of Rest			
					0	1	2	3-5
2016 Playoffs	63%	80%	59%	73%		62%	71%	88%
2016 Reg. Season	74%	71%	74%	72%	69%	71%	82%	90%

James also called out the team's focus and attention to detail, suggesting they'd become complacent. That was no surprise to anyone who had seen them. Even without Irving they seemed to coast through stretches of the game without always putting in full effort, failing to grind their boot heel into an opponent's windpipe when given the chance to put them away early.

"We expect that we're a great basketball team, and we're not," James said. "We have too many down periods during the game mentally. You can't play down to the competition because we're not better than nobody in the league. We got so much work to do at this point. We shouldn't feel entitled. We're not entitled to a win. We're not entitled to being Eastern Conference champions. That was last year."

Cleveland returned home on November 19 to avenge the Bucks loss, ambushing them in the second quarter with LeBron on the bench and Love leading the reserves. They put together a 15-6 run keyed by Love's nine points, giving the Cavs a ten-point lead, which ballooned to 21 before half.

Milwaukee fought back in the third, cutting the lead to 86-79 at the start of the fourth, but the Cavs hung tough 115-100, aided by nine second half points from Anderson Varejao, his season high. Blatt had been hesitant to use Varejao, who still hadn't fully recovered from his off-season Achilles injury.

It became a necessity when Mozgov strained his right deltoid and left early in the second quarter. (He'd be sidelined the next 10 days.) Andy played 11 minutes and said he felt good, but would only manage that many minutes for Cleveland a dozen times during the year.

The Cavaliers maintained their momentum in a blowout of the Atlanta Hawks that started out innocuously enough. The Hawks were up 17-16 with five minutes to go when Cleveland made an 11-2 run to close the first up 27-19. The lead grew to 15 at half and 26 with six minutes left in the third.

That's when Jared Cunningham threw LeBron James—posted up on the right block—an entry pass two feet from his grasp. James became so frustrated he simply walked off the floor and took a seat on the bench. Nobody could recall ever seeing anything like it. Certainly not when up by 26, and after the Cavs had hit five of their last six shots!

"I blew a gasket," James said. "I apologized to my teammates for it."

Cleveland received a technical, and Blatt made light of it in the postgame presser. "He thought we were playing hockey," Blatt joked. "LeBron is a lot of things, a lot of great things, but probably we're not going to see him out there playing for the [New York] Rangers. I understand his frustration but obviously he shouldn't do that."

Blatt noted before the Magic game that the team wasn't "playing right," and the team obliged by going out and demonstrating what he meant. Cleveland allowed Orlando to shoot 56 percent in the first half and hang close, 59-55, despite 27 first half points by Kevin Love, including five three-pointers. He finished with a season-high 34.

"We were sort of running alongside the game defensively in the first half. In the second half we imposed our will and that was the difference," said Blatt.

The Cavs outscored Orlando 33-21 in the third quarter behind 11 points from Smith, who finished with 26 (one off his eventual season high). That was his first game of 20+ points on the season. It would be five weeks before he had another (coinciding with Kyrie's return).

After the game, James was told he'd joined Oscar Robertson as the only players among the NBA's top 25 in both career points and assists. "For me all I care about is winning," he said, unimpressed. "I have enough stats."

Cleveland's penetration issues flared again in Toronto the day before Thanksgiving. Matthew Dellavedova sat with a calf injury and Cunningham got the start while Williams contributed 15 points off the bench. Even without starting center Jonas Valanciunas, Toronto shot 59 percent at the rim and beat the Cavaliers 52-28 on points in the paint. Cleveland's three-point shooting (14-of-29) kept them in the game.

The back-and-forth game featured 19-2 runs by each team. The Cavaliers went up 84-82 on Williams' 19-foot pull-up with just under nine minutes left. They didn't make another basket until Williams hit a floater with 3:15 left. By then the Cavs were down 94-87. They'd never get significantly closer, though two Smith three-pointers in the last 30 seconds offered a more respectable 103-99 margin.

Toronto's backup big man, Bismack Biyombo, who started for Valanciunas, figured in an animated postgame locker room discussion helmed by LeBron James. Biyombo had six rebounds and six points in the final frame, including two uncontested dunks in the last minute.

LeBron and James Jones led a(nother) postgame players meeting to discuss the team's lack of physicality, will, and defensive presence at the end of the third and into the fourth. Blatt made excuses. ("We are very shorthanded," he said. "I thought our guys played hard. I thought we ran out of gas.") But James expected more.

"We have to hold each other more accountable, we got to play better, and we will," James said, demonstrating this by proceeding to discuss the defensive breakdowns of Love, Williams, Smith, and Jones during the second half with them as the media stood within earshot.

Going into Charlotte on November 27, Cleveland had lost three straight road games. The Hornets were hot after opening the season with three losses; they'd won nine of 12 and seven in a row at home. James, however, had won his last 20 games against Charlotte.

The Cavs defense did a decent job containing Kemba Walker (10 first half points, 18 points and four assists for the game), but lacked ball movement on offense, producing six assists against six turnovers, and trailed 52-50 at half.

Cleveland trailed by seven midway through the third when LeBron flipped the switch. He scored 11 over the next five minutes, sparking a 15-10 Cleveland run. But Charlotte got off to a quick start in the fourth and pushed the lead back to seven

It was another case of the Cavs waiting until the last moment to hit turbo and flash that checkered-flag horsepower. With 10 minutes left Blatt inserted Dellavedova for Williams to lead a small lineup featuring Jefferson, Thompson, and James in the frontcourt. They ended the game on a 20-6 run to prevail 95-88.

Afterward, James commented on his 11-point outburst. "I was just trying to be aggressive," he said. "[Assistant] coach Lue told me to be aggressive, and I just tried to answer the call."

This comment weighs heavier in retrospect. Lue had lots of interaction with players as the Cavs' defensive coordinator, yet James credited his *offensive* encouragement and not Blatt, recalling James' prior perceived sleights of his head coach.

Not yet a team to build on past wins, the Cavs followed that hard-fought Charlotte road victory with a bare-knuckle ride against one of the league's worst teams, the Brooklyn Nets. It took a LeBron runner from the right elbow over 7-footer Brook Lopez's outstretched arm with seconds left to seal the 90-88 home win.

Afterward James expressed his appreciation for his teammates to sideline reporter Allie Clifton. "I know I get on them a lot," James said. "But I get on them so much because I love them and I want them to be great. They allow me to make plays like that."

Though the Cavaliers led the Eastern Conference they had shown a disturbing tendency to save their best for the fourth quarter after three quarters of intermittent intensity.

"[We're] not as focused in different areas of the game on both sides of the ball as we need to be," Blatt said. "That's part of disciplining themselves, but we try to play at a high level all the time."

On the positive side, Kevin Love was thriving as the number two option with 19.8 points and 11.8 rebounds a game, coupled with strong shooting percentages (46 percent field goal, 41 percent three-pointers). Mo Williams had stepped up as a third option (13.7 points, 50 percent field goal, 35 percent three-point), and Dellavedova was averaging 5.9 assists a game off the bench. Unfortunately, the impending return of Iman Shumpert and Kyrie Irving would impact all three.

5

NO INSTANT OATMEAL

WHILE THE CLEVELAND Cavaliers ended November sitting somewhat complacently atop the Eastern Conference with their 13-4 record, the defending champion Golden State Warriors set upon the 2015-16 season like a sand-specked Charles Atlas. They were frustrated by the perception that their 2015 title was fluky or lucky.

They'd avoided perceived powerhouses—the San Antonio Spurs and Los Angeles Clippers—who faced off against each other in the first round due to the preferential seeding granted to division winners (since changed). Then the Clippers became just the eighth NBA team ever to choke away a 3-1 series lead, losing to the Houston Rockets.

Meanwhile, every team the Warriors faced in the 2015 playoffs struggled with crushing injuries to their starting point guard (Jrue Holiday, Mike Conley, Patrick Beverley, Kyrie Irving), the player putatively tasked with blanketing the Warriors top weapon, Steph Curry. This while Golden State enjoyed perfect health all postseason and opponents endured injuries to other contributors as well, such as Tyreke Evans, Tony Allen, and Kevin Love.

Perhaps stung by skepticism, Golden State began the year on a mission. They broke the record (15) for most wins to start the season and took aim at the most wins in a row (33). Counting four wins from the prior year, they made it to 28 before losing in Milwaukee. The loss came on the last night of a two-week, seven-game road trip, on the back end of a back-to-back, after a double-overtime win over the Boston Celtics the previous night.

If the Warriors hadn't lost to Milwaukee, a Christmas Day win would've tied the NBA record of 33 straight regular season wins in a row. Even without that incentive the Warriors' efforts loomed over the Cavs, who went from presumptive preseason favorite to an also-ran.

After the November loss to the Pistons, James belittled the Cavs' effort, saying, "We lost in the Finals. We didn't win. And the team that beat us looks more hungry than we are. It shouldn't be that way."

A week later, James would laud Golden State's consistency while also hinting the Cavaliers hadn't been nearly so fortunate health-wise.

"The most impressive thing is the way they've been playing at a high level for so long," James said. "They've been the most healthy team I've ever seen in NBA history, and they have great talent. Those guys all play for one common goal and that's to win."

In a *New York Post* quote in early December, James almost evinced a note of jealousy toward Curry. "I'm very impressed with just the way they continue to play the game the right way," he said. "They move the ball, share the ball, play at a huge tempo every single night. The head of the snake is Steph, and *everyone falls in line.*" [Our emphasis.]

Curry had won the 2014-15 Most Valuable Player Award, and with the Warriors' ascendance he increasingly appeared to be the new face of the NBA. He grinned with insouciance that echoed his equally effortless confidence and long-range shooting prowess.

It's interesting to note their different backgrounds. Curry was also born in Akron (March 18, 1988) when his NBA dad, sweet-shooting Dell Curry, played for the Cavaliers near the beginning of his career. Stephen wasn't a great physical specimen in high school, weighing 160 pounds soaking wet, and didn't generate a lot of recruiting fanfare. His father's alma mater, Virginia Tech, wouldn't offer him a scholarship, so Steph attended Davidson.

Curry starred at Davidson and was an All-American as a sophomore (second team) and junior (first team), leading the Wildcats to the Elite Eight and second round of the NCAA tournament, respectively, before turning pro. He was selected seventh by Golden State in the 2009 NBA Draft. Though no longer unsung, he wasn't a player anyone expected to win back-to-back MVPs.

The teams seemed to reflect their different personas. Curry and backcourt mate Klay Thompson keyed the Warriors' loose, free-wheeling vibe with carte blanche to shoot whenever and wherever they chose. Everyone shared the ball and moved without it. Reporters genuflected at their feet like the Warriors had unearthed basketball nirvana.

Meanwhile Cleveland had LeBron James, who catalyzes traffic-stopping media cacophonies at a pitch similar to dropping an alkali metal into water. James is arguably the most relentlessly driven player in basketball, and nobody holds higher expectations for himself or his teammates. It's possible to imagine where that intensity could create a tense atmosphere at times.

"If you're here for any other reason than to get better and help us win, then you're here for the wrong reason," J. R. Smith told *GQ* in their December issue. "And he'll tell anybody that—he doesn't care. You could be mad at him or whatever. If you're not here to win? Time for you to go."

Smith, who the article notes was once rated the NBA's hardest partier based on his performances on Sunday versus the rest of the week, claims city nightlife isn't even a consideration once you've joined James' Night's Watch.

"You would never go out and party on this team," said Smith. "Once you're on a team like this, you're just so locked in. When you see someone like LeBron in the gym around the clock? Usually it's the guys who want to get better so they can get more playing time who are always in the gym. But if you've got four MVPs, two championships, two Finals MVPs...?"

Smith put it in perspective for *Akron Beacon Journal*'s Marla Ridenour during the playoffs. "For me he's the crossing guard," he said. "Nobody goes without him saying, 'Go,' and nobody stops without him saying, 'Stop.'"

Three Game Skid. Tuesday, December 1, 2015, Cleveland. (13-4)

Cleveland greeted December like the patsy to a crime, dull-eyed and befuddled. Continuing a gnawing habit of slow breaks out of the gate, the Cavs fell behind Washington 10-0 in the game's first two and a half minutes before Blatt called a timeout.

They battled back to trail 27-24 after one, and the lead was still three when James caught a breather with eight minutes left in the second. Two and a half minutes later the lead had grown to 10, and to 52-41 by half. (The Cavs suffered all season when he left the floor; they were +11 per 48 minutes when James was on the floor and -4.8 when he wasn't.)

Goateed Wizards center Marcin Gortat repeatedly abused Timofey Mozgov for 10 first quarter points, resulting in Mozgov's benching at the six-minute mark. This was his third game back after sitting 10 days with a shoulder strain, but to watch him play you might have wondered if he'd been out a month.

Mozgov had as many turnovers as points (10) in 44 minutes across those three games, which incredibly included a back-to-back. It was another case where the hardworking Russian leviathan showed more courage than wisdom in pushing his body.

For years he'd dealt with a cyst behind his knee, an issue that grew more painful as the season wore on. The off-season surgery to remove it had been deemed a success, but he still had pain in the knee. Just normal, post-surgery breakup of scar tissue, he was told.

But its persistence wasn't normal, and by season's end it'd be rumored that Mozgov would need to go back under the knife. He probably should've rehabbed more cautiously and not returned so quickly, but it was a contract year and Blatt wanted his big man. Mozgov's difficulty reaching the previous year's playoff level haunted the Cavs and informed their approach the second half of the season.

The Wizards fastbreaked off turnovers, rebounds, and even made shots. Their pace and John Wall's propensity for pushing the ball unnerved the Cavs. But it wasn't like the halfcourt defense gave him trouble either. The Wizards guard finished the half with 21 points and four assists.

Like many recent opponents, Washington roasted the Cavaliers in the high pick-and-roll, exploiting the defense of starting guard Mo Williams. Mozgov was supposed to provide rim protection, but his help rotations were slow and ineffectual. Without vintage Mozgov, Williams' inability to stay in front of his man could be debilitating, though Dellavedova didn't fare any better with Wall.

Mozgov came out to start the second half and immediately fumbled a potential James alley-oop, traveled, and committed an offensive foul in his first three possessions. The only thing missing from the fiery carnage was Herb Morrison saying, "Oh, the humanity."

"I don't think we have him at his full strength and conditioning level in order to give us the things he normally does," said Blatt after the game. "He has to push the envelope and we want to push it, to get him back to where he needs to be. A big part of that is going to be in-game play."

Blatt ultimately exiled Mozgov to the bench but by then the lead was

17; it would balloon to 69-47 early in the third. The Cavaliers got no closer than 12 the rest of the way.

"We didn't play with pace," Blatt said. "We didn't get back on defense and we didn't take care of the ball. Washington is a team that does extremely well when you don't do those two things."

They got off to a better start three days later against New Orleans, taking a 27-21 lead thanks to five first quarter three-pointers by J. R. Smith. Blatt made Dellavedova the starter, a move that might've angered Williams. Delly responded by scoring in double figures five of the next seven games and averaging almost five assists. He had eight points and four assists against New Orleans.

The Pelicans outplayed the Cavs in the middle quarters, shooting 63 percent and outscoring them 63-50, to take a seven-point lead into the fourth. New Orleans led 94-81 when James staged a solo blitzkrieg.

He made eight of nine in the final six minutes for 21 points. Seven of those baskets were at or near the rim. The one miss was a runner from the left elbow that would've won it in regulation. The Cavs lost in overtime, after they called on players to shoot that really hadn't touched the ball since LeBron took over. While Love scored his only post-halftime points in overtime, he and Smith were a collective 1-of-5 in OT as New Orleans won 114-108.

"We did not play a 48-minute game," said James. "It's either one or two guys that break down and it breaks the whole team down. Until we find the right matchups, the right lineups that guys are going to play 48 minutes or when they're on the floor they'll play their minutes the right way, we're going to continue to have stretches where we let guys get to the rim or make shots on us and then we have to dig ourselves back out of that hole."

Cavaliers announcer Austin Carr zeroed in on a different issue. He noted that the Cavaliers struggled defensively at the point of attack, allowing guards to penetrate the lane and cause havoc in the pick-and-roll, particularly the high pick-and-roll, occurring at the top of the key/three-point arc. Making Delly the starter appeared an attempt to address this shortcoming.

"They do not defend the high pick-and-roll well," Carr said. "There's always a small team and that's what they run—the high pick-and-roll—and if they're doing that it's part of the scouting report, because it happens every game. When [the Cavaliers] try to blitz, [opponents] just back out and run it again until the Cavs eventually let them have a driving lane. They have to find a way to slow that down because that's become a major problem."

The late game meant Cleveland's plane didn't land in Miami until 5 a.m. The early morning arrival and 45 minutes James logged against the Pelicans prompted Blatt to sit LeBron, allegedly displeasing his star.

The Cavaliers fell to 0-4 playing without either James or Irving, losing to the Heat 99-84 in a game in which they trailed by 17 late in the first quarter and didn't get closer. The Miami loss marked the end of Thompson's eight-game streak of double-figure rebounds. It coincided with Mozgov's shoulder injury and was the longest such streak of Tristan's career, regular or postseason. He seemed to have reached game shape after missing training camp with the holdout.

The defense's penetration troubles continued at home versus the Portland Trailblazers, led by the quick, high-scoring guard tandem of Damian Lillard and CJ McCollum. The Blazers opened the game by hitting seven of nine shots, and started the second quarter making nine of 10. Mozgov sat after seven empty minutes in the first quarter, never to return. Down 37-21 with three gone in the second, Blatt brought in Dellavedova for Williams, teaming him with Jared Cunningham. They proved sturdy enough at the point of attack to stop the bleeding.

Cunningham is a former first round draft pick from Oregon State who played for the Mavericks, Hawks, and Clippers, but never saw much time. He stuck after training camp because of his willingness to dig in and defend, abetted by enough quickness to handle point guards and size to handle off-guards. Flashes of driving ability were a bonus.

A small run at the end of the second that cut the 16-point lead to nine gave the Cavs a boost, and Cleveland started the second half purposefully. They came out physically, opening the quarter with an 18-5 run fueled by Jefferson, Smith, and Dellavedova threes. James had half of the team's 28 fourth quarter points while Cleveland held Portland to 38 percent shooting to wrangle the 105-100 victory.

The Gang's All Here. Friday, December 11, 2015, Orlando. (15-7)

Cleveland finished a quick two-game road trip to Orlando and Boston by positively blowing out the Magic again on December 11, and beating the Celtics behind a dominant second half defensive performance the next night. After (again) falling behind in the first half—as they had eight of their last 15 games—the Cavs held the Celtics to 26 percent shooting in the second half while shooting above 50 percent themselves.

Mozgov rebounded from the bad Portland game with two of his best games to date. He scored 17 points in the Orlando blowout and then scored nine points, grabbed 10 rebounds, and blocked three shots versus Boston. Shumpert returned against the Magic and scored six against the Celtics. The injury issues didn't dissipate immediately, though. No sooner had Shumpert returned than Williams injured his thumb late, forcing him to sit the next two games against Boston and Oklahoma City.

The injury struggles and related lack of continuity manifested in a poor second quarter defense (mostly the reserves' fault, but partly the starters' too, in fairness). Cleveland was 29th in defensive effective field goal percentage (54.5) and allowed the seventh highest free throw rate during the second quarter to that point. While Kyrie's imminent return offered hope, James squelched the idea that it would solve everything.

"There's only one guy ever in the world that everything is going go be all right when he comes back and that's Jesus Christ," James said. "Other than that you can't bank on nobody being okay."

The Cavs returned home to face the Oklahoma City Thunder, owners of the third-best record in the Western Conference (17-8) behind the Warriors and Spurs. Shumpert and Williams both sat, leaving the Cavaliers shorthanded again. Fortunately others stepped up, including Cunningham, who played 13 scrappy minutes, many of them on cruise missile Russell Westbrook, and Richard Jefferson, who added 13, including a trio of threes.

Even Mozgov played well, replacing Kevin Love after he picked up his second foul with four gone in the second quarter. Over the next five minutes the Thunder could manage only a single point while the Cavaliers ran off 18, including 14 by Smith and Dellavedova, to take a 47-46 halftime lead.

Oklahoma City took a 10-point lead in the third before the Cavs tightened the defensive vice, holding the Thunder without a basket for seven minutes across the third and fourth quarters, outscoring them 22-7. Nick Collison hit a reverse layup that cut the lead to 83-80, but the Cavs answered with an 8-0 run featuring threes by Cunningham and Jefferson to push the lead to 11. The Thunder couldn't recover, thanks in part to James' defense on Durant, who shot 1-of-5 in the last frame.

"Each time that we went down eight, 10 points, we never let them get away from us," said Blatt. "They had us a few times and we didn't break. Coming back at the end of the third and then coming out well in the beginning of the fourth was significant emotionally and mentally…to me that was what was the difference."

Kyrie Irving returned to the lineup on December 20 with 12 points in 18 minutes of the Cavaliers' 108-86 home win over the Philadelphia 76ers. When Williams returned for the game against New York two days later, the Cavs finally had their full complement of players for the first time, 26 games into season. (Irving still hadn't been cleared for back-to-back games.)

Despite a full roster, the absence of injured star Carmelo Anthony (sprained ankle) from the Knicks lineup accompanied a Cavaliers letdown. It wouldn't be the last time Cleveland lost focus when an opposing star sat. New York rallied behind strong play from Derrick Williams, Arron Afflalo, and talented Latvian 7-foot rookie Kristaps Porzingis, taking an 82-80 lead with four minutes left.

The Cavs closed the game with an 11-2 flourish, with seven of the points by LeBron James, who finished with 23. Kevin Love added 23 and 13 boards, while Irving was dreadfully off with 1-of-7 shooting in his first start, playing just under 20 minutes.

After the game the team boarded a plane to Golden State for a Christmas Day rematch against the Western Conference's top team. It was not only that day's marquee matchup, but the kickoff to the dreaded four-games-in-five, all of them on the road. The Cavs would return for two home games and then leave again for a six-game, ten-day road trip, which concluded with their only home game of the season against the Warriors.

While Irving was obviously still rusty after only two games back, and Shumpert hadn't found his rhythm, at least they were all back. The Warriors were actually shorthanded, playing without starting small forward Harrison Barnes, but they were playing at home, where they'd won 49 of their last 50 regular season games.

Both teams came out with good energy. Blatt's plan, like in the playoffs, was to slow the game down to limit Golden State's transition opportunities. Cleveland ran motion sets to start the game, and it remained tight early on. Mozgov made a couple nice defensive plays early, but came up Lilliputian in every other way, going scoreless, missing five shots (three of them blocked), making three fouls, and fumbling a LeBron under-the-bucket dish out of bounds.

After falling behind 28-19 at the end of one, the Cavaliers made a 9-0 run early in the second to tie the score at 35. They took a 40-37 lead before the Warriors put a Draymond Green layup and Klay Thompson tip-in around four free throws to retake the lead 45-42 at half. Irving opened the third quarter with a 20-foot pull-up jumper to close the deficit to one, but Cleveland never got closer.

Six times in the second half the Cavaliers pulled within three points but couldn't get over the hump. Their shooting deserted them, as they shot 32 percent for the game including 17 percent (5-of-30) from behind the boundary.

The Cavs' best chance came with 90 seconds left. They trailed 81-77, and LeBron stood at the line for two free throws. He missed them both, and on the following possession Curry scored on a layup to push the lead to six. A Smith three would halve the lead, but again Curry darted through the lane for a layup.

With the Cavs down four again with 20 second left, James could only convert one of two free throws. Cleveland fouled Iguodala, who missed both of his shots, creating another opening, but James missed another three and the Warriors made the rest of their free throws for an 89-83 win. Outside of Smith, Cleveland was 1-of-22 from the arc.

The Cavs only stayed in it by dominating the offensive boards (17 offensive rebounds) and limiting their turnovers (11 to the Warriors' 16). As a result the Cavs had 17 more shots, but only two more baskets. Their chance for vengeance lay less than a month away in Cleveland.

That Jefferson didn't play or Mo Williams only saw four first half minutes—yielding their time to Shumpert and Dellavedova whom Blatt trusted defensively—took on added significance a month later.

"For the first time, for a long period of time, we had some different lineups out there," said James. "Against a championship team like this, it's hard to do that on the fly. We're not making excuses—we still got to be a lot better, still got to move the ball, got to share the ball, get it moving from side to side—but offensively we were all out of rhythm. You credit their defense, for sure, and then our lack of detail."

Hangover or Sabotage? Saturday, December 26, 2015, Portland. (19-8)

If the Cavaliers suffered from a lack of detail against the Warriors, somebody positively shook the Etch-a-Sketch before the Trailblazers game the next day. Portland was missing Damian Lillard, who sat with plantar fasciitis in his left foot, and as against the Knicks three days earlier, the Cavs let down in the star's absence.

The media would later focus on this game as a possible "work strike" by disgruntled vets, though no one said anything to that effect until weeks later. Whatever the cause, it acted upon the squad like a trash compactor: They came out flat.

With Kyrie Irving sitting out the back-to-back, Matthew Dellavedova got the start over Mo Williams, who'd been the starter before Irving's return. Calling their defensive effort halfhearted does an injustice to the truly ambivalent, but perhaps it was the offense that was really to blame.

The Cavs had shown a characteristic tendency to let their defense slip when shots weren't falling. Their offensive frustrations would manifest in step-slow close-outs on three-point shooters, slower help on drives, and lackluster transition defense. While they didn't commit a lot of turnovers as a team, their opponents did convert a high percentage into points. Those are just a few of the things that went wrong as the Trailblazers blasted the Cavaliers 34-12 in the first quarter on their way to a 105-76 victory.

"We didn't take particularly good shots in the first half," Blatt said. "We took a lot of hurried shots. We got behind fast and tried to make it all up at one time, and that forced us to play out of any kind of rhythm. We didn't really do anything right in the first half. Nothing."

Jefferson discounted the emotional hangover or mental lapse, saying they simply didn't come out with the right energy. "We made them feel way too comfortable," said Jefferson, who played 26 minutes after sitting the entire Warriors game. "They had zero turnovers and I think only five free throws. That means we weren't aggressive. We didn't foul them and didn't make them uncomfortable, and that's pretty much what our defense is predicated on."

However, James was still fixated on the lineups, which were even more confusing for the moment because Irving couldn't play back-to-backs.

"The first eight weeks we built chemistry. We knew who was playing. We knew who wasn't playing. Coach had rotations down," James said. "So we have to get back to that. We have no rhythm. We have some guys who don't know if they're going to play of if they're not going to play and it's hurting our rhythm a bit. The only thing that can help it is practice and then games."

The player(s) must've relayed their dissatisfaction to the coaches, as well as the media, because a reporter asked Blatt about rotations after the game, which seemed a strange thing to ask about in a 29-point loss where no one looked good start to finish.

"That was something I just talked to the coaches about," Blatt said. "With the lineups changing a little bit, it's natural that things get a little bit out of whack, and just between games and playing there is no other way because obviously we got to get guys in shape and got to get guys into the flow. But one thing you can always do is play hard and play right. I don't think in the first half we did that."

The Cavs recovered against Phoenix two nights later with a great first half where they shot 11-of-19 from three. It wasn't so fun in the second when the long-distance chucking yielded a more sobering 6-of-22. They were just 6-of-15 within the arc.

The Suns fought hard but Blatt deployed the minutes-restricted Irving at the end of the quarters, giving Cleveland an extra boost at the end of the third and fourth. Irving sank a three-pointer with 20 seconds left for a 99-95 lead in a 101-97 victory. Again Williams failed to make it off the bench, while Blatt benched Mozgov in favor of Thompson.

"I just felt like we needed to be a little faster on the court to start the game, a little more mobile and just to shake it up a little bit," Blatt said. "I just wanted to inject some more energy…potentially for a while, [but] I don't see it happening forever."

In their fourth game in five nights, the Cavaliers turned to James, who paced the team with 24 points and (oddly) his lowest assist total of the season (two). All season long James had been going hard to the basket and abjuring the mid-range jump shot, which NBA analytics gurus had isolated as having the lousiest return in basketball.

In one year James cut the average distance of his shot from 12.6 feet to 9.6 feet, well below his 12-foot career average. This coincided with his worst three-point shooting percentage (31) since his rookie year, as was his percentage from three to 10 feet (36 percent vs. 43 percent career). Suddenly,

46 percent of his shots were coming inside the restricted circle, where the previous year only a third did (35 percent career).

James closed the 2015 calendar year on a positive note by rediscovering his jumper against the Nuggets, sinking 6-of-9 midrange shots and finishing 13-of-24 with 34 points. Shumpert was the team's second-leading scorer with 16 points including two threes and two steals, while Love suffered through a tough night, going 4-of-16 and finishing with eight points.

Afterward Blatt made a strange comment about needing to get James going. This, of course, ran counter to what James had said early in the season about being able to get his points as needed—LeBron's pretext for Love being the "focal point." It sounded suspiciously like Blatt was catering to his star for some reason.

"[James] got into a good rhythm early and it was something that we wanted. I felt maybe the last couple games we maybe didn't help him get into an early rhythm. Tonight we made an effort to do that and he responded extremely well," he said. "He got into a good rhythm, really shot well, really played well all around the court, and we needed him to have a good game to carry us to this win."

James had been doing extra shooting before the games, which continued for the next couple weeks. This followed a tweet by NBA.com writer John Schuhmann of "The worst high-volume shooters from outside the paint, a list topped by LeBron James & Kobe Bryant."

Lowest FG% from outside the paint, 2015-16 (among 64 players w/ 200 FGA)

Player	Mid-Range			3-point range			Total outside the paint			
	FGM	FGA	FG%	3PM	3PA	3P%	FGM	FGA	FG%	eFG%
LeBron James	38	119	31.9%	27	109	24.8%	65	228	28.5%	34.4%
Kobe Bryant	61	172	35.5%	53	207	25.6%	114	379	30.1%	37.1%
Andrew Wiggins	57	168	33.9%	18	74	24.3%	75	242	31.0%	34.7%
Joe Johnson	33	102	32.4%	38	124	30.6%	71	226	31.4%	39.8%
Trevor Ariza	12	37	32.4%	60	185	32.4%	72	222	32.4%	45.9%
K. Caldwell-Pope	40	107	37.4%	44	148	29.7%	84	255	32.9%	41.6%
Zach LaVine	39	113	34.5%	35	109	32.1%	74	222	33.3%	41.2%
D'Angelo Russell	35	98	35.7%	50	155	32.3%	85	253	33.6%	43.5%
Jimmy Butler	57	163	35.0%	33	103	32.0%	90	266	33.8%	40.0%
Monta Ellis	50	136	36.8%	27	90	30.0%	77	226	34.1%	40.0%

Through Dec. 28, 2015

Note: If min. set to 150 (114 players), Mudiay (39-164, 23.8%) would rank last, then James.
NBA.com/stats

LeBron reached his nadir in December, shooting 28 percent from midrange for the month. From the point when Schuhmann's tweet ran through the Cavaliers' championship victory in June, James made 39 percent from midrange and 36 percent from three. James certainly isn't faultless, but he'll do his damnedest to correct them.

Cleveland returned home after New Year's and made the Orlando Magic disappear in a puff of smoke, taking a 55-32 lead at halftime and cruising to a 104-79 victory. James had 29 on 11-of-18 shooting and was 4-of-7 from three with no turnovers. Kyrie was the next highest scorer with 13 in 21 minutes.

This narrative of getting the King going reappeared as if the greatest player in basketball needed a jump-start. This time it was Love mouthing the meme.

"In the first quarter in some games you look at the stat sheet and he doesn't—we weren't necessarily making it a point to get him going and we do need to do that," Love said. "We feel he's the best player in the world and that's what we need to do. We feed off of him. When he sucks in the defense and it brings so much attention, it allows other guys to step up and hit big shots."

On a side note, Williams showed up an hour before the start of the Magic game, the same time the team allows media access to the (nearly empty) pregame locker room. (Most players avoid the press' allotted half hour by receiving treatment in the inaccessible training room, when not taking part in their pregame shooting.)

Williams responded two days later, explaining among other things that, "there is no particular time we have been at the arena. My routine has just changed—that's all." Still, he never arrived that late again.

Toronto visited the next night, hoping to reprise November's home victory when they exploited the penetration of Kyle Lowry and shooting acumen of DeMar DeRozan. The pair combined for 28 first half points on 11-of-18 shooting. The Raptors shot 60 percent and were continually able to get the ball "downhill," driving toward the basket like water down a drain.

Midway through the third, with the score knotted at 69, Cleveland adjusted its pick-and-roll defense. Rather than dropping the roll man into the lane to defend the basket, known as "icing" the pick-and-roll, the Cavs sent both defenders aggressively after the ballhandler, what's called "blitzing." It forced the ballhandler to give up the ball. Cleveland employed it primarily on DeRozan, a more limited passer and dribbler than Lowry.

The Cavaliers went on a 17-7 run to end the quarter, taking a lead they'd never relinquish. Over the next 18 minutes they held Lowry and DeRozan to just one basket and seven points. The Raptors managed just 44 points in the second half and shot under 40 percent.

It didn't hurt that the Cavs shot 17-of-33 from beyond the boundary, led by J. R. Smith's 8-of-14 shooting. Irving shed some rust with 25 points on 10-of-16 shooting and eight assists while James had 20 points on a hyper-efficient 7-of-11 shooting with seven assists.

The better second half defense had been a Cavaliers characteristic. Whether it was Lue's defensive adjustments or the team's better second half focus, Cleveland finished with the best second half defensive efficiency (points allowed per 100 possessions, pCp) in the league, more than a point better at 95.7 than the second place Miami Heat (96.9).

"We're a team that feels out the game a little bit. We start getting a little rhythm in the late second quarter and it trickles down into the second half," said James. "I wish we would start off better, but I wouldn't like it in the reverse way, where we're the best first half team and in the second half can't stop nobody." (That would change, for a time, soon enough.)

Despite the team's variety of niggling issues, their second half defensive efficiency hinted at what the Cavaliers were capable of when properly motivated and displaying an appropriate sense of urgency. Now they were about to embark on a road trip that would in some sense define their season. They were good but still needed to discover what it takes to be great.

6

SWORD OF DAMOCLES

LEBRON JAMES HAS not just led on the basketball court; he's taken the lead in talking about gun violence. The "creative" side of the entertainment field (musicians, writers, actors, directors) has enjoyed far less compunction speaking their mind than professional athletes. Muhammad Ali paid for his activism as did 1968 Olympic medal winners Tommie Smith and John Carlos.

There had long been the sense among players that you don't bite the hand that feeds you. In 1996, Chicago Bulls guard Craig Hodges filed a lawsuit claiming the NBA blackballed him for his outspoken views. Hodges arrived for the Bulls' 1992 White House visit in a dashiki and handed President George H. W. Bush a letter expressing his scorn for the treatment of poor and minorities in this country.

The world champion Bulls cut Hodges while he was the reigning three-time champ in the All-Star Game's three-point contest. Nobody else wanted him. He defended his three-point title at the All-Star Game, becoming the only free agent to ever compete. Hodges had accused Jordan of "bailing out" by claiming ignorance about the riots in Los Angeles after the Rodney King decision that April.

It's been widely reported that Jordan explained his failure to support Harvey Gantt, an African American Senate candidate from North Carolina who ran against Jesse Helms in 1990 and 1996, by saying "Republicans buy shoes too." When Helms died in 2008, Jordan took the opportunity to clear the air.

"What I said was true," he explained. "Republicans buy sneakers. And usually full retail. But I've since realized that there are more important things than money, or market share or the Jordan brand." As the only African American NBA owner, Jordan had significantly less to worry about by then.

Buck Williams, head of the NBA Players Association at the time of Hodges' suit, told the *New York Times*, "It's well known through the league that there may be repercussions if you speak out too strongly on some sensitive issues."

However, that was two decades ago and the climate has changed. Basketball had its first openly gay player before any of the other major sports, and the league moved its 2017 All-Star Game from Charlotte to New Orleans because of North Carolina's anti-LGBT "bathroom law."

LeBron James might not fear the NBA blackballing him, but as an enormous brand, he had more to lose. Yet in the wake of the Trayvon Martin shooting in March 2012, James and his Miami Heat teammates donned hoodies and posted a picture of solidarity on Instagram with the hashtags #Stereotyped and #WeWantJustice.

On November 24, 2014, a grand jury failed to indict the officers involved in the death of Michael Brown of Ferguson, Missouri. History repeated 10 days later when another grand jury failed to indict those responsible for the chokehold death of Brooklyn's most notorious loosie vendor, Eric Garner. Three days later, on December 6, Derrick Rose wore a T-shirt bearing the phrase "I Can't Breathe" in warm-ups. Several football players followed suit the next day.

On Monday, December 8, James, Kyrie Irving, Jarrett Jack, Kevin Garnett, Deron Williams, and Alan Anderson wore shirts bearing the phrase during the pregame warmups in Brooklyn. Later James posted an inspirational picture of Brown and Martin walking arm-in-arm on Instagram.

"Violence is not the answer and retaliation isn't the solution," James said after the game. "As a society we know we need to get better, but it's not going to be done in one day."

President Obama credited James for his actions a week later in *People* magazine, saying, "LeBron is an example of a young man who has, in his own way and in a respectful way, tried to say, 'I'm part of this society, too' and focus attention…. I'd like to see more athletes do that—not just around this issue, but around a range of issues."

When Muhammad Ali passed during the 2016 NBA Finals, LeBron called him the "the first icon" and mentioned how much of an inspiration and a guide the boxer had been in finding his own voice, and understanding his role beyond that of sports figure.

"For an athlete like myself today, without Muhammad Ali, I wouldn't be sitting up here talking in front of you guys," James said. "As I got older and started to be more knowledgeable about sport in general and about the guys who paved the way for guys like myself, I understood that he is the greatest of all time, and he was the greatest of all time because of what he did outside of the ring."

On October 1, 2015, during the Cavaliers' training camp, a stray bullet from a drive-by shooting killed five-month-old Aavielle Wakefield in Cleveland. It was the third child under six felled by a bullet in the past four weeks. James spoke up.

"There's no room for guns, first of all, but then for violence toward kids or anybody. I see the news go across my phone and I'm sitting there in front of my three kids, so it automatically just hit me," he said. "It's not just in Cleveland. It's the whole nation that goes through this as well. We all hurt from it."

On December 28, 2015, it was another grand jury and another failure to indict cops, this time in the death of Cleveland 12-year-old Tamir Rice. It was revealed over the New Year's weekend in an obvious attempt to limit coverage and political damage. (No matter, county prosecutor Tim McGinty lost his battle for reelection anyway.)

James returned to Cleveland five days later, but stayed on the sidelines. "To be honest, I haven't really been on top of this issue. So it's hard for me to comment," James said. "The most important thing that we all need to understand…this issue is bigger than me. It's about everyone. And gun violence and tragedies and kids losing lives at a young age, some way, somehow, we need to understand that that matters more than an individual."

There's no critiquing James' concern for the welfare of children. He has never forgotten where he came from or the odds he beat. After leaving for Miami he decided to really do something about it. Perhaps there was guilt mixed in, but James always felt he owed a debt to Akron and the community that supported him and his family.

Indeed, his greatest legacy may be the LeBron James Family Foundation

(LJFF) and the kids it helps as a mechanism for long-term change in Northeast Ohio. The nonprofit works with Akron public schools to identify third graders at highest risk of dropping out, offering the child and his or her parent(s) an opportunity to join his Wheels for Education Program. Parental participation is an essential aspect in building a shared investment.

Once these third graders (and a parent) complete the We Are Family orientation, they're able to stay in the program until the child graduates high school. In 2015 James promised that every student that completes the program has a guaranteed scholarship to the University of Akron, worth $9,500 a year. More than 2,000 kids are already eligible, though the program's first kids are entering eighth grade.

The program takes kids on excursions to amusement parks and cultural events to broaden their horizons. There are catered "hometown hall meetings" at area schools where parents are invited to ask questions and give the Foundation feedback, while the kids are honored and door prizes given away, ranging from new tablets to James' shoes and uniforms from his last practice. He encourages the kids with personal letters and even phone calls. As the kids grow older, they become involved in local service projects.

It's an ambitious effort headed by an all-volunteer organization, but there's little doubt about James' dedication or personal investment. It would've been as easy for James to make a token effort as it would've been to bypass sensitive social subjects. Kobe Bryant even criticized James for what he saw as a kind of knee-jerk black nationalism.

"I won't react to something just because I'm supposed to, because I'm an African American. That argument doesn't make no sense to me," Bryant said. "You want to talk about how far we've progressed as a society? Well, we've progressed as a society, then don't jump to somebody's defense just because they're African American. You sit and you listen to the facts just like you would in any other situation."

No one imagines themselves capable of impacting such issues, but James has taken that responsibility seriously. That made it difficult to hear Samaria Rice criticize James.

"It's quite sad that LeBron hasn't spoken out about my son," Rice said on January 6. "I'm not asking him to sit out a game. I know his kids got to eat too, but you can at least put on a shirt or something. Some of the other athletes, some of them have said something."

That's the hazard in speaking out: Whatever you say, it may never be enough.

The Calm Before the Storm. Wednesday, January 6, 2016, Washington. (23-9)

The Cavaliers' torrid shooting continued in Washington, on the first leg of their six-day road trip, half of it spent in the Texas Triangle (Dallas-Houston-San Antonio).

Cleveland led most of the game, including a dozen at halftime and by 17 points midway through the third before they lost the thread completely. Washington proceeded to outscore the Cavaliers 34-17 as John Wall perpetrated identity theft, taking the same drive-and-kick techniques the Cavaliers favor to resurrect the Wizards.

When Washington knotted the score at 95, Irving took over. He scored 12 points in a 15-2 run and finished with 19 in the frame as the Cavs beat the Wizards 121-115. Irving (32 points), James (34), and J. R. Smith (25) combined for 91 points and shot 36-of-60 (60 percent) collectively.

On defense, the Wizards had success switching everything, taking away the openings afforded by a screen or pick. When the offense screens the defender, he stays with the screener, removing the usual advantage of the ballhandler's man fighting over the screen to follow him.

Teams usually avoid switching because it leads to positional mismatches, such as bigs defending guards or vice-versa. Far enough from the basket, the ballhandler can beat a slow-footed big to the basket while bigger players typically thrive posting up smaller guards.

As the league's grown more athletic, more teams have experimented with lineups capable of more or less defending any player. It's effective in thwarting many of the usual ways basketball teams create open shots. That leaves offenses trying to beat slightly mismatched players one-on-one, while the off the ball movement created by picks and screens slowly withers.

"Washington went small and they were switching every pick-and-roll and every screen," said Blatt. "It's difficult to move the ball in a normal fashion and play the same type of offense maybe we were playing earlier. We had to depend on some of the one-one-one skills our players have.... We got good shots but it didn't come after a lot of ball movement."

The Cavs made it three games in a row scoring over 120 points by crushing the Timberwolves 125-99, in a game in which Shumpert set his season high with 23 and J. R. Smith led Cavs scorers with 27. So naturally two nights later in Philadelphia, Cleveland got overconfident and almost fell to a scrappy 76ers team that since signing free agent point guard Ish Smith had won three of six. Before that they'd won once in 34 games.

The Cavaliers held eight- and nine-point leads in the second and third quarters but could never extend it. The young Philly squad battled back every time. When the Sixers pulled to within two, 81-79, on a three from Ish Smith, James announced, *"No soup for you."* He took control, scoring 12 points in a decisive 14-0 run, including a layup, a dunk, and three jumpers in the 95-85 victory. James finished with 37 points on 15-of-22 shooting with nine assists.

They reprised the last-minute theatrics two nights later in Dallas. In the first half the Cavs allowed the Mavericks to shoot 58 percent, while shooting 35 percent themselves, yet somehow managed to stay within five, 52-47. Dellavedova had a trio of three-pointers and LeBron had two more as they made four more threes than the Mavericks, grabbed five more offensive boards, and made five fewer turnovers.

It was a strange but encouraging truth—even when the Cavaliers failed to shoot or defend, they found other ways to stay within reach.

Cleveland went down 10 with four minutes left in the third, then played with the kind of intensity they seemed to reserve for the last quarter and a half of a game like special stock. That's when Cleveland made half their shots, outrebounded the Mavericks 17-8, had nine assists on 14 buckets, committed just two turnovers, and held future Hall of Famer Dirk Nowitzki scoreless.

The lead passed to and fro. With a chance to go ahead, Nowitzki was isolated on Shumpert just inside the top of the key. He made his move with five seconds on the game clock, dribbling right and then spinning back left for the fallaway. As Nowitzki spun to his left and raised the ball Shumpert jabbed his hand in there, poking it away before Dirk could elevate and send the game into overtime.

Down 103-100 with two minutes left, after Nowitzki's second three of the extra session, the Cavs outscored the Mavs 10-2 (before a meaningless bucket by Williams at the buzzer), thanks to five points each from James and

Irving. The Cavaliers were six for nine and LeBron chipped in three assists in overtime as Cleveland snuck away with the 110-107 win.

On January 11, a practice day before the Dallas game, James tweeted, "No RESPECT for time! #PetPeeve." Blatt allegedly engendered that tweet by showing up late to practice, something anonymous sources would suggest had happened in the past.

Cleveland had won eight straight going into San Antonio, but hadn't necessarily looked sharp all those games. Still, LeBron's teams tended to elevate their play against the upper echelon. Sure enough, the Cavs opened with real purpose against the Spurs. They took limited threes (making 5-of-9), shot 53 percent from the field, and held the Spurs to 36 percent shooting over the first 23 minutes of the game.

With Cleveland up 50-38, Tony Parker carved up the Cavs' pick-and-roll defense like Christmas ham the final sixty seconds of the half. Three times Parker left Irving velcroed to a pick while slicing through the heart of the defense like Christiaan Barnard, scoring over the outstretched hand of Kevin Love, caught guarding him on the switch.

J. R. Smith scored the Cavs' first two buckets of the second half, cutting to the basket on a feed from James and dropping a three for a 55-46 lead with 10 left in the third. Kawhi Leonard contribute seven in an 11-0 run that gave the Spurs their first lead, 57-55. The lead kept changing hands. Cleveland took a 73-72 lead when Irving beat the double-team and found Dellavedova in the right corner for a buzzer-beating three to end the third.

The Spurs amped up their defense in the fourth while the Cavaliers forgot how to pass. On the Cavaliers' first 15 possessions there were 11 (frontcourt) passes. Most possessions featured switches into favorable matchups, then a one-on-one attack off the dribble.

While it's good to attack a mismatch, like Duncan on James, it's a Spurs victory if it only results in a long three by James. Since taking over, Blatt seemed to be on the losing end of a tug-of-war between the motion-based, ball-movement style offense he wanted to play and an isolation game dictated by the skills (wills?) of his two stars.

As Irving and James attacked the paint their teammates stood around, watching and waiting like extras on a movie set. Without such movement it's much easier for the defense to anticipate and stop one-on-one play with late help from off the ball.

"We stopped moving the ball as well as we were earlier and of course they picked their defense up," said Blatt. "It's always important to move the ball. It's also important to utilize the strengths you have in ISO [-lation] situations but it's absolutely critical to move the ball."

Six different Spurs scored as San Antonio outscored Cleveland 15-2 over the next five minutes. But those crazy Cavs seemed to fight hardest when the odds were the longest. They pulled within four on an Irving three with 12 seconds left. Tony Parker cracked the door when he missed two free throws, but LaMarcus Aldridge grabbed the offensive rebound to seal the 99-95 win.

"Obviously the way we started we seemed to know what we were doing and have a plan, and we did get away from what we were doing earlier—that was pretty clear," Blatt said. "My guys played hard. I just think they need to be a little more determined to play throughout the game with good flow and good pace."

The Cavaliers' first back-to-back of the road trip came the next night in Houston and didn't start well. The Rockets hit five of their first six shots for an 11-4 lead that prompted a Blatt timeout. On the next possession James Harden stole the ball and took it in for a layup.

From that point fierce defense became a point of pride for the Cavs. Over the last eight minutes of the first, Cleveland held the Rockets to 2-of-16 shooting. The offense wasn't clicking, but the defense was on point. Kyrie scored nine in a 13-7 run to push the lead to eight in the second quarter, and they led by 11 at halftime.

The Cavaliers held the Rockets to 10 points the first 10 minutes of the third to take a 21-point lead and there was no looking back. Irving paced the team with 23, while James added 19 points, seven boards, and seven assists. Love added 11 points and 13 rebounds. Mozgov got the start against Howard, and kept it for five games, making just one turnover in that span. His defense had improved and he'd started to iron out his offensive inconsistency, though his swagger still wasn't close to "A Boy Named Sue."

The Last Roundup. Monday, January 18, 2016, Cleveland. (28-10)

The team returned home on Saturday, January 16, having been away from home for 18 of the last 23 games. Indeed, after playing Golden State on Monday they would be on the road again to Brooklyn before settling in for a four-game homestand. The Cavs had won 15 of their last 18 since that three-game losing streak during the beginning of December, and were rounding into form.

While the Warriors remained impressive, they came into Cleveland having lost consecutive road games to the Denver Nuggets and Detroit Pistons (sandwiched around a home win over the hapless Lakers). Given how well the Cavaliers had played Golden State on Christmas Day with a still-rusty Irving, the Cavs had reason to believe vengeance was within reach. (Damn 3-D glasses!)

Still, the Warriors were 37-4 overall and barely slowed entering Quicken Loans Arena. They laid thick black rubber all over the court and backs of Cavaliers players, tearing out to a 12-2 lead by making their first five shots. A mini Cavs run cut the lead to 15-11, but by the end of one, Golden State led 34-21.

Early in the second and still up 13, the Warriors went on a 19-7 run, pushing the lead to 25. It happened so quickly with so little resistance you could nearly hear an audible hiss as the Cavs' will seeped away. They wouldn't get any closer, losing 132-98.

"We were slow and we were late and we became frustrated when things weren't going our way," offered Blatt. "I don't know if it was the effort or if it was our inability to overcome our own frustration, part of that stemming from us just not executing and doing the things that we normally do, or being able to, against a team that really played us tough and hard and challenges us the way they did. We didn't raise our level to that."

The Warriors shot 65 percent in the first half (26-of-40), led by Stephen Curry with 21, and Draymond Green had 11 points, five boards, and six assists. J. R. brought it, shooting 6-of-8 for 14 points in the first half, but the rest of the Cavaliers shot 13-of-33 (39 percent).

"It started with Draymond," James said. "Draymond did a great job of attacking our scheme and putting pressure on our defense to assist, score, or make plays, and obviously Steph hitting the shots that he hit."

The team came out flat, according to Blatt, but he didn't shirk the blame. "We could've played anybody and I don't know that we would've had a vastly different result. Obviously their quality will make it that much worse," he said. "They played the kind of game they wanted to play. They played our coverages well. They defended us extremely well. We didn't find answers at either end. And again, I'll take responsibility for that."

Little did he know how true that was.

The Cavaliers took care of business two days later by beating the Nets in Brooklyn, 91-78, and returned home to meet the Los Angeles Clippers, who boasted the fourth-best record in the Western Conference (behind Oklahoma City, San Antonio, and Golden State). The Cavaliers moved the ball much better against both the Clippers and the Nets than they had in recent weeks.

They amassed assists on 15 of their first 20 baskets, and took only 10 first half threes while shooting 15 free throws. The Cavaliers held a one-point lead with just under four minutes left in the second quarter and then went on a 14-6 run, building a lead they'd never relinquish.

"We moved the ball extremely well from side to side. Against very good defensive teams, you have to do that," said James. "We've been harping on that the last couple games and we executed that, and I think defensively we were in tune with the gameplan, and even though they made some shots we stuck with it."

The Cavaliers didn't just shoot well (42-of-83 from the field, 13-of-28 on threes), they also flattened the Clippers on the boards, 47-35, including 14 offensive rebounds that they turned into 24 second-chance points—the most all season.

"The regular season all I care about is the process," said James. "We took two or three steps backwards on Monday [against Golden State] and a couple steps forward these last couple games and that's all that matters to me. We have a lot of time. Not as much as I would like, but enough time to prepare and get ready for each and every game and we've done it well the last two games."

Before the game, Blatt made a long plea, defending his record and the team's play. It seemed strangely out of character and overly strident.

"We didn't get where we are right now by being a bad team or by having all these problems that suddenly surface when we have a bad game like we had," Blatt said. "We had to work very hard to get where we are this year. Very hard. And we have a ways to go, but I told everyone here in the very beginning of the year that it was going to take us time.

"We weren't a homogenous unit from day one, with all our guys out and not having a real preseason. But we're okay. We've got to get better and we will, but it shouldn't be overlooked what we have done so far." he continued. "There are going to be times that seemingly nothing goes right. But your effort level and your consistency in terms of your approach, those are the things you want to see more than anything else, and I think we've seen that… I don't think that [the effort in the Golden State game] has been the norm here at all."

It would be Blatt's last lengthy address. The Cavaliers fired him the next afternoon, making him the first NBA coach ever dismissed with the best record in his conference.

7

WHEN THE WHIP COMES DOWN

UNIVERSALLY FETED IN Europe, David Blatt received warm praise from his players. He won at the highest levels of international play, including the EuroCup, EuroLeague, and Olympics.

Blatt was born in the United States and attended Framingham High School in Massachusetts, where he was class president. After four years at Princeton he graduated with an English literature major (his thesis was on Bernard Malamud's *The Natural*) and went abroad to play professionally. He never came back until signing with the Cavaliers. His family stayed in Israel when he became coach of the Cavs.

Blatt played abroad for a dozen years, and after retiring became an assistant coach for the Israeli team Hapoel Galil Elyon. Before long he'd ascended to the top position, kicking off a 20-year coaching career culminating with an improbable EuroLeague Championship for Maccabi Tel Aviv in 2013-14, after which the Cavaliers signed him.

At the time, the team was unaware that James was considering his return. The organization believed they'd need to assemble a winning team before LeBron would consider wearing Wine and Gold again. Blatt was seen as a good coach to guide a young team, with time to acclimate himself to the manners and mores of the big leagues, surrounded by former NBA head coaches including onetime player Larry Drew (Atlanta, Milwaukee) and Jim Boylan (Chicago, Milwaukee).

"We all kind of thought [LeBron] was a year away from being ready to do that," Griffin told Adrian Wojnarowski after the Cavs' title run. "Just in terms of us showing that we were capable of being a winner and he would come back."

While Blatt had a difficult time admitting it, his first year in the league was a real learning process. He bristled at the idea that he was a rookie coach, feeling it ignored his two-decade international pedigree.

During his first season, when reporters would ask if he'd "ever seen anything like that," brazenly fishing for descriptive quotes about LeBron or whomever was the star of the game, Blatt would explain that he'd seen a great many things in his 20 years of coaching basketball.

There was no end to such questions, which often amounted to nothing much more specific than, "Wow, that LeBron is something else, huh?" At worse, they fell into trivialities such as LeBron's headband or whether the team might get an extra playoff boost seeing their injured comrade before the game. (Sports journalists apparently have watched *Brian's Song* and *Knute Rockne, All-American* far too many times.)

Blatt earned a reputation for "thinking he's the smartest guy in the room," to quote one of my colleagues, who graciously allowed a moment later that "he just might be." Asked what he thought of a particularly scintillating performance by Kyrie Irving, Blatt replied, "Probably that same thing you thought. I'll leave it to your creative abilities to describe what you saw."

It was the type of reportorial trolling that San Antonio coach Gregg Popovich has elevated to an "arch form." Popovich can get away with it because he's won five championships and is a Phil Jackson-size legend. His contempt for dumb, pointless questions is legendary, but he's earned it in their eyes, and Blatt hadn't.

This initial adversarial relationship helped turn the small cadre of local beat reporters against Blatt. Only five reporters traveled regularly with the Cavaliers, and four were new to the sport/coverage or town when James returned. Three were with the same paper and mapped their coverage together to avoid quote or subject overlap.

A certain amount of groupthink is probably inevitable, and Blatt's haughty tone only amplified the us/them disconnect, opening the door for them to carry water for those who would like to see Blatt gone. This persisted through the first year before the Cavs PR department took steps to bridge the divide with offers of better access, while Blatt softened his tone.

While those negative voices were largely mollified in the local press, Blatt's detractors extended beyond the media. Without friends in the NBA coaching fraternity or those who'd worked with him in the front offices, he found little support from the league's old boy network (until he was dumped, at which time they gnashed their teeth at his fate, fearful of the precedent it set).

Blatt was Dan Gilbert's guy. David Griffin had preferred Tyronn Lue, who played with Kobe and Michael Jordan (during his Wizard years) and coached under Doc Rivers in Boston and Los Angeles. However, Blatt liked Lue too, and aggressively pursued him. The Cavaliers made him the NBA's highest-paid associate head coach, which necessarily put Lue at the center of rumors when Blatt's job security first came into question in January 2015.

While James was taking a two-week break to recuperate from a facet injection in his back, rumors abounded that Blatt was on the brink of losing his job. Griffin went public, calling the talk ridiculous and pointing to the injuries that had held the team back. Later he revealed that he had discussed pulling the plug with Gilbert, but instead triggered the trade that turned around that season.

At the time, most calls for change allegedly came from James' confidantes, including his agent, Rich Paul, who represented one rumored Blatt replacement, Mark Jackson, the ex-Warriors coach turned ABC color commentator. According to Wojnarowski, "Once James' camp realized that Jackson would never be considered as coach...Lue became a compromise choice for James' group."

Strangely, the rumors persisted through the 2015 playoffs, abetted by James sometimes peremptory behavior toward the coach. James would countermand plays and check himself in and out on his own accord, according to several reports. Of course, other stars routinely changed plays or contradicted their coaches in the huddle, but to some observers, LeBron took it to another level.

During the Golden State series, ESPN writer Marc Stein recalled watching LeBron from behind the bench, and seeing him "shaking his head vociferously...amounting to the loudest nonverbal scolding you could imagine," compelling Blatt to draw up another play. Elsewhere he noted how often James huddled with Lue, "often looking at anyone other than Blatt."

Blatt dismissed such breaches of protocol as harmless, describing it as the spirited emotions of someone who wanted to win as badly as he did. But it seemed clear that the Blatt-James relationship wasn't on the steadiest ground. Blatt admitted to *USA Today*'s Jeff Zillgitt during the 2015 Finals, "I know I said many times the game is the game. Well, it's not. It's different. It's different in many, many ways.

"The learning curve was greater than I thought it would be," he continued. "It's a lot of things on and off the court, because the whole off-the-court picture of the NBA is so much more significant than it is in Europe that it's almost indefinable, and the on-the-court aspect, too, is very, very different."

One cardinal difference between Europe and the NBA is that overseas coaches are the superstars and the players must defer to them. In the NBA that's reversed. Blatt perhaps didn't make that adjustment quick enough to avoid playing catch-up.

The only significant attributed quotes after Blatt's dismissal came from former center Brendan Haywood, who hadn't been with the team all year and might've had an axe to grind. He was one of several veterans who groused about lack of playing time the year before, after racking up only 199 minutes all year. The solitary thing that kept him on the team was the value of the last $10 million non-guaranteed year of his contract as potential salary relief (since he could be traded for someone of up to equal salary and then waived).

During an appearance on CBS Sports Radio's *The Doug Gottlieb Show*, Hayward accused Blatt of failing to critique James during film sessions and catering to the star to curry his favor.

"I remember we had James Jones [talk] to coach about how, 'Hey, you can't just skip over when LeBron James makes a mistake in the film room.' Because we all see it," said Haywood. "Slowly but surely, that respect started chipping away where he would kind of be scared to correct LeBron in film sessions. When he would call every foul for LeBron in practice. Those types of things add up. Guys are like, 'C'mon, man, are you scared of him?'"

While presumably those first-year issues had largely cleared by the second year, the truth is murkier. A few days before the decision, Griffin reportedly sat in on a film session and called out James for failing to get back on defense, a particular LeBron bugaboo.

Wojnarowski reported at the time that after the first loss to the Warriors, "James had become increasingly vocal in his opposition of Blatt in recent practice sessions and game environments," though LeBron took great pains during the year to avoid sharing such complaints in public or with the media. Yet behind-the-scenes issues remained.

"It's not like he got fired because he can't get along with people or because he was a hard person to deal with or he was difficult," Haywood said. "He got fired because they didn't believe he had the pulse of the team. I don't think LeBron really was that cozy with him."

Mo Williams was another alleged source of discontent after he went from starting to hardly playing when Irving and Shumpert returned. It's been suggested his late arrival to the Magic game was an expression of his frustration.

Some players such as Smith, Dellavedova, Varejao, Mozgov, Sasha Kaun, and Irving expressed support for Blatt before and after the move, while others were more circumspect. Jefferson described Blatt as being "in an unfortunate situation" but denied ever having any of the concerns about playing time attributed to frustrated vet(s) by reporters after Blatt's firing. Love in particular couldn't find anything to say about Blatt when asked to compare him to Lue during the playoffs.

In December Griffin spoke to me about how he envisioned Williams' midrange pull-up game and three-point range helping the team come playoff time. This is one example of a rumored disconnect between coach and general manager. Blatt's aversion to Williams was based on his red-caped tendencies on the other end. Like Bartleby, Blatt decided he'd rather not.

A similar occurrence happened the year before in the playoffs. Despite being severely shorthanded, Blatt never played the veteran bench help Griffin had acquired. Not just backup bigs like Haywood, but once solid-greats—Kendrick Perkins, Shawn Marion, and Mike Miller—who gathered splinters even though the Cavs were badly shorthanded with injuries and by the end of the Finals exhausted.

(It was a lesson Lue learned, playing a deeper bench down the stretch and specifically referencing this issue. "I wanted to play 10, 11 guys because you never know when a guy goes down and you need to be ready to play," he said. "Last year I felt it kind of burnt us, not playing guys and keeping them in the rhythm.")

In the end, Griffin laid most of the team's inability to perform passionately or consistently on Blatt's shoulders.

"I'm in our locker room a lot, and I knew there's just a disconnect there right now. There's a lack of spirit and connectedness that I just couldn't accept," he said while announcing his decision. "We need to build a collective spirit—a strength of spirit and a collective will. Halfway through this season, we have not yet developed [a clear] identity, and each step forward, unfortunately, I think we've taken two steps back. Frankly, pretty good is not what we're here for."

He cited the investment in the team and suggested a goal like a championship didn't leave room for half measures. "You could look at a lot of different analytic measures of our team and we're pretty good right now and that's not what we're in the business to be," Griffin said. "I'm not leaving an unprecedented team payroll and all the efforts of everyone that works in this organization to chance."

As Griffin would reiterate every time he spoke about Blatt, it wasn't a question of his abilities as a coach as much as his fit for the team. Though Griffin refrained from stating specifics, who was going to have an easier time communicating with LeBron James? A former NBA player with championship rings, raised by a single mom in the small town of Mexico, Missouri, or a worldly East Coast-bred Princeton English lit major/Euro baller with a Jewish heritage and zero NBA experience?

That might be a tad disingenuous. Blatt had communicated with players from widely disparate circumstances and cultures in Europe. Some of what it came down to may have been that Blatt hadn't won key players over enough to avoid them scapegoating him for their losses and the players' failures. So long as Blatt was there the team would never own up to their own culpability. Without Blatt, there could be no excuses.

Of course, some of this had to do with Lue as well. He already had James' respect. In the end, Lue's communication skills and inner confidence filled Griffin's bill for what might cure symptoms he saw of an ailing team.

"The voice and the attitude he brings to this is a little bit different. That's not implying what we had was bad, but every situation calls for something unique," Griffin said at the time of the firing. "We have to have group buy-in and team-first habits in order to become the team we intend to be."

Speaking after the season with Wojnarowski, Griffin amplified those thoughts a bit.

"We probably didn't understand what it meant to come together and play for each other," he said. "So when Ty Lue took over he brought that mindset of sacrifice for one another, and that was the element we were missing. We were a bunch of individually talented guys that liked each other but we weren't a team that was willing to sacrifice for each other, and once we sort of became that we untapped our full potential.

"We've got a team that responded really well to being told it can't and there was a real 'we'll show you,'" he said, referencing 2015's playoff run under Blatt. "But when we were told we were supposed to, we didn't deal well with the pressure and expectation of that."

While some hypothesized that Lue had been gunning for Blatt's job, nothing could be further from the truth. When Griffin called to offer him the position, Lue told the GM, "This is fucked up, Griff," and spent the next few minutes trying to talk him out of it, according to the *Plain Dealer*'s Chris Haynes.

Indeed, according to other reporters, Lue had been performing the same balancing act with LeBron and his mates, encouraging them to give Blatt a chance. His loyalty was never truly in question, and that fair-handed manner worked for the team.

When Griffin called the players to tell them about the move, the initial sentiment of several players was that there had been a trade. Griffin called them not just to deliver the news, but for the frank discussion James Jones facilitated after he left.

The players' meeting echoed issues Griffin raised in his presser, notably the absence of accountability. Irving, James, and Love agreed to do a better job calling each other out and accepting such criticism. They shared their expectations for themselves and their teammates, owning up to past mistakes and recommitting to the team. (Again.)

In the presser Griffin also cited a general lack of joy in the locker room after a recent victory. Lue made this one of the first things he focused on. He hammered home this idea about appreciating your moment in the NBA the first time he spoke to them.

"I don't think they're enjoying it," Lue said. "No matter how great LeBron is and Kyrie and Kevin, the game will pass you by. In 20 years, the only time they'll be recognized or talked about is if there's a record [broken].... I want them just to enjoy the moment now. It's a long journey, I know. We got a lot of young guys and they don't really understand that. But the game will pass you by."

He explained that he wasn't going to do things differently than Blatt, but "better." While disrespectful on the surface, the truth lies lower, where Lue was largely continuing the policies and ideas of Blatt with the hope of implementing them more effectively. First and foremost that meant demanding accountability where Blatt maybe didn't feel he could.

"I talked to Bron," Lue said after taking over. "I told him: 'I got to hold you accountable. It starts with you first. And if I can hold you accountable in front of the team and doing the right things, then everybody else has got to fall in line, fall in place.'"

That particular dynamic would play out in the coming weeks as reports would surface of Lue calling out James. One instance in particular grabbed media attention, as James tried to assert himself during a team huddle and Lue told him point blank, "Shut the fuck up, I got this." While Lue criticized the team before, he vowed to step that up now that it was his name on the door.

"I didn't want to overstep my boundaries with Blatt because, like I said, he did a phenomenal job," Lue said. "I didn't want to make it look like I was doing more than I was supposed to, but now I think I have to be even more hard on these guys."

He talked about balancing the team's ball movement and isolation basketball, and minimizing it until the moments to when it was truly necessary, usually the last two-thirds or half of the final stanza. The threat of stagnation is much less perilous at the end of the game. Lue understood that Cleveland had two of the best one-on-one players in the league with Irving and James, and he had to use them.

"Last year we were number one in offensive efficiency, but we played a lot of ISO basketball," Lue said. "I've just got to find that line, just try and stay with it, preach to our guys ball movement."

The most intriguing thing Lue said in the first few days was about relieving Kyrie of his playmaking responsibilities. Lue wanted Irving to attack the basket and look to create for himself before creating for others. This was an interesting nod to Irving's talents.

Kyrie is a particularly gifted penetrator off the dribble or the bounce, as they say. When in a pick-and-roll he attacks aggressively. Traditionally you wait for the screener to roll to the basket, but Irving typically doesn't, going quickly against the defending big and his own trailing man, forcing the action, and he's extraordinarily good at it.

Lue felt encouraging Kyrie to think "attack" would diminish tentative decision-making by allowing him to play more instinctively. He could create based off his aggressiveness and how the defense reacts, not necessarily with a set play.

Lue also wanted more aggression from Love. If things weren't going his way offensively and/or he wasn't receiving the ball, Kevin had a tendency to drift out to the three-point line, stop posting up, and stop calling for the ball.

Under Lue, not only did Love start setting more screens for Kyrie and James—continuing the season's trend—but also started to see the ball more on the elbow. That's where he had done his most damage while with Minnesota.

By season's end that particular set would fade from the playbook, with Love receiving even fewer elbow touches than before. He got 3.8 elbow touches a game under Blatt, and 5.5 a game under Lue until the All-Star break. After the break he got 2.8 elbow touches a game.

While great in concept perhaps, it made more sense to get Love in the post, where he was more efficient. (Love averaged .98 points per possession on post-ups and finished in the 83rd percentile according to Synergy's numbers.) James, however, would make keen use of these same elbow sets in the playoffs with Dellavedova to devastating effect.

The team also continued to explore options to feed LeBron working off the ball and cutting toward the basket, increasingly taking the ball out of James' hands and letting Love become more of a distributor.

Though Love averaged the same number of shots a game (12.7) before and after the break, he had one more free throw after the break, emblematic of the team's effort to get him the ball around the basket.

The other thing Lue emphasized was playing with better pace. Blatt had also been preaching that, as James noted after the Brooklyn win, saying,

"Coach has been pressuring us about pushing the tempo, pushing our pace, and getting up the floor. I think we did that tonight."

It wasn't necessarily about playing a faster game like the Golden State Warriors do. Pace only nudged up a little under Lue, as measured by the number of possessions a game. Prior to his ascension, the team averaged 95.05 possessions a game, 28th in the league. It went up to 95.5 in the 11 games prior to the All-Star break. After the break it was 96.05, 26th best during that stretch.

What Lue was really looking to do was to take better advantage of the best transition offense in the league, which was middle of the pack in frequency (15th at the end of the season). In general even if you don't get a transition hoop, pushing the ball can force the backtracking defense into bad matchups, and it allows the offense to attack before the defense gets set in place.

Over the first half of the season 28.8 percent of the Cavaliers' possessions occurred in the first eight seconds of the shot clock. After Lue took over, that increased to 33.6 percent without compromising any offensive efficiency. During that time they went from scoring 105.6 points per 100 possessions (known as offensive efficiency or rating) to 110.6 under Lue. (Unfortunately, the defense also jumped more than five points.)

New Jack City. Saturday, January 23, 2016, Cleveland. (30-11)

Cleveland lost its first game under Lue to the Chicago Bulls, who were playing their second game in two nights. The Cavaliers got off to a quick start, outscoring Chicago 14-8 in the first seven minutes. The Bulls outscored Cleveland 13-0 the rest of the quarter as the Cavs missed 15 straight shots, including five by James.

The Cavs managed to pull to within two a minute before half, and got as close as four with eight left in the third quarter. From that point Cleveland was outscored 21-7 before a Dellavedova three at the buzzer. Pau Gasol and Nikola Mirotic did much of the damage, scoring 17 during the run. They went on to win 96-83.

The ball movement wasn't that great. According to Lue the issue was that when the pick or screen didn't work on one side, the team wasn't reversing it to try it on the opposite side.

"The guys tried to play for each other and tried to move the ball," Lue said. "We're just not used to playing to the second side yet. Once we [swing the ball] to the second side, it gets stuck and we get lost."

Lue also complained that the team wasn't in good enough shape to play up-tempo yet, and that they got tired in the third. That may be understandable for Irving and Shumpert, returning from injuries, but it was an indictment of the rest of the team. The Cavaliers would ultimately reap the benefit of their improved conditioning in the Finals.

Play improved two days later against the Timberwolves as Cleveland turned 11 turnovers into 21 points and garnered 30 assists on 45 baskets. Thompson got the starting nod over Mozgov (going forward) and was an energizing force. He had 19 points and 12 rebounds, seven of them offensive. James showed up strong as well with 25 points on just 15 shots, while Delly scored 18 off the bench.

As well as the Cavaliers played offensively, they didn't give the same effort on defense, as the Timberwolves mostly avoided the three (4-of-16) while making their shots inside the arc (37-of-68, 54 percent). Minnesota pulled within 94-91 with six minutes left, and was only down three with 16 seconds left, before James hit two free throws to ice the 114-107 win.

"What we've been doing is taking teams out of making their three-point shot—running guys off so they're getting easier twos and pull-ups," Lue said a few days later. "We'll have to live with that. But nowadays in this game the threes hurt you, so we want to limit guys' threes and live with our rim protection."

It would take six more weeks, but Lue would have to tweak the defense because they were simply giving up *too many* open midrange twos. Meanwhile across the country, the Warriors were busy destroying the San Antonio Spurs in Oracle Arena by 37. Popovich cracked after the game, "I'm just glad my general manager wasn't in the locker room. I might have gotten fired."

The Cavaliers began having more success pushing the ball, which was like grease for their offensive engine. Fastbreak situations elicit good ball movement in part because that's the best way to press a numbers advantage such as two-on-one, three-on-two, etc. If the transition hoop doesn't materialize, the ball's already moving and flows naturally into the offensive set.

Cleveland produced strong offensive nights against Phoenix and Detroit. It was defense sparking offense against the Suns as the Cavaliers scored 33 points off turnovers and held them to 43 second half points in a 115-93 win. "We got stops and pushed the ball. You could see in the open floor we're pretty devastating," Love said.

After the game, Lue talked about something he had put on the chalkboard, noting the team's success based on the number of passes that preceded the shot. "With no passes we shot 27 percent. One pass we shot 32 percent. Two passes it was like 40 percent, and three or more passes we're shooting 52 percent from three," Lue related. "So I put that in guys' minds before the game and we did a good job of moving the ball."

The offense hummed for three 30+-point quarters in Detroit, then stalled in the fourth quarter to let the Pistons back into the game. While the Cavs continued to do a good job defending threes, holding the Pistons to 7-of-23, their defense inside the boundary was less stellar (33-of-61, 54 percent). But James, Irving, and Love all scored over 20 points for the first time of the season to lead Cleveland.

"They scored a lot easier than we wanted to so we couldn't get out and run like we wanted to, but that's going to come once we get our legs in shape and we can get more defensive stops," said Lue, new head trainer for Move Your Ass Cavs.

During the game James surpassed the 26,000-point mark, becoming the youngest player to do so at 31 years, 30 days. He also broke into the NBA's top 20 in career assists, passing Derek Harper.

Cleveland replicated the 66-point first half they put on the Pistons the very next night against the San Antonio Spurs, who rested Tim Duncan but otherwise had their full contingent. The Cavs shot 57 percent for the half and had 17 assists on 15 baskets as they jumped out to a 17-point halftime lead and never let the Spurs back into the game.

Lue showcased a new defensive wrinkle against San Antonio. When Parker received picks from David West and LaMarcus Aldridge, the bigs covering them stepped out to "show" (also called "hedging") before recovering to their man. This kept Parker from gathering momentum as he detoured around the big, giving his defender time to catch up.

In the last game against the Spurs the Cavs' bigs hung back, allowing Parker to take it right at them. They would begin to use this hedging tactic more frequently—particularly without Mozgov on the floor as much—and explore even more aggressive defenses against playoff opponents' explosive guards.

"Last game they took advantage of us being on drops [where the defender drops into the lane] and ISOs, and Tony went one-on-one against our bigs a lot the whole night," Lue said. "So coming into this game we decided we wanted to show and make them veer out, and then play one-on-one against our guards, and it was effective for us tonight."

Coming on top of a string of strong offensive performances, the Spurs game suggested the Cavs had turned a corner. It took time for people to realize it was an oval track and they'd turn a lot of corners before the season ended.

Attention Deficit Disorder. Monday, February 1, 2016, Indianapolis. (34-12)

Cleveland opened the month with their third straight 60-plus point first half. They shot 62 percent to help overcome 10 turnovers. The Cavs had four starters in double figures—in just the first half—including LeBron with 17 on 11 shots. But after a great first quarter, ball movement diminished steadily. The Cavaliers got eight assists on 15 baskets (15-of-22, 68 percent) in the first, then had four assists and five turnovers in the second. They simply had no patience for success.

In the third the Pacers came out aggressive and outscored the Cavaliers 30-15. Cleveland shot poorly (5-of-19) and made five turnovers in the quarter, while Myles Turner grabbed four offensive rebounds over Tristan Thompson and seven total in the quarter.

"We just couldn't get stops," said Lue. "They had like a 30-point quarter, so they got a lot of offensive rebounds. That stopped us from getting out in transition. They made us play halfcourt offense, and we didn't trust, and we didn't move the ball the way we're capable of."

When the team frittered away its 11-point halftime lead, Lue stood by and watched. He refused to call a timeout, pulling an old Phil Jackson trick of forcing them to pull themselves out of it and show their mental toughness.

"I just told the guys after the game we can't resort back to bad habits when things get tough," Lue said. "Coming out in the third quarter they made it tough for us and we went back to our old habits of one-on-one, holding the ball, dribbling around. Then they wanted me to bail them out and I wasn't doing it."

Cleveland came back with a strong fourth quarter and overtime, but it wasn't with ball movement. The Cavaliers just kept running pick-and-rolls involving small forward (or "3") LeBron James and point guard ("1") Kyrie Irving. The Pacers had trouble defending it, as Irving scored 15 in the last stanza and extra session, including eight of the Cavs' 15 overtime points.

"We went to the 1-3 action and they had trouble stopping it all night," Lue said. "You put Kyrie and LeBron in a pick and roll, you gotta pick your poison. So they have to show because they can't go under on Kyrie if they switch it now you have LeBron posting a point guard and you can get any shot. So we kind of stayed with that and it pulled us through for the game."

While the isolation worked, it wasn't their preference. The team's passes/touches bottomed out at 66.9 percent, the lowest mark of the season. The trust to give up the ball and believe in your teammates was still lacking. Firing the coach didn't suddenly change lingering issues like ball movement, transition defense, and consistent effort.

"Obviously, we all wish it could happen overnight like instant oatmeal. But it's not gonna happen that way," James said. "The best teacher in life is experience. When the game gets tough and we have some adversity, we can't resort to our old ways. We've got to continue to work on our offense."

That same offensive stagnation set in two nights later in Charlotte, against a Hornets team missing post threat Al Jefferson and starting point guard Kemba Walker. There were flashes of ball movement in the 35-point second quarter, where nine different guys scored 12 buckets (nobody more than two) with seven assists and zero turnovers.

However, bad habits returned in the third as the Hornets blasted Cleveland 33-17, as the Cavs managed just seven baskets (on 23 shots) and a single assist. There was no fourth quarter comeback for the Cavs, who fell 106-97 after Jeremy Lin scored six in an 8-4 run to ice it.

"Things that are working, we have to stick to it and continue to move the basketball," said Irving. "Obviously we have the talent to go one-on-one, but we want to get away from that and save it for the fourth quarter when we need to be in that mindset."

It was another second half disappearing act for Kevin Love, who in a typical performance had nine first half points on nine shots, and scored only three points on three shots the rest of the way. James and Irving took 24 second half shots, suggesting Love's membership in the Big Three was more of a limited partnership.

On February 5, facing Boston at home, the Cavs burst out of the blocks to a 14-2 lead, which grew to 15 points. It was a game of runs and Cleveland suffered a power outage, leading 45-31 midway through the second. They were outscored 12-4 in the last half of the second and 11-2 to start the third, allowing the Celtics to take a three-point lead.

Poor starts to the third quarter had been an issue that Lue had addressed of late, a great irony given their fine second half play under Blatt. "We've been talking about it a lot," he said after the game. "We've got to be better. We've got to come out with more energy and more effort, and if not we have to find guys that can in the third quarter."

The Cavaliers made a run of their own to take an eight-point lead going into the fourth, despite losing Love late in the third to a left thigh bruise. Unfortunately, the Celtics scored 39 points in the fourth, including 10 in the final 48 seconds while down 99-94. Time and again down the stretch the Cavaliers surrendered offensive boards.

First Tyler Zeller put back an Isaiah Thomas floater to cut the lead to three. J. R. Smith rebounded a bricked James three (0-of-5 in the game, extending a stretch of 18 straight missed triples) and fed Irving, who was fouled and converted his free throws. Jared Sullinger returned the favor, rebounding a missed three by Avery Bradley and finding Jae Crowder to cut the lead to two.

Two more Irving free throws with seven seconds left were followed by Evan Turner's slithering drive past Smith, which drew a ticky-tack foul call. Turner missed the free throw. Mozgov had a good shot at the rebound, but Crowder hooked his right arm. The ball hit Mozgov's left hand and bounced over LeBron's knee and out of bounds.

Down two with four seconds left, Thomas drove and kicked out a little to the left of Bradley, who had to grab the loose ball and then hopped behind the line while Iman Shumpert closed. But Shumpert swatted at the ball rather than contesting and Bradley got a good look, which he sank for the victory. Shumpert often attempted the theft rather than contest, possibly contributing to his opponents' relatively high shooting percentage.

"It's not over until the horn sounds," said James. "We relaxed just a little bit. He shouldn't have been that open to get a shot off like that. Not up two. If we give up a layup, that's OK, we go into overtime. But not a three."

It was another case of the Cavaliers playing well for a good stretch of the game but proving unable to sustain the focus—or maybe something else.

"I wouldn't say mental focus. I'd say the desire to perform and execute with urgency," said James Jones. "This is a group that's always had to play and which thrives under pressure when we're down. But we struggle to deal with success and to play at a high level once we've had some success. At the end of the day it's a desire to be on point every single possession, and right now guys just aren't exhibiting that."

They didn't let the loss linger, beating the New Orleans Pelicans convincingly, 95-84, despite what Lue figured were "tired legs." Love sat with a quad injury and Mozgov got a start. Again they turned in a weak third quarter, getting outscored 27-20, allowing the Pelicans to pull within four. However, Cleveland stiffened, holding New Orleans to 14 points in the fourth to win going away.

After the game, Lue complained that the team didn't know the play calls, 50 games into the season.

"I tried to call 'slice' a few times tonight and we couldn't run it right. Tried to call 'punch,' we couldn't run it right," Lue said. "What's happening after makes [when we can't push the ball] is we're kind of drifting into random…. When we hold the ball and the ball sticks, it's because we're in random and we don't know what we want to run, because we don't have anything to flow into."

Cleveland entered the All-Star Break scoring 120 in consecutive games against the Sacramento Kings and Los Angeles Lakers, though even the latter hapless opponents caused a moment of pause. The Lakers put together a 37-point fourth quarter to close a 20-point gap, before ultimately falling 120-111. Irving showed his improving form by topping 30 in both games. He'd made at least half of his shots in seven of his last eight games and scored at least 25 point in five of the last six, highlighting his improving form.

It was that same ADD issue as before. They just couldn't stay focused and playing the right way for 48 minutes, preferring to freelance and relax, drifting away from the fundamentals that got them there in the first place.

"I don't think we take it seriously all the time," said Lue after the Lakers game. "I think we get up and then we make the fancy pass or take a bad shot and the score's gone from 20 to 12. We have to be more professional in what we're trying to do. We're trying to build better habits and build something here, so guys have to be better."

8

THE LONG-AWAITED GRADUATION

THE NBA REGULAR season is only a preliminary heat. More than half the league—16 of 30 teams—makes the playoffs, and so there's a diminishing return to regular season victories. Sure, the top four seeds get homecourt advantage and that's useful. Home teams have won 60 percent of individual matchups in recent years; that's down from two-thirds a quarter century ago. The team with homecourt advantage wins 75 percent of playoff series and an even better 80 percent of playoff Game 7s.

But the season's grind wears down teams, and exhaustion increases the potential for injuries. Recognizing this and the somewhat limited advantage of home court, teams began prioritizing safeguarding their players for the playoffs, particularly toward the end of the season by limiting minutes and distributing days off for no other reason than rest.

By the All-Star break many playoff seeds are largely determined. Winning a few more games to move up a slot often isn't worth the risk. San Antonio coach Gregg Popovich has pushed harder than anyone in resisting league norms, resting players even early in the season before the break and against lesser opponents. Many have since followed suit.

Griffin suggested the team might have internalized this thinking, eliciting Cleveland's chronic bouts of dolor and indifference before inferior teams.

"I worry that we blew too many opportunities to get better because we weren't always playing hard enough," Griffin told *Plain Dealer* reporter Terry

Pluto at the end of the season. "We were sort of jumbled. At times, we lacked continuity and it showed."

Perhaps it wasn't injury-fear tentativeness so much as overconfidence, like a gifted kid who succeeds with the least effort possible, turning that lowest bar boundary into a game of chicken. Often the Cavs waited until the fourth quarter to shift into fifth gear, or the third quarter when down double digits. Opponents missing key players engendered such a subconscious downshift that Cleveland often couldn't compensate for the head start in effort.

These were Lue's challenges in taking over from Blatt—getting an underperforming team atop the Eastern Conference to play with greater intensity and consistency when it could be argued they'd done plenty well without it.

Lue's ascension had a positive impact on the offense. Under him they were scoring 5.7 more points on 5.1 more shots. Many of these were of the open (closest defender four to six feet away) or wide-open variety (closest defender more then six feet away)—27 and 18 under Lue, respectively, versus 23 and 16 under Blatt. That's six more open or wide-open shots a game!

The crazy thing is that the Cavaliers were making nearly 20 fewer passes per game than they were under Blatt (306.1 to 288.6), even with more overall possessions, yet even so they somehow had more assists (23.5 to 22). This was probably due to early offense creating better shots that players starting making with better frequency. In an example of an equal and opposite reaction, the defense went backwards nearly as quickly as the offense went forward, allowing 5.2 more points on defense.

"Our defense is worse," Lue said just before the break. "We're scoring a lot of points now. We're playing faster and we're playing with pace. But in doing that, guys are not in great shape yet, so now we're saving it for the offensive end and not competing on the defensive end. So now we've got to try to get both ends of the floor."

One challenge was a lack of preparation time. Lue only had two proper practices in the three weeks leading up to the break. As holders of the best record in the Eastern Conference, Lue and his staff had the honor of coaching the East in the All-Star Game.

Lue had initially suggested his old boss Blatt might still coach the game, but the league nipped that in the bud. The West won a typical NBA

JAM-style arcade game 196-173, but Lue accomplished his only goal—playing James two fewer minutes (20) than any other starter on either team.

Trade Deadline Day. Thursday, February 18, 2016, Cleveland. (38-14)

The break energized Cleveland, fueling its nine-point victory over Chicago. The Cavs jumped out to a 17-point lead before a 16-5 Bulls run to close the second quarter trimmed the deficit to 48-42. The Cavaliers struck back with a 30-point third and cruised to the 106-95 win.

It was bittersweet because before the game it was announced that 12-year Cavalier veteran Anderson Varejao had been traded with Jared Cunningham and a 2018 first round pick for 33-year-old stretch big Channing Frye. Varejao was frustrated to leave.

"It wasn't easy for me because of my history with Cleveland being there for 12 years, went through a lot of stuff there—good teams, bad teams—and we fought through a lot," Varejao said.

In addition to Orlando, the trade involved Portland, with the salary cap/landing space for Varejao, getting the first-rounder in return. The Blazers subsequently waived him.

"All of a sudden I don't have a team and I didn't know what's going to happen," he said. "But soon enough phone calls started to happen and I had good teams calling me and I had the privilege of making a decision to come [to Golden State]."

For the Cavaliers, Frye offered a versatile, sweet-shooting big with a lifetime 39 percent shooting percentage from three. He could play the 4 or 5, and had a long friendship with Richard Jefferson going back to high school and their shared year at the University of Arizona. Their camaraderie proved infectious.

"It's tough for Channing," Jefferson observed. "He's no longer the funniest guy on the team."

Frye had signed a four-year, $32 million deal with the Orlando Magic the year before, and had been a target of Griffin's before James came into the picture. Griffin knew him from the Suns, where his career finally got untracked after a couple years with the Knicks and the Trailblazers.

A heart issue stole one Phoenix season, and after a successful 2013-14 comeback he signed with a Magic team looking for veteran help. Yet with Orlando treading water it was time to move on from Frye, who pairs a sweet three stroke with some back-to-the-basket and post skills.

Defense was his weak spot. While Frye uses his length well enough to handle merely athletic (Biyombo), more brutish (Andre Drummond), and unathletic stretch 4s (Ryan Anderson), he's just not quick and agile enough to pose much resistance for the current crop of superstar 4s (DeMarcus Cousins, Anthony Davis, Blake Griffin, Draymond Green, LaMarcus Aldridge).

He excels at pulling slow, rim-protecting bigs away from the basket and toasting them golden brown. That obviously meshes well with accomplished drivers like James and Irving. If bigs collapse, Frye and Smith will rain wide-open jumpers all night long.

Not only is Frye close with Jefferson, but he credits James Jones with playing a role in his growth as a player. "James was always in my ear about things that I needed to do and how to be professional," Frye said. "It's more about consistency, what you're supposed to look at, how you're supposed to approach each day with your mental attitude.

"The season is long and when you're young you always think I'm supposed to play great every single game," he continued. "But really there are only two or three guys that play like that every single game. Say you play four games in a week. You play two and a half good games, your bench should help you out for a game and a half. Or someone else should help you out. When you think about it like that it takes off some of the pressure."

That pressure may have contributed to what sidelined Frye in 2012, when he showed up with a heart abnormality and had to sit the entire season. He used the time productively, embracing yoga and a more peaceful way of thinking.

"I was a super perfectionist. It helped me a lot not to have so much anxiety about things I can't control," Frye said. "The year I had to take off because of [air quote] my heart issue [air quote], for me it helped me just embrace the moment. It helped me just take a second and breathe. I'm kind of a web thinker—I think of a situation and every response I could have to that situation—so for me just being in the moment and being able to focus has not only helped me outside the court but it's helped me in the game."

Frye had a role to fill for the Cavs on and off the floor, but it'd take time to gain Lue's trust and master the offensive and defensive sets.

The Cavaliers traveled next to Oklahoma City for another match with the Thunder, whom they had beaten by four in December. The Cavaliers came in shorthanded, minus Iman Shumpert, who sprained his shoulder against Chicago, and Mo Williams, who was still nursing a sore left knee that would trouble him the rest of the season.

Meanwhile, Dellavedova had missed five games early in the month due to a hamstring injury and was still on a minutes restriction (25). Midway through the first quarter Kyrie Irving went to the locker room to throw up, and did not return. Then halfway through the second quarter J. R. Smith picked up his third foul and had to sit.

That's when, for whatever reason, the Cavaliers slipped into gear. Perhaps the odds had finally turned enough against them to merit their full attention and effort. It was tied at 39 with seven minutes left when Love received the ball from LeBron at the elbow, and threw right back to him at the left wing arc where James dropped the three for the lead.

That three inaugurated a 56-30 run that extended almost to the end of the third. During the run Cleveland shot 17-of-29 from the floor and 17-of-19 from the line as Love did a number on the Thunder in the post. He was 11-of-12 from the line with 17 points during the run while James also added 17, including two of three from distance.

The Thunder never got back in the game, losing 115-92. Love finished with 29 points and 11 rebounds; James added 25 points and 11 assists. This started some silly whispering about Love and James being better without Irving, which ranks with "the moon is made of cheese" on the scale of logical syllogisms.

Postgame, Irving attributed his sickness to late-night hotel guests. "Just imagine how freaked out you'd be if you saw friggin five, big-ass bedbugs just sitting on your pillow," said Irving, who lay awake the rest of the night on the couch (instead of getting another room?). "I woke up itching and I'm just looking around and I'm like, 'Are you serious right now?' It was 3 a.m. and I was so tired at that point."

Back home for the second half of the back-to-back against the Pistons, the Cavaliers ran out of gas. It started like a drag race, each team blasting off the line shooting a combined 15-of-22 in the first six minutes of the game. After falling behind six in the second, Irving scored 10 in a 12-4 run to take a brief lead.

But a 14-5 run to end the half gave the Pistons back the lead, and they never relinquished it again, beating Cleveland 96-88 in a game that wasn't really that close most of the second half. Love had another strong game with 24 points. Irving had a bounce-back 30-point game, but James had just 12 on 5-of-18 shooting. Afterward Lue lamented that he hadn't trusted his gut and rested James.

The Cavs rediscovered their swagger against the Hornets, winning 114-103 thanks to a 40-point second in which they finally looked liked world-beaters. Entering the quarter down 24-23, Cleveland outscored the Hornets by 12 while shooting 16-of-23 and sharing the ball. Eight different players scored, five took three or more shots, and nobody took more than five. Irving and Smith hit all seven of their combined shots while Channing Frye had his first breakout game with 15 points.

"I thought for the most part all the guys played good," Lue said during the postgame. "The thing I like the most is we went up by 14-15, they made a run, and we didn't hang our heads and get mad and we built the lead back up again."

Still Leaky at the Point of Attack. Friday, February 26, 2016, Toronto. (41-15)

That resilience didn't last long as the Cavaliers then lost consecutive road games to the second-place Toronto Raptors and Washington Wizards in a game that Lue rested James.

In Toronto, Kyle Lowry became the third consecutive point guard (Reggie Jackson, Kemba Walker) to score over 20 on the Cavaliers, dropping a career-high with 43, on 15-of-20 from the field and 11-of-15 from the line, while dishing out nine assists and making four steals.

Lowry was a one-man army (apologies to late voice legend Don LaFontaine), slicing up the Cavs in the high pick-and-roll like Hannibal Lecter. His drives helped Toronto win points in the paint, 50-34. Thirty-five of 73 Raptors shots came at the rim, including a perfect 7-of-7 over Kevin Love.

During one stretch early in the second quarter, the Raptors made 10 straight shots, though the Cavaliers led much of the game—by four at halftime and nine at the end of three. The Cavs led 91-82 with five and a

THE LONG-AWAITED GRADUATION

half minutes to go on a LeBron James alley-oop from Love. Then the wheels came off. Toronto outscored the Cavaliers 13-1 over the next four minutes.

"We gave up a couple threes, a couple unfocused plays not following the gameplan. And it burned us," said James. "When you lose the way we lost—mental mistake after mental mistake—those hurt more than anything when you can play better mentally. We get so caught up in the physical thing but we lack the mental."

The Cavs almost pulled it out. Down three, Love hit one from long distance and then converted a couple free throws for a short-lived two-point lead with 68 seconds left. Lowry beat Dellavedova in the high pick-and-roll (natch), backing him into the middle of the lane before sinking a five-foot half hook to even it at 97.

Smith missed a three and Lowry ran down the shot clock before hitting a 23-foot pull-up for the 99-97 victory. Lowry scored 18 of the Raptors' 30 fourth quarter points. Not Shumpert, Dellavedova, or Irving could stop him.

"Down the stretch Kyle Lowry took over the game," Lue said. "That's the second time he's done that to us, so going forward we've got to get somebody that can guard him."

The Cavs faced off next against the fastest-paced team in the league, the Washington Wizards. The Cavaliers had struggled in transition defense all year long, but kept their turnovers low to minimize its potential to hurt them. Whether worn out from the Raptors game a couple nights earlier or just hurting too much without James on the floor, Washington smoked them.

The Cavaliers' defense gave up 35 first quarter points, but fought hard enough in the second to stay within nine, 63-54. The Wizards came out of the third quarter locker room like Roman Christian gladiators one step ahead of the lions. They hit 10 of their first 11 shots, comprised of four layups and five threes, including three straight triples by Otto Porter to open the quarter. The Wizards led by as many as 30 in the third before a rally by Cavs third-stringers made it a more respectable 113-99 loss.

"Today was one that was very uncharacteristic of us," Love said. "We need to lock in sometimes. We're so talented that we're able to get away with a lot of stuff on the offensive end. We might put up a lot of points, but when we play on the other side of the ball we're so much better."

The Cavaliers took losing three out of four to heart and ran off a three-game win streak, beating the Pacers at home the night after the Wizards loss, and avenging both the Wizards and Celtics losses in blowouts.

The Pacers game was a back-and-forth affair that came down to the very end. James scored a very efficient 33 points on 22 shots, but down the stretch played facilitator instead of scorer. After going down 94-91 on a Monta Ellis layup with 90 seconds left, LeBron fed Dellavedova for three and Thompson for a five-foot fallaway in the lane. Irving hit four free throws in the last 10 seconds to ice the 100-96 victory.

"When our backs are against the wall, that's when we tend to play harder," said Lue afterward. "It's annoying, but when you have a team like we have with great individual players, they can turn it on at any point in time. Sometimes it can come back and bite you, but I have to get that effort out of those guys for 48 minutes. When we play the good teams, we do that. But when teams don't have a great record, we tend to kind of let up."

The four days off before the Wizards rematch gave Lue time to incorporate some new offensive wrinkles, such as playing Irving off the ball and running him off baseline screens like Ray Allen used to do. There were more sets with Love at the 5 and LeBron the 4 with J. R. initiating the offense and post-ups to James on one side, with Irving and Love teaming on the other.

After crushing the Wizards with small ball 108-83, the Cavaliers almost took a step backwards at home against the Celtics. Cleveland fell behind the Celtics 35-17 at the end of one before the second team's defense took over. The Cavs went small, and though Love and James went a combined 1-of-8, the rest of the team was 6-of-10 and Cleveland closed the second on a 26-12 run to end the half down only one.

"We had a heck of a second quarter spearheaded by Kyrie and our defense," James said. "Once we settled in, we got a little more physical on defense and also offensively we turned the game around."

James and Celtic point Isaiah Thomas traded three-pointers, tying the score at 70 with six left in the third before Cleveland closed the quarter on a 21-13 run, capped by a Shumpert three. He finished with 12 points, a career-high 16 rebounds, four assists, and two steals as the Celtics never got closer than 10 after that.

Faulty Ignition Switch. Monday, March 7, 2016, Cleveland. (44-17)

Two days later the Cavs demonstrated their strangely unerring tendency to read news of opposing players sitting out as "attendance optional." The Memphis Grizzlies were missing damn near their whole team—Zach Randolph, Marc Gasol, Mike Conley, Matt Barnes, and Chris Anderson—so naturally the Cavs arrived late.

The Cavaliers went down nine at halftime and trailed almost the entire second half, but Irving scored 14 of the team's 29 in the fourth. The Cavs took the lead back twice in the final two minutes, before essentially losing on a seven-foot Mario Chalmers floater with 25 seconds left, making the score 101-100. The Grizzlies held on for a 106-103 win.

Tony Allen scored 25, while JaMychal Green, Chalmers, and Lance Stephenson posted 17. Even Vince Carter's ghost turned corporeal for 15 points. James and Irving combined for 55 points as well as 11 of the 25 turnovers that led to 29 Memphis points.

"We just could have done a better job of respecting the game," said Love, admitting the team held back maximal effort until the end of the game. "We have a luxury of being able to turn it on, but it shouldn't have to be like that."

After embarrassing themselves before the Grizzlies scrubs, the Cavs flew to California for three games in Sacramento and Los Angeles. Cleveland played a disinterested first half against the lowly Kings, falling behind 16 at half. They rallied in the fourth behind the defensive play of Tristan Thompson, who neutralized DeMarcus Cousins down the stretch while carrying five fouls in the 120-111 victory.

The Cavs beat the Lakers 120-108, building a double-digit lead in the second that they never relinquished. Irving scored 26, his sixth straight game with over 20, his best stretch of the year, including the playoffs. Channing Frye—increasingly taking time from Mozgov—got the start while Love rested and scored 21, as six Cavs hit double figures.

"I was talking to Richard [Jefferson] about defense, and I was like, 'Wow, we have 70 points and LeBron has nine—who's scoring?'" Frye recalls. "He's like, 'Channing, you have 21.' I was, 'Oh crap, do I?' I don't know. I don't pay attention. I'm always into what's happening now and what is the other team going to do."

Three days later the Cavaliers overcame a shaky first quarter against the Clippers, running away from them in the middle quarters 70-49, shooting 60 percent from the field, and going 12-of-20 from three. The ball was moving and Cavs were hitting their open shots. James paced the team with 27 points on just 15 attempts as again six Cavs scored in double figures.

"We're not thinking about it anymore, who's getting the shot or anything like that," Irving said. "We're not just a one-sided team anymore. We're driving close-outs. We're getting the ball to the weakside. We're driving second-side pick-and-roll. We're getting to our secondary actions. That will be very important for us going forward."

He wasn't kidding. For his part, James was happy that his teammates didn't succumb to the temptations of Los Angeles and kept focused on the work despite the long stay.

"Guys understood what this trip was about," James said. "This is a business trip and they get an opportunity to be in a great city, but at the end of the day we knew what the main thing was, and that was to continue the momentum that we've been on. We came out and took care of business."

Cue the sad trombone, because no sooner had they said it than they ended the road trip with an uninspired effort in Utah, against a Jazz team missing its leading scorer, Gordon Hayward. Instead, Rodney Hood (28 points, just off his career high of 32) and Shelvin Mack (17 points, 10 assists, seven rebounds) hurt the Cavs with big nights.

Mozgov started against the Clippers and for most of the road trip, while still averaging less than 15 minutes a game. Lue probably wanted to cut Thompson's minutes as the postseason approached and give Mozgov a last chance to show him something.

Mozgov's knee had improved without being better, and so had his defense (relative to the year before). He was providing good rim protection, but to some extent the Cavaliers had moved on from those schemes. Instead of protecting their back line, Cleveland was pressuring the perimeter, and that more aggressive approach may have even helped them start games quicker. It also offered a preview of the Cavs' playoff defense trump card.

Back home against Dallas on March 16, before departing again on a two-game Florida road trip, the Cavaliers took a six-point halftime lead and pushed it to 20 in the third before losing interest. The Mavericks outscored the Cavaliers 30-15 and pulled within two before a couple turnovers in the last 40 seconds cost them the comeback, as the Cavs held on 99-98.

Even the Magic, who had fallen to Cleveland by 14, 35, and 25 their last three matchups, put the Cavaliers to the test two nights later thanks to inconsistent effort. There was one sweet stretch in the second where Cleveland outscored the Magic 36-19, making 12-of-15 shots, eight of them assisted, with six different players with assists. Love was the focal point with 11 points including a trio of threes. After surrendering the lead in the third quarter the Cavs battled back in the fourth to take it 109-103.

The next night Miami brutalized Cleveland 122-101, as the Cavs' lead over Toronto for the conference's top seed shrank to 1.5 games. Lue experimented again with the small lineup featuring Love at the 5 and James at the 4. "I kinda went with my gut and went small to see how it'd work out," he said. "It didn't work out so well."

The team held its own until Love picked up an offensive foul (his second) and was replaced by Tristan Thompson with Miami leading 11-9. For another three minutes the Cavaliers hung close. Cleveland trailed 18-15 when the Cavaliers hit their frequent mid-first quarter swoon.

The Heat closed the first on a 13-4 run and never looked back. The lead ballooned as large as 33 points, despite the fact that the Cavaliers shot 53 percent and committed only 14 turnovers.

"As usual when we struggle, we hold it, and when we hold it we don't get good opportunities for everyone to get involved, and end up in isolation too much," said assistant coach Jim Boylan, in a straightforward halftime diagnosis of the Cavaliers' offensive issues.

The defense was the issue, allowing Miami to shoot 61 percent through three quarters while dominating points in the paint (56-14) and second-chance points (19-4). Through three quarters the Heat were beating the Cavs 31-14 on the boards, with 10 offensive rebounds. That physicality, as embodied by the rebounding numbers, was lacking.

"When we're physical and we're the aggressor to start the game offensively and defensively, we're at our best," said Lue. "When we're on our heels to start the game it's tough to try to come out of that."

Re-Dedicated (And If Feels So Good). Monday, March 21, 2016, Cleveland (49-20)

The loss to Miami proved a turning point for the team, not so much because of the loss per se, but the attention on LeBron James. Though he played a pretty good game with 26 points on 13-of-20 shooting in 26 minutes on the court, some players were displeased with the way James and Dwyane Wade hung out during halftime warmups.

That wouldn't happen in the old NBA where fraternization was discouraged, but times had changed. While Miami players suggested lifelong friendships transcend the game, some Cavaliers players felt frustrated. This incident and a comment to the press about one day hoping to play with banana boat buddies Carmelo Anthony and Chris Paul prompted separate discussions with David Griffin and Tyronn Lue, according to *Plain Dealer* reporter Joe Vardon.

At the point the Cavaliers were 19-9 under Lue compared to 30-11 under Blatt, and people were suggesting that Lue hadn't done enough to change the team's personality or faltering attention span since taking over. With just 13 games left, some wondered if it were even possible.

If those meetings took place as Vardon suggests, they might have been responsible for James switching into "playoff mode" early. The year before he'd turned up the intensity several games before the season finale. In response to criticism, it would appear LeBron turned it on a couple weeks early.

There were other changes aside from James' "Eye of the Tiger" behavior. Lue announced the Cavaliers had scrapped the defense they'd installed when coach Mike Longabardi came aboard, replacing Lue as defensive coordinator.

Cleveland had been challenging ballhandlers deeper in the frontcourt, forcing the picks much farther from the basket. When the Cavs' bigs retreated into the lane to defend the basket, the distance of the drops and rotations was affording too many open midrange jumpers, upon which opponents had been feasting.

"We were trying to do some different things," Lue said, explaining their return to the coverages he used as defensive coordinator. "It's just getting back to the basics and doing what we're accustomed to doing."

The Cavaliers annihilated the Nuggets 124-91, accumulating a season-high 38 assists. Shortly after the break, during the game in Washington,

Longabardi commented during a halftime interview with Fox that the key to the defense was going to be playing better offense.

This seemed a strange thing to say, but it's because when they make baskets, other teams can't get out in transition, and must attack the Cavaliers' set halfcourt defense, where they're much better. Frye reiterated this point after the Nuggets game.

"If you notice when we get easy baskets now the offense's flowing a lot easier. 'Okay we got three layups so now; someone's feeling rhythm, now we get J. R. a shot,'" he said. "It's really those one or two stops that are getting us going. Now we feel like we can get stops—there's not as much pressure on us to make these shots."

The Cavaliers posted another strong performance against the Bucks on March 23, other than an awful second quarter that all but erased a ten-point first quarter lead. After allowing 61 first half points, the defense stiffened, allowing just 43 in the second half by forcing turnovers and keeping the Bucks off the line. (Milwaukee shot 50 percent in the second half, but made just one three.)

The Cavaliers then lapsed back into indolence in Brooklyn against the sorry Nets. Cleveland fell behind in the second, battled back in the third, and then the game slip from their grasp. The Cavs held a 92-90 lead on a Dellavedova three with six minutes left, before the Nets outscored them 14-0 down the stretch. Cleveland missed 10 straight shots, discounting a meaningless Jordan McRae three at the buzzer.

"With our backs against the wall in the third quarter we tried to come back and played hard. It just wasn't enough," said Lue. "The third quarter we come out, we're aggressive, we're getting into the ball, and we're scrambling. We hold them to 21 points in the third quarter but our backs were against the wall—instead of coming out from the start of the game, focusing and playing the way we're supposed to play."

The loss prompted a team meeting, one of probably more than a dozen during the year, though this one proved especially productive.

"I just think the Big Three sitting down and getting on the same page of understanding what they need from each other on a nightly basis and understanding that they have to trust each other and also trust the team," said Lue, several weeks later. "We had that talk in front of everyone, and everyone kind of gave their opinion and kind of talked about what they expected and what we needed to do better."

After the meeting the roles of the Big Three of Irving, James, and Love became better defined, as Lue successfully challenged Love to be more aggressive, and for Irving and James to consistently get him the ball, not just in the first half.

"Kevin Love has really benefitted from that day," Lue explained weeks later. "Talking to him in front of everyone and letting him know that, 'Be aggressive. Look to score the basketball. And you're one of the top 10 players in this league.' So when you're open, tell LeBron, 'I'm open.' Tell Kyrie, 'I'm open.' Demand the basketball and be aggressive. And once we had that meeting, I think the team understood what we needed from each other to win, if we wanted to win."

Bad habits don't change overnight—not when they've been building all season. In their next matchup with the Knicks, the Cavs took a 24-point halftime lead, holding New York to 32 first half points, then surrendered a 40-point third quarter, though they still won comfortably, 107-93.

James sat at home against the Rockets, but the Cavs still built a 19-point lead at half, and held a 13-point lead at the end of three. Houston outscored the Cavs 35-15 in the fourth, handing Cleveland a dispiriting, if by now not entirely surprising, 106-100 loss. Smith, Shumpert, and Dellavedova went 0-of-10 in the final frame as the Cavs shot 26 percent.

The March 29 loss to the Rockets was something of a wake-up call for the Cavs. They won their next four, their longest win streak under Lue since before the All-Star break, including a gutsy 110-108 overtime victory over the Hawks in Atlanta on the back end of a back-to-back (preceded by a 20-point home vengeance killing of the Brooklyn Nets).

One of the game's highlights was James passing Oscar Robertson, a personal inspiration, for 11th place in NBA all-time scoring with a layup in the third quarter on which Al Horford was charged for goaltending. That bucket gave him 26,711 points, and he reflected on it after the game.

"I wish I could've had a triple-double in passing him as well, that would've been the perfect thing," James said. "Any time I'm linked with the Big O, it's an honor for myself. I understand and know how much he meant not only to the game of basketball but what he represented off the floor."

Individual accolades are great, but the Cavs were closing out the regular season still unable to maintain any semblance of consistency. After demolishing the Bucks 109-80 on the front end of a road back-to-back, they lost 123-109 to the Pacers in a game in which James sat and the team surrendered 70 first half points. Three days later they suffered another dispiriting loss, 105-102 to the Chicago Bulls in their final regular season road game.

The Cavs took a 10-point lead with three and change left in the third, and a three-point lead to start the fourth on a James buzzer-beating three. Then the Cavaliers spent the first eight minutes of the fourth looking for their first basket of the quarter. Down 12 with four minutes left, Cleveland mounted a furious comeback to pull within two with eight ticks left. J. R. Smith missed his second free throw, recovered the rebound, and passed to Love, who found Delly at the boundary. He airballed the three, and the Bulls prevailed 105-102.

Kyrie Irving was particularly upset about his play at the beginning of the fourth when he made three grievous turnovers and missed several shots including a layup. He took the blame after the game for letting the team down while Love and James were on the bench. Indeed, he felt so bad that he texted James that night, promising to improve.

"[The text] was just about being better and being a better leader of that second unit when he's on the bench. I know we expect a lot from one another. We have to hold each other accountable," Irving explained a couple days later. "I had to take that responsibility. I couldn't go home without feeling like that fourth quarter could have gone different if I would have played better."

This was just the type of accountability the team hoped to breed, with the faith that such honesty and humility can be contagious. They won their next game at home against Atlanta 107-93, outscoring the Hawks by 19 in the middle quarters thanks in part to a 39-point third quarter. James was spectacular, scoring 34 on 16 shots, while Irving added 35 points and five assists against six turnovers.

The victory clinched the Eastern Conference's top seed, with one game to spare. It would allow Cleveland to sit their starters in the final regular season game against the Pistons, whom they'd face a few days later in the first round. "It's a credit to this team when we needed to win, we won," said Lue.

Of course, that was sort of the problem, putting themselves in must-win situations in the first place. Against higher-caliber playoff foes, digging big early holes could prove fatal.

"We had lots of those games this year where we would go and get a very, very good win and we would follow it up by just laying an egg," said Jefferson during the playoffs. "We still won 57 games. That's a lot of games. But we felt personally that we should have been in the mid-60 range if we'd been locked in."

POSTSEASON

Carmelo Anthony and LeBron James tussle in high school.
Photo by Lou Capozzola/USA TODAY Sports

*Top: James Jones (foreground),
Iman Shumpert and Kyrie Irving
get shots up during pregame.*

*Right: Kyrie Irving demonstrates
grip on his hair-trigger release.*

Photos by Emanuel Christian Wallace.

Top: LeBron James' ideal jump shot form is also a gun show.

Above: J. R. Smith likes to keep his pregame shooting ritual incognito.

Photos by Emanuel Christian Wallace.

Top Left: LeBron James beats Kobe Bryant in the post with an up-and-under move to get baseline in the fourth quarter.

Top Right: James missed the finger roll and the follow tip. It was Kobe's final visit to Cleveland on February 2016.

Above: LeBron James keeps the ball locked in the triple threat position, while wondering, "What you talking 'bout, Stanley?"
Photos by Emanuel Christian Wallace.

Top: Kyrie Irving uses his soft touch to float it over Detroit's Reggie Bullock in the 2016 Playoffs.

Above Left: Kevin Love and Richard Jefferson share an exuberant moment finishing in the lane against Detroit.

Above Right: LeBron James introduces himself to the Atlanta Hawks with authority and extreme prejudice.

Photos by Emanuel Christian Wallace.

*Top: James exudes confidence sinking this fallaway
over Atlanta's Al Horford.*

*Above: LeBron James and Tristan Thompson compare
game faces while Kyle Korver schleps toward the exit.*

Photos by Emanuel Christian Wallace.

Top: Shooting should be fun; just ask Kyrie Irving.

*Above: Tristan Thompson cleans the glass like Windex,
while James takes a "Hell Yeah" position.*

Photos by Emanuel Christian Wallace.

Opposite: Pompeii a moment before eruption. James with the Deus ex machina moment.

Above: Kevin Love gets thwacked more than the jukebox from Happy Days, but that's just life in the lane.

Photos by Emanuel Christian Wallace.

Top: LeBron takes baseline the way fathers steal their kid's nose.

Above: James has spent enough time airborne to earn his pilot's license, and enjoys turning Toronto into his runway.

Photos by Emanuel Christian Wallace.

LeBron James makes "The Block" on Andre Iguodala, averting a goaltending call my inches.
Photo by Eric Risberg/AP Photo.

Top: Moments before "The D," Kevin Love made another
good contest on the Warriors' Stephen Curry.
Photo by Bob Donnan/USA TODAY Sports.

Above: Kyrie Irving hits the historic game-winner over
Stephen Curry, sealing the 93-89 championship victory.
Photo by Kelley L Cox/USA TODAY Sports.

Top: *The night The Curse ended and the Factory of Sadness ran out of juice.*

Above: *Stare into the eyes of champions, and always, always, Believe.*

Photos by Emanuel Christian Wallace.

J. R. Smith's shirtless rampage ran so long, President Obama sought to intervene.

Photos by Emanuel Christian Wallace.

Top: LeBron's bracelets could be military bars. After nine Cavs' tours of duty, James can smile, "Mission Accomplished."

Above: Kyrie Irving basks in parade euphoria while sporting the latest J. R. Smith topless style.

Photos by Emanuel Christian Wallace.

Cleveland's borne witness, now they're champions.

Photos by Emanuel Christian Wallace.

9

PISTONS FIRE BUT CAVS BULLETPROOF

L EBRON JAMES IS more judicious with his energy these days given the miles on his odometer. Yet when he switched to playoff intensity for the last 13 games of the 2015-16 season (playing in 10 of them), his play hinted at the MVP-level he keeps in reserve.

James finished the year averaging 25.3 points, 7.4 rebounds, 6.8 assists, and 3.3 turnovers a game, while shooting 52 percent from the field (a personal best in a Cavs uniform) and just under 31 percent from three, his lowest rate since 29 percent his rookie year.

Over his last 10 games he averaged 28.4 points, 8.0 rebounds, 8.5 assists, and 3.7 turnovers, while shooting 62 percent from the field and 52 percent from three, in addition to shooting 80 percent from the free throw line. Of particular of note is the increased assists, as James focused even more on finding his mates.

James was able to shoot that ridiculous field goal percentage because he began taking everything to the rack. During the year James shot 45 percent of his shots from within three feet, higher than his career rate (35 percent) or his prior highest (40 percent). Over those last 10 games he took a startling 68 percent of his shots there. (He made 73 percent of them, a little above career and year-long rates.)

This different intensity energized the team, though inconsistent effort continued to dog the Cavs through the regular season's end. Coming into the playoffs there was a legitimate question whether they could play hard and with purpose all game long.

Love got going after Lue implored him to behave like a "Top 10" player in Brooklyn. After that game he shot 43 percent from three and averaged as many points as Irving, despite four fewer shots. His rebounding, as always, was strong, as he averaged a double-double over the last three weeks.

Irving, however, struggled. Over the last 10 regular season games, Kyrie shot 39 percent from the field and 33 percent from three while making almost three turnovers a game. He asked to play that final regular season game against Detroit to work on his offensive rhythm, though Lue kept him on the pine.

Like many quick lead guards, Pistons point Reggie Jackson gave the Cavaliers fits in the pick-and-roll during the regular season. He came to the Pistons the year before at the trading deadline from the Thunder, where he'd thanklessly toiled behind Russell Westbrook.

Given a chance to start, Jackson showcased an explosive first step and enough skill running the pick-and-roll (.88 points per possession, aka ppp, 77th percentile according to Synergy) to lead Detroit in scoring with 18.8 points a game. Though only an average three-point shooter (35 percent), he had a good midrange jump shot (40 percent), and maintained a better than two-to-one assist-to-turnover ratio.

Cleveland began first game of the series by blitzing Jackson, pushing him toward the sideline and generally forcing him to give up the ball without driving. Then the defending big retreated quickly to defend the lane and prevent lobs to athletic Pistons 7-footer Andre Drummond.

Thompson's quick feet kept Jackson bottled up until his man recovered. "I think we frustrated Reggie Jackson a little bit because he couldn't turn the corner on Tristan," said Lue. "He's our best defensive big and we can do a lot of different things with him."

While he's a skilled defender, Drummond's offensive arsenal is limited. He shot just 42 percent in the paint beyond the restricted area and 11-of-48 outside of 10 feet. With the Cavaliers taking the ball out of Jackson's hands and packing the paint on Drummond, the Pistons had to rely on other players and their ability to make jump shots—which they did, at first.

E. C. Quarterfinals, Game 1. Sunday, April 17, 2016, Cleveland. (Even)

Marcus Morris hit three jump shots for six of the first eight Pistons points. Two came during a stretch where the Pistons hit seven straight shots and sprinted out to an 18-11 lead. The last seven points coming from third-year shooting guard Kentavious Caldwell-Pope, who finished with a team-high 21 points.

Morris wasn't lucky to hit those jumpers. He's a 36 percent career three-point shooter who's extremely proficient at knocking down long jumpers (15-19 feet), finishing the season shooting over 44 percent from that range. Only a dozen players averaged as many shots and shot a better percentage, including Kevin Durant, Karl-Anthony Towns, Chris Bosh, Dirk Nowitzki, and Pau Gasol.

Morris was as good as Kevin Love at post-up during the season (.99 ppp), and if not a great rebounder did play physical defensively. He's a versatile young player (26) who had only been available to the Pistons (for a second round pick, no less!) because he, twin brother/teammate Markieff (traded to Washington at trade deadline), and three friends allegedly assaulted an old acquaintance in January 2015.

The Cavs responded to Detroit's hot start with their own 10-2 run. Irving popped out for three while Tristan Thompson backscreened his man. Caught in a double-team, Irving kept from dragging his pivot foot before finding James steaming down the baseline for a reverse layup. Dellavedova hit a floater while attacking the close-out from a James kickout and Smith hit a three when LeBron found him coming off a weakside screen.

Suddenly the Cavs were back up one, 21-20. On the J.R. three, James attacked a mismatched Jackson and appeared to push off with his arm before making the pass. Later, refs called Jackson for a foul that could've gone either way, frustrating the Pistons.

"A couple calls have upset our guys. They've got to understand, LeBron is LeBron," Pistons coach Stan Van Gundy told ABC's Lisa Salters. "They're not going to call offensive fouls on him. He gets to do what he wants." (The NBA fined him $25,000 for his comments.)

The Cavs finished the first up 27-25. James had 10 points, all in the paint, and four assists, but having played 11 minutes he sat to open the second. The second-team offense, led by Irving, failed to create any breathing room while the Pistons remained hot. Detroit bolted to a 39-33 lead with four minutes gone before Lue called a timeout.

When the starters returned, Cleveland went on an 8-0 run to retake the lead. Love had a couple buckets and a free throw, punctuated by an Irving transition three after James picked Tobias Harris' pocket on a drive. Harris was a recent addition acquired by the Pistons from Orlando at the trade deadline in February. Though a talented scorer (16.6 points per game) from anywhere on the floor, Harris wasn't very physical or particularly tough defensively.

The Cavaliers continued to put LeBron and Kyrie in pick-and-rolls that ended in Jackson checking James in the post. Eventually someone had to come double, and that was how James found Love for the three that knotted it at 50 with 2:16 left in the second.

The Pistons stayed in it thanks to Morris, who hit three consecutive threes off a slow rotation, an unusual 4/5 screen from Drummond, and a slow close-out by Love. Morris scored another couple on free throws when James fouled him on an inbounds play.

The Pistons closed the half on a 6-1 run for a five-point lead. Detroit shot over 60 percent from the field and 63 percent (10-of-16) from beyond the arc. Seven of those 10 threes came in transition or early offense, as they often took advantage of cross-matches and poor close-outs. The Pistons helped their cause with assists on 15 of their 21 buckets while the Cavaliers shot just 43 percent.

The only thing keeping Cleveland in the game was its ballhandling (just one turnover to the Pistons' six) and eight offensive boards. They parlayed that into a 10-2 lead on points off turnovers and a 13-2 lead on second-chance points, not to mention doubling the Pistons' points in the paint, 24-12.

"Our gameplan was to pack the paint so Drummond couldn't get any lobs, and when they spread out for three, we have to be able to get back and contest," said Coach Lue. "We closed out with our hands down, giving up dare shots.... I thought in the second half we did a way better job of getting back in transition, and we did a better job of getting after shooters, contesting and trying to run them off."

The Cavaliers Big Three appeared in force, scoring 44 of the team's 53 first half points, led by Love with 18, followed by Irving 14 and LeBron with 12. Morris led the Pistons with 19, followed by University of Georgia product Caldwell-Pope with 13.

Irving came out on fire, scoring eight points in the first 65 seconds of the half to give the Cavs a brief three-point lead. It began with Kyrie running left to right, past baseline screens by Love and Thompson to get an open three. On the next possession Irving crossed Jackson over in transition, setting up a 14-foot jumper from the right elbow. James setup another, stealing a Harris pass and quickly passing upcourt to Irving, who buried the transition three.

"Our third quarters haven't been the best this season, but coming into the playoffs, we know that possessions really matter," said Irving. "Guys just did a great job setting screens coming out in the second half. Picking up the tempo a little bit. For me as a point guard, sometimes I need to take it upon myself or come into a 1/3 pick-and-roll with LeBron. Anything to get our guys going coming out of halftime, so they get open looks and we feel good going into the fourth."

It was back and forth the rest of the quarter. A Drummond tip-in was followed by an alley-oop where Love or James failed to provide help. The Cavaliers answered with a 7-0 run, culminating in an Irving drive-and-dish to Smith in the weakside corner for three.

But after Tristan Thompson tipped in a missed Irving layup (his only shot of the game) for the 74-71 lead, Cleveland went cold. They shot 1-of-9 over the final 3:55 of the third as ball and off the ball movement stalled.

The Cavs opened the fourth down 78-76 with both Irving and James on the bench. Lue called a timeout 55 seconds into the quarter when Harris hit a midrange pull-up and backup point Steve Blake found swingman Reggie Bullock for a transition three. Boom, the Pistons had their largest lead of the game, 83-76.

"[Coach] made a couple changes, both from a personnel standpoint and also what we wanted to do offensively and defensively," James said. "The group that went in at that point was able to make a run. For the most part, we just used our crowd, we used our ability to be able to come out of a timeout and execute."

Lue went small, bringing James in for Thompson and sliding Love over to center, forcing tough rotations for the Pistons' slow, bearded big Aron Baynes. Love drove to the rim, forcing Harris to collapse on him, leaving Jefferson alone in the weakside corner where Kevin found him for three.

On the next possession the Cavs whipped the ball around the perimeter, driving and kicking, moving it side to side and making 10 passes before Dellavedova's foot-on-the-three-line bucket.

"We understand how demoralizing it is for a defense when you're passing like that and they're rotating because we have a lot of good shooters on the team," said Jefferson. "When we play unselfishly it makes it extremely tough on a defense. It takes a little starch out of the defense, which helps us make a run."

On the next possession James screened for Dellavedova around the free throw line and then rolled to the basket, where Delly gave him an alley-oop, which he laid off the backboard. The refs called a foul before the shot, but Cleveland ran the same play again. This time the defense hung with James, leaving Dellavedova a layup. He missed, but James had the putback to tie it at 83.

"We manufactured like 10 points in a row by running that play alone, so it was a big play for us, and putting Kevin at the 5 was a big adjustment for them," Lue said, noting the different options they'd used off the same basic set. Midway through the fourth Lue called a timeout after Reggie Jackson hit a pull-up three over Iman Shumpert in transition to tie it at 88.

Coming out of the timeout Cleveland ran a high pick-and-roll above the top of the key twice with Love screening Jackson. The first time both Drummond and Jackson followed Irving into the lane as he threw the no-look, behind-the-back pass to Love for three before Drummond could possibly recover.

The second time Drummond got to the arc in time, but Love pump-faked past him. He fumbled the drive but recovered it, and threw to Shumpert in the left corner. Shumpert swung it to James, who drove the lane and hit Love retreating to the right weakside corner for a three as the shot clock expired, giving the Cavs a 94-90 lead with 4:48 left.

After the game, Van Gundy mentioned that possession. "We had several good defensive possessions in there," he said. "The one that sort of broke our back as we had a good defensive possession, a loose ball. We had played it down to 24 and the ball goes out to Love in the corner and he hits a three."

The Cavaliers almost blew that lead. Caldwell-Pope drove the lane and in the air switched from his right to his left, eliciting an Irving foul. Caldwell-Pope hit them both. Then James found Love alone under the basket, but the

Pistons collapsed before he could shoot it and Harris stole his pass, sparking a fastbreak the other way.

However, as Harris tried to lay it up over James, Irving tipped the shot away from behind. It generated a fastbreak back the other way on which James drew the foul and cashed both freebies. Next time down Jackson missed a pull-up, and lost his composure arguing Shumpert had fouled him. He complained loudly to Derrick Stafford, who gave him a technical foul. Irving hit the foul shot for the 97-92 lead.

A Jackson crossover through his legs left Shumpert flailing, as he converted the and-one to cut Cleveland's lead to 98-95. Irving answered by slaloming between defenders and slicing past Baynes for a layup, making it 100-95. (Van Gundy sat Drummond moments before the Jackson lay-up, presumably because of his poor foul shooting and trouble guarding the Cavs' small lineup with Love at center.)

Morris drew a cheap foul on James for contact coming around a screen, but he hit only one of the free throws. (After scoring 19 in the first half, that was his only point of the half.) "I thought we got into Morris' space and made him drive the basketball," said Lue. "I thought in the second half our defense really picked up."

LeBron made the Pistons pay on the other end, when again Jackson switched onto James. He backed RJax into the lane, turned, and shot over him as easily as if it were his Mini-me. That made it 102-96 with 84 seconds, and the Pistons never challenged after that, falling 106-101.

Irving led Cleveland with 31 points and six assists, followed by Love with 28 points and 10 rebounds, and James with 22 points, 11 assists, six rebounds, two steals, and two blocks. Love's 22 shots were his most in two years with the Cavs.

"We could never get their three main guys under control," Van Gundy lamented. "Then down the stretch in the game I didn't think we got great shots."

The Cavaliers' defense tightened at the end, holding the Pistons to 36 percent shooting in the last quarter, while Cleveland shot 50 percent, the only quarter all night the Cavs shot better.

"In the second half, we did a way better job of getting back in transition and we did a better job of getting after shooters, contesting and trying to run them off [the three]," Lue said, before evaluating the offense. "Our main objective in this series is to attack. We don't want to bail them out with jump shots. We want to attack, get downhill, get into the lane, and then we can kick out for threes. The Big Three did a phenomenal job of doing that. Kevin set the tone early posting up in the paint, getting deep, and it all started from there."

The Cavaliers looked rusty, and by all accounts blew numerous defensive assignments, particularly in the first half. The Pistons' offense took what the Cavs were giving them—jump shots—and thrived until the Cavaliers' defense and resolve stiffened in the fourth. The Pistons had to take solace in the fact that they'd outplayed Cleveland three of the four quarters, just not when it counted most.

E. C. Quarterfinals, Game 2. Wednesday, April 20, 2016, Cleveland. (1-0 Cavs)

The Pistons started Game 2 looking to get Thompson in foul trouble. Detroit's very first possession went to Drummond in the low post for a short hook over Thompson. The next two times the Cavaliers missed, Detroit pushed the ball and found a rim-running Drummond near the basket. They continued to post up Thompson until eventually the refs obliged with Thompson's second foul on a Drummond dunk with two and a half minutes gone in the first. In came Timofey Mozgov.

"Stan did a great job of going at Tristan early trying to post him, and get him in foul trouble," said Lue. "We had Timo come in and give us eight or nine minutes just to put a body on Drummond because we didn't want to wear Kevin down early."

The Cavaliers went to Love in the post as in Game 1. The first time Detroit sent a double; the second time they didn't and Love hit a fallaway jumper over Morris. They continued to change up the help and timing of rotations while trying to get more physical with Love to throw off his rhythm and move him off his favorite spots.

"I think he was just too comfortable. His confidence was too high. We've definitely got to get him out of that rhythm early," said Morris between games. "We're definitely going to push up a little harder on him, maybe foul him a little harder, things like that."

Irving answered a Caldwell-Pope three by scooting to his left behind double screens from Mozgov and Love above the right break. When Jackson went under, Irving lined up a straightaway three before Jackson could get there, making it 11-7. Detroit would continue to go under screens all series, daring Irving to take threes. (He made half his catch-and-shoot trifectas and 42 percent of his dribble pull-up threes in the series.)

With Thompson out, Detroit attacked Love. Jackson answered with a step-back jumper over Love after he switched a Morris screen. Drummond denied James' alley-oop pass to Mozgov in transition, knocking it out to halfcourt where Jackson picked it up and pushed the other way. James' defense hindered Morris' reverse layup, but Tobias Harris made the putback. Next time down Harris drew a foul on Love, and converted both free throws for a 17-7 lead with 6:22 left in the first.

Irving led the Cavaliers right back with eight straight points. He stepped to his right around two beefy Mozgov screens for threes, and sank a pull-up 18-foot jumper for the third bucket to close the lead to 17-15 with 4:15 left.

"Just reading and reacting out there, seeing the way they're playing me and playing other guys and coming off and being aggressive," said Irving, asked to explain how he scored 13 of the team's first 15 points.

On the very next possession Love received a questionable loose ball foul on a Drummond rebound, his second foul, even though replays showed that the Detroit big pushed Irving aside before leaping for the ball. Shumpert entered for Love and the Pistons staged a 9-2 run.

Detroit was able to hide Drummond on Shumpert defensively, daring the flat-topped wing to shoot the three while the Piston big hung around the lane preventing penetration. Rookie forward Stanley Johnson had five in the run, including a transition three from the right corner to give Detriot a 26-17 lead with just under two minutes left.

Lue called a timeout and pulled LeBron. Love and Thompson were already on the bench with foul trouble, so it was like an early appearance of the Irving-led second quarter squad. Lue figured he'd sit James and bring him back to start the next quarter.

The move looked good when Mozgov poked away a Drummond pass, knocking it to Shumpert, who drove the lane and dished to J. R. Smith above the break for the transition three. Next time down, Smith drained a straightaway three to close the lead to 26-23. A couple Morris freebies made it 28-23 at the end of one.

James directed an 11-2 run to open the second. Like Game 1, the Pistons struggled to stop the Dellavedova/James pick-and-roll from out of the high-post/elbow set. The first play produced an alley-oop slam by James when everyone left with Delly and nobody followed the King. Indecisive weakside help afforded Richard Jefferson an open right-corner three the next time they ran it.

Blatt had used James with the second team much of the previous year, but the injuries and Irving's minutes restriction prevented the second team from developing much continuity during the first half of the season, and Lue fiddled much of his half-year trying different combinations.

Lue felt the team needed two starters on the floor to close quarters because of its importance, and decided that Love and Irving could handle it, letting James helm the second squad after Game 2's experiment proved so successful.

"LeBron and Delly have a great chemistry together, and I just thought it'd be better for the second unit to get more shots, spread the ball out and spread the floor," Lue explained later. "It worked out and so we stayed with it."

Bullock beat Shumpert on a baseline backdoor play out of a timeout. LeBron responded by posting up first Johnson and then Bullock after a switch and scoring in the lane over both with a short fallaway and a layup, respectively. "I have to do a better job with the lineups," Van Gundy said. "The second quarter, those first couple minutes, that's on me."

Channing Frye blocked a shot by Australia's answer to Grizzly Adams, Aron Baynes. Shumpert retrieved the loose ball and almost overthrew James, who chased down the bounce pass and laid it off the backboard ahead of Baynes' swipe. A minute later, Delly drove the lane and hit James cutting to the hole from the weakside for a demonstrative dunk to give Cleveland a 36-30 lead with seven and a half left.

Love returned as did Smith, who provided all the Cavaliers offense for almost five minutes with a trio of three-pointers. Meanwhile the Pistons hit seven straight shots, including three consecutive hoops by Jackson and three more by Drummond.

Drummond beat the Cavaliers down the middle of the lane when Smith failed to help from the weakside. It was a Pistons adjustment from Game 1 when the Cavs trapped Jackson. Drummond was now going to the front of the rim before help could arrive, something they corrected at the first opportunity.

"Weakside, J. R. missed three [help rotations] and Drummond had dunks. I showed him at halftime, like, 'You know J. R., we have to be better,'" Lue said. "We did a great job of making multiple efforts in the second half, pulling in, they make the pass, we make it back out, and run them off the three-point line."

The Cavs made something other than a three when James slipped behind Morris and Love threw him an alley-oop coming down the right baseline. That tied it at 47. The lead changed hands several times, with Delly and Smith contributing additional threes and a James putback of a Jefferson missed three giving the Cavs a 55-53 halftime lead.

Cleveland finished the first half 22-of-42 (52 percent) and 11-of-20 (55 percent) from three, led by J. R. Smith (5-of-7) and Kyrie Irving (3-of-4). Detroit got the Cavs in foul trouble but hit only 11-of-20 from the charity stripe thanks to Drummond's 3-of-12 shooting. (Drummond had just set a new NBA low, making just 35.5 percent from the line, breaking the old record, 38 percent, held by Wilt Chamberlain since the 1967-68 season.)

Like in Game 1, the Pistons got off quickly in the third, scoring the first seven points while the Cavs missed their first five shots. Jackson exploited a Smith/Irving miscommunication for a layup, Caldwell-Pope sank a three in James' face, and Drummond hit a hook over Thompson from the left block, prompting a Lue timeout.

"It happened last game. We got down, called a timeout, came to the bench, and no one had their head down," Lue said. "We had to pick it up. I thought in the first half, we had a lot of defensive breakdowns that weren't normally us."

Whatever he told them, he might want to bottle it because over the next seven minutes the Cavaliers outscored the Pistons 21-4. Irving, Love, Smith, and James all dialed up long-distance, collectively going 5-of-6 from three and 7-of-9 from the field, while forcing four turnovers for more transition opportunities. (Three of the five triples occurred in transition or early offense.)

"We felt we needed a better focus on the defensive end and we did that," said Love. "We created more turnovers. Our rotations were great and that led to a lot of great offensive possessions for us, let us get out on the break, opened up a lot of threes for us."

The Pistons didn't do themselves any favors, frequently settling for dribble pull-ups early in the clock, notably Harris and Jackson. The Cavaliers turned a five-point deficit into a 12-point lead in seven minutes. James sat and Cleveland carried an 82-68 lead into the fourth.

"We were maybe too aggressive in not taking good shots and making the extra pass. We were trying to force the ball to the basket, taking some really really bad shots," Van Gundy said. "Their runs sort of took our minds for three minutes at a time where we just stopped doing what we were supposed to do, especially on the defensive end."

James came back to start the fourth, and like in the second Dellavedova used a LeBron screen or the threat of one to twice get to the rim. Then Caldwell-Pope airballed a three from the right break; LeBron grabbed the rebound and sprinted upcourt, going right by a flatfooted Morris, who fouled James for the and-one. It gave the Cavs an 88-70 lead, and Detroit wouldn't get any closer, succumbing 107-90.

"In the second half, we came out and held them to 37 points. We just have to do a better job in the first half of locking down and bearing down on our defense," said Lue. "We did a better job defensively in the second half, especially of running their guys off the three-point line, making them drivers, then trapping.... The second half was really how we want to play to start the game."

LeBron led the Cavs with 27 points, six rebounds, three assists, three steals, and five turnovers. Kyrie had 22 points, four assists, two steals, and one turnover, and J. R. Smith added 21. Love had 16 points and 10 boards. Dellavedova was huge off the bench with eight points, nine assists, a steal, and one turnover in just 22 minutes.

The Cavaliers tied the record for three-pointers in a playoff game, making 20 (out of 38), set earlier by the 2011 Mavericks, 1996 SuperSonics, and 2015 Warriors. Drummond missed 12 of Detroit's 32 free throws, and the Pistons shot only 4-of-17 from three, a yawning gap that the Pistons couldn't fill.

"I don't care if you're left by yourself, 20-of-38 is pretty good three-point shooting," said Van Gundy. "I didn't think our close-outs were good, and I didn't think we did a very good job identifying shooters in transition. So there's no question that we could have done a better job, but they shot the ball very, very well."

Kyrie Irving described the record number of threes as a byproduct of moving the ball and playing right, not aping some West Coast team's style of play.

"We don't want to become too reliant on [the three], but when we have great shooters on our team that space out the floor really well, we're going to continue to make those guys make plays on the weak side," said Irving. "We have Channing Frye and J. R. and myself, guys that space out the floor and great passers, willing passers. It just makes the games a lot easier."

J. R. Smith delivered the evening's best comment, which will undoubtedly be the centerpiece of his future book, *Zen and the Art of Aerial Bombing*. "I was open so I shot the ball. It's kind of simple for me," he explained. "I have some great teammates that are willing to make the open pass and I was just one of the guys in that situation to make them."

CAVS LEAVE PISTONS WISHING THEY HAD A V8

THE CAVALIERS TRAVELED to Detroit for a pair of weekend games, having taken care of business at home. The Pistons had out-played the Cavs in the first halves of both games, scoring 111 points before halftime and 80 after Cleveland's defense awoke.

The Pistons couldn't stall the two-headed driving machine of James (49) and Irving (53) or really any of their corollary weapons, on the port and starboard sides of the ol' drive-and-kick vehicle. Detroit had played two fine halves of basketball, but returned late from lunch and found that someone had eaten theirs.

Lue deserves credit for remaining unfazed against a 20-year veteran that had coached two conference finalists and an NBA finalist. After Game 2, James praised the wise-beyond-his-years rookie coach.

"Coach is even-keel. He doesn't let the moment get the best of him," James said. "He trusts that over the course of his career he's learned from some of the best and he puts us as players in positions to succeed. It's up to us to do it. We're happy he's at our helm."

Pistons 20-year-old rookie Stanley Johnson forgot that a microphone wasn't Twitter, and proceeded to shoot his mouth off after Game 2, offering that he was "definitely in James' head." This despite the fact that according to ESPN Stats and Information, James had scored seven of the nine times Johnson had covered him during the two games. Still, the rook took exception to the way the four-time MVP trash-talked.

"He jabbers. He moves his mouth sometimes. Their whole team does, kind of like they're little cheerleaders on the bench," Johnson offered. "Every time you walk in the right corner. They're always saying something like they're playing basketball, like they're actually in the game. There's only seven or eight players who play—I don't see why the other players are talking. They might as well just be in the stands, in my opinion." (Van Gundy spoke to Johnson afterward, and rest assured there was no more of that.)

LeBron refused to respond to Johnson's taunts. "The game is played between the four lines and that's my only concern, to go out there and help my guys execute our gameplan as well as I can," James said. "That's all I can worry about."

"They're doing a good job at times of getting us unbalanced, and we're a step slow on some of their actions so we want to key in on that," James continued. "If they're able to score over the top of our defense or when we're in the right position, then so be it. But we want to be there and not get lucky when they miss a couple open shots."

E. C. Quarterfinals, Game 3. Friday, April 22, 2016, Cleveland. (2-0 Cavs)

The Cavaliers got off to a slow start and had fallen behind the Pistons 19-13 midway through the first when things got chippy. Morris fouled James on a drive, swiping at the ball from behind while raking his elbow across LeBron's skull. Three times in the first two games James caught elbows without getting the call and this time complained demonstratively. The referees called a common foul, inbounded on the side.

"I know what [a flagrant foul] is when it happens to someone else," James said sometime later. "When it involves me I have no idea what [the difference between] a common foul and flagrant foul is."

James took the ball right at Drummond. He missed, but the fact that Drummond challenged the shot opened up Thompson for the offensive rebound and putback. After Morris went by Love again off the bounce, the Cavs went back to Kevin, who beat the double on the left wing by throwing crosscourt to J. R. in the right corner for three (with help from a Thompson backscreen). The Cavaliers' run helped close the lead to 21-20, and they trailed 27-24 at the end of one.

"The crazy thing is Kevin told me before in the timeout it was going to happen and demonstratively. you're going to be open,"referees called a common foul, said Smith. "I was like, 'Yeah okay, Kevin. You'll shoot it off the glass and make it. I'm going to say great shot.' Then sure enough it was there and I made the shot."

Lue experimented with a different second squad featuring Frye, James, Jefferson, Shumpert, and Dellavedova, spelling the end of Mozgov's meaningful postseason minutes. Shumpert clanked consecutive midrange jumpers before stealing a Pistons pass and sinking a three on the ensuing possession. It energized the squad.

Next time down, Shump drove baseline and threw it into the right corner. The ball quickly swung to Dellavedova, who sank a straightaway three. Cleveland hit a third consecutive three on the next possession when Delly drove the lane out of a James pick-and-roll. Instead of throwing to LeBron, who was checked by Drummond, Delly found Shumpert in the left corner for the three and a 33-31 lead with nine minutes left.

Detroit battled back and took a 45-40 lead when Lue struck back by going small again, using a three-guard lineup of Dellavedova, Irving, and Smith, with James and Love up front. Cleveland immediately ran pick-and-rolls with Love that resulted in an Irving three, as well as an Irving drive that he kicked out to J. R. Smith at the left wing. As Jackson ran out at him, Smith swung it into the left corner, where Delly drained another three.

The Cavaliers intentionally fouled Drummond the next time down the court—he made one out of two—then he committed an off the ball foul, his second foul, and Van Gundy pulled him for the rest of the half. Absent his rim protection, Delly was able to drive and score on a short floater. Love was also able to go down low, posting up Johnson, drawing a foul, and cashing both freebies. Kevin scored again off a pick-and-pop the next time down for a 47-46 lead.

"With KLove we're running a 3/4 pick-and-roll and they're switching and putting KLove on the block and letting him work on guys that are a little bit smaller and he's doing his thing, he's playing great," Thompson explained. "When Kevin's rolling early, that's good for our team. You know LeBron and Kyrie can get going because they dominate the ball, so if Kevin's playing at this high level it's exciting to watch."

Johnson came right back, hitting a wide-open three when Love didn't close him out properly. Love tried to take Johnson baseline on the next possession, but the Arizona rookie got his hand in his wheelhouse, upsetting Love's shot.

While Kevin looked askance of the officials, Johnson sprinted the other way, receiving a pass at the arc and taking it to the hole for the flush. That was his ninth point and gave the Pistons a 51-47 lead with two and a half left. On the other end, Thompson gathered two crucial offensive rebounds, creating second-chance buckets for Irving and James that helped Cleveland take a 54-53 halftime lead.

The Pistons finished the first half up 26-12 on points in the paint and shooting 60 percent from the field. While the Cavs' defense may have been below par, the offense was, shooting 55 percent from the field and 6-of-13 from three, with a 19-12 rebounding advantage. Irving led the Cavs with 13 points, while Love and James had 11.

"It is a good sign we're up one point with them shooting 60 percent, but we've got to do a better job of containing the basketball off the dribble," assistant coach Larry Drew told Fox's Allie Clifton at half. "We're putting ourselves in a little bit of a predicament with the close-outs. They're attacking the close-outs. It's something we've worked on—we just need to be better about it."

Both teams got off to a lackluster start in the third. The Pistons didn't score for the first three and a half minutes, and the only Cavaliers bucket came when Irving dominated a possession attempting to take Caldwell-Pope off the dibble, finally beating him on the right baseline. He also sank a technical foul shot on Drummond for pushing James to the ground moments after refs had called a foul on LeBron.

Detroit missed its first six shots before Morris beat the double-team, finding Drummond underneath the basket for a layup and-one (which he missed). Love again posted up Harris, who Kevin owned like a friend's Netflix password ("use as you please"), banking a 16-footer off the backboard, facing him up when Detroit didn't send a double.

With the score squared at 67, the Cavs worked the ball to Love on the left block, now guarded by Morris. When the Pistons sent the double, Love found James weakside. LeBron touch-passed it to Smith in the right corner for three. Harris hit a pull-up 15-footer to cut the lead to 70-69. Then Love flared out of a baseline screen that initially seemed to be for Smith, confusing the Pistons, who left Kevin open for his night's only three.

"I have to continue to be aggressive. These two guys over here [James and Irving] have been constant on me about that. So, when they're coming to the double-team I just face up to see what they are going to give me and make a play," Love said. "A lot of times, I was looking weakside when I was able to get to the middle, split the double-team, kick out to LeBron, kick out to Dellavedova. We can get the swing-swing action."

Thompson got a putback on a wide-open left corner three by James, and the next possession cut baseline as Irving rolled down the lane, receiving a perfect feed for the slam and-one (which he missed). That made it 77-71, and the Cavaliers would lead 79-73 to start the fourth.

James came out with the same squad as the second quarter and continued to screen for Delly and roll to the hoop. The great timing of Dellavedova's feed allowed LeBron to catch, step, and finish without having to dribble while drawing the foul on Johnson.

"Having [James] at the 4 spot and putting him in pick-and-rolls as the roll man, he's such a dynamic roller and he can catch anything and he can finish, but he can also kick it out for threes so he's pretty dangerous as a roll man," Dellavedova said. "And [as a screener] he's somebody people don't want to help off of much because they don't want to leave him so it's pretty effective."

Caldwell-Pope answered with his own layup and-one call on Shumpert, but James got those points right back running a pick-and-flare, sinking his only three of the night. He was 1-of-6, after confessing the game before, "We have shooters. They are deadly snipers…and I'm not one of them."

That gave the Cavs a nine-point lead until six minutes left, when Detroit went on an 8-0 run. Harris hit a pull-up jumper from the left elbow, then on the other end poked the ball away from James, who grimaced as though fouled. Jackson passed to Morris out of the pick-and-roll, who drove the lane and finished through contact with no call. Morris got the call next time down and cashed both free throws. After James missed yet another three, Harris received the ball in the left corner and attacked a Love close-out, drilling a 14-foot baseline jumper to cut the lead to 87-86.

After the Cavaliers called a timeout, Irving ducked behind a Thompson screen for a straightaway three, as Detroit again dared him to beat them from long. Cleveland intentionally fouled Drummond, who missed both. Van Gundy pulled Drummond at that point.

"I gave him one possession," Van Gundy explained. "We're behind. We can't go down and play for zero points. Even though we did. We just can't do that. And Tristan Thompson had eight offensive rebounds. Hardly a dominant performance. He had offensive energy."

After Morris and Irving traded turnovers, James drove the lane and dropped it off at the last second to an unguarded Thompson beneath the basket. Tristan missed but Love tapped it in for a 92-86 lead.

The Pistons weren't done, though. Missed jump shots by James and Irving turned into transition offense the other way. Jackson rebounded both misses and pushed the ball, leading to an open pull-up 18-footer by Harris and a breakaway slam by a streaking Caldwell-Pope. Suddenly it was 92-90 with four minutes remaining. Lue called a timeout. (The Pistons were great when they could get out in transition or create early offense, going 19-of-33 with between 18 and 22 seconds on the shot clock.)

"We did some things differently defensively when we came out of that timeout," Lue said. "Credit to the guys. They executed the plan, we were able to get stops, and held them to that one free throw."

Irving drove the lane and dished to James cutting in from the right wing. LeBron passed to Smith in the right corner, who pump-faked Jackson away, took a rhythm dribble to the left, and calmly drained the shot with four seconds left on the shot clock to make it 95-90. Several empty possessions ensued for both teams.

With 43 seconds on the game clock and .7 on the shot clock, Cleveland inbounded. LeBron set a backside screen for Irving near the free throw line and then rolled to the bucket. The Pistons were so conscious of the rolling James that they missed Kyrie flaring to the right corner. Dellavedova whipped the pass almost across the entire court to Kyrie, who elevated and stuck the right-corner three for a 98-90 lead. They won 101-91.

According to *Plain Dealer* reporter Chris Haynes, Cleveland designed that play 24 hours earlier as a counter for Detroit's attention to James' cuts and rolls on the inbounds, which made him the perfect decoy. "We wanted our best players involved in that with Kyrie and LeBron," Lue said. "Dellavedova has two reads on that play and made a great read, and Kyrie made a great shot."

When the shot went through, LeBron looked like he received one of Willy Wonka's golden tickets. His grin was Cheshire-wide as he greeted Kyrie. "The crazy thing is Ky practices that shot all the time and Bron is always, 'Why you practicing that shot?'" Smith related. "This situation it worked."

The Cavs got 26 from Irving and a very efficient 20 from Love on just 10 shots. He also contributed 12 boards. Dellavedova added 12 points and five assists. James had 20 points, 13 boards, and seven assists, but also five turnovers.

"It's been the best I've seen them play all three together," Lue enthused. "LeBron is just being LeBron. He's taking the defensive challenge of trying to hold Tobias and Morris in check, and Kyrie and Kevin have carried the load as far as scoring the basketball for us."

James shot 8-of-24, 3-of-11 in the second half, including way too many jumpers, stalling the ball with excess dribbling and deliberating. In three postseason games LeBron had taken 20 shots where he held the ball for six or more seconds; 11 came in Game 3.

"It took everything we had. We had runs, they had runs," James told Fox's Allie Clifton. "They took the lead, we took the lead. We're a group that's growing. And this was another step in our growth. We kept our composure through 48 minutes and Kyrie was spectacular. Kev was great. Everyone picked me up. I needed it with the off-shooting night that I had. They picked me up and I just tried to affect the game in other facets."

For the third straight game, the Cavaliers clamped down like a third world dictatorship in the second half, bullying Detroit on the boards (27-20) and torturing them in the halfcourt offense (12 of 18 hoops were assisted). For the third game in a row, the Cavaliers held Detroit at or below 40 points and 40 percent shooting in the second half.

"We didn't make plays down the stretch," Van Gundy said. "We went to our stuff we always close with and we didn't do a great job."

For the Cavaliers it was a matter of attention to detail and bringing the right mindset.

"We're not doing anything different other than trying to be more consistent, and be more efficient," James Jones said. "We had some mistakes in the first half, and a lot of them were effort-based. Once we got back in at halftime and locked in, we could focus on executing our schemes and being in the right places and be able to live with them making shots."

E. C. Quarterfinals, Game 4. Sunday, April 24, 2016, Cleveland. (3-0 Cavs)

Game 4 was about pride for the Pistons. Barring an *It's A Wonderful Life*-size miracle, the Pistons weren't going to win the series, but they'd played the Cavaliers tight every game, and hoped to come away from the series with something more than an empty handful of moral victories.

"We're in a great flow, as far as us three," said James. "We understand what we all want. We understand what we want individually and what will help the team. Guys are picking their spots. First of all, we're going to Kev a lot in the post. We want Kev to continue to be aggressive, put pressure on the defense, and we want Kyrie as well to be aggressive on pick-and-rolls, and when he's able to get his shot, we want him to take it."

The Cavaliers didn't start off particularly attentive defensively, and their early inability to hit shots let Detroit exploit them in transition, taking a 10-2 lead, prompting a Lue timeout with not three minutes gone in the first.

Irving drew a shooting foul on Drummond with a transition pick-and-roll featuring Thompson out of a timeout, then Love drew another, sending Detroit's big man to the bench early. A little later Love posted Harris and the Pistons sent a double. Love passed out to Kyrie as the ball swung left to right twice before reaching the corner, where J. R. Smith drained it before the defense could rotate, cutting the deficit to 12-10. (Smith made 17 of 33 threes in the series.)

Neither team made much headway until Blake and Harris hit threes for Detroit late in the quarter, helping the Pistons take a 28-25 lead after one. Love finished the quarter 1-of-8 as the Cavaliers shot 35 percent. Love did get nine first quarter rebounds as well as four of the team's seven free throws. Harris led the way for the Pistons with 10 points and six rebounds.

Frye opened the second by knocking the ball away from Drummond. Shumpert recovered it and tossed ahead to James for a breakaway dunk. LeBron also drew a shooting foul, sandwiched around a Jefferson runner in traffic and corner three, as Cleveland opened the second on an 11-5 run to take a 34-31 lead with 8:30 to go in the second.

The Pistons would tie it at 34 and play some of their most inspired offense of the game. Over the next four minutes Detroit made six of seven shots and three free throws. Morris scored half of Detroit's 16 points in the stretch. In the middle of the run the Cavaliers sent Drummond to the line twice (he made two of four) to try to break the Pistons' rhythm.

Yet Detroit only held a 50-49 lead thanks to three Irving or James layups and three Smith or James threes over the same stretch. "A few of the shots I felt a little gas come out, but they came right back down," said Smith, crediting the Pistons' moxie. "They played hard; they're just a young team. Time will come. They will be very good."

Detroit took a 52-49 lead on a Drummond drive, but Irving and James scored the last two buckets of the half for a 53-52 lead. James had 16 points, four rebounds, and four assists in the game while Smith had 12 points and Irving 11. On the other end of the spectrum, Love was 1-of-10. Morris led the Pistons with 18, 12 in the second quarter, as the Pistons outshot the Cavaliers 48 percent to 43 percent.

"From the other close-out games, the first half is when the team really gives everything they've got in the tank," Thompson said before the game. "It might get a little chippy. It might get a little physical, but you just have to stay the course."

In some sense the first half duplicated the blueprint for the entire series, with the Pistons landing blows all half and outshooting the Cavaliers but finding themselves in a one-point ballgame. Every time Detroit made a run, the Cavaliers had the poise to staunch the bleeding before their blood pressure dropped and they lost consciousness.

"We were able to take a hit and keep moving forward," Lue explained. "We've been harping on that all season—not to drop our head, not to have bad body language when teams make runs...that's the biggest growth in this team right now, just staying with it and not giving in when things get tough."

The Cavaliers opened the third with a blistering run. On the first two possessions they went into the post to Love, not shying away despite his first half struggles. He converted one of two—a short fallaway in the lane— sandwiched around a James pull-up baseline fallaway over Harris.

Detroit tried to stay with Cleveland as Morris hit two contested dribble pull-ups, the Pistons' only baskets for almost the first five minutes of the third. Meanwhile, Irving put together a personal 10-0 run that took just 85 seconds.

"It starts with me as a point guard continuing to get rebounds or steals or anything like that to continue to push the pace, especially coming out for the third quarter," Irving said. "Getting these guys going offensively and defensively. Just let them know we have to get going. We can't continue to have third quarters like we did in the regular season."

It began with a catch-and-shoot three from the wing, followed by a transition layup, a 19-foot dribble pull-up from the right baseline, and another three where he dribbled horizontally from one side of the floor to the other, almost fumbling away the ball, before grabbing it back up and hitting an improbable three with the shot clock nearly extinguished. Yes, he passed the heat check. Suddenly it was 67-56 Cleveland, with eight left in the third.

"Kyrie bailed us out. We struggled a bit getting the ball to Kev, getting Kev going, and Kyrie just came up big," said Smith. "Everybody knows him as a scorer, but he's such a willing passer. He makes plays for everyone else, and he doesn't get enough credit for that."

Unfortunately, the Cavaliers drifted back into bad habits and left the door cracked. After Love drained a three off an Irving pick-and-pop dime for a 72-63 lead with five left, the Cavs went through a three and a half minute scoring drought. They missed seven shots, despite four offensive boards, and committed a turnover as the Pistons made a 9-0 run that cut the lead to 72-71 with 90 seconds left in the third.

"We went down by [11] where it looked like they were going to take over the game," Van Gundy said. "I looked around at that point. What is this team really made of?... We talked about finding a way to compete and find a way to try to win. It says a lot about this team, no matter what situation we're in. Backs against the wall, nobody wavered. We took their best punches and we kept swinging back."

That's when Dellavedova stepped up with perhaps his best stretch of play in the playoffs. On a possession where Love chased down two offensive rebounds, Delly beat Blake to his right and got to the bucket ahead of Baynes' help for the layup and his first points of the game.

"I tried to get downhill more. They weren't leaving LeBron on the roll so I had to be a bit more aggressive," Dellavedova said.

The next time down—after Caldwell-Pope's second three of the quarter—Delly again beat Blake to his strong hand, going right and drawing the foul. Detroit came back with Baynes tipping in a missed three by Caldwell-Pope, followed by another pair of Dellavedova free throws on a Blake reach-in.

Harris got a driving layup in transition to tie the game with three seconds left in the third.

Emblematic of the Pistons' fortunes, Irving took the inbounds and advanced it to halfcourt, where he gathered himself and dropped the 41-foot shot at the buzzer for an 81-78 lead. All series the Pistons had been a moment late and dollar short. Delly opened the fourth with a runner and a three-pointer, extending the lead to 86-78, while scoring all of his 11 points during a two-minute span across the quarters.

That was the last basket the Cavaliers would score for nearly the next five minutes as Cleveland got three-crazy looking for the knockout punch. They missed seven shots, five of them threes, including two questionable ones by the King. Their only points were a pair of Irving free throws before James rebounded an Irving breakaway as three Pistons defenders flew by, leaving him alone under the basket for the putback. That gave Cleveland a 90-85 lead with 6:32 remaining.

The Cavs started taking the air out of the ball. Irving banked a midrange shot, Smith a three from at least four feet beyond the arc (his fifth), and James got to the rim, all with the clock's last ticks. Detroit closed to 97-93 on a Harris turnaround jumper in the lane over a mismatched Irving, his 23rd point, with two and a half minutes left.

James settled for contested three despite having the much smaller Jackson on him. He missed. (On the prior possession LeBron took RJax to the left block, turned, and shot over the 6-foot-3 Piston.) However, Love recovered the offensive board and Lue called a timeout to set up a proper play. Irving got an open straightaway three, but like everyone else, he was tired and front-rimmed it.

Dellavedova and Jackson fought for the loose ball, which went out of bounds off Detroit. James again got the mismatch on Jackson. LeBron took Jackson right but as he prepared to spin back left, Jackson hooked his left arm, preventing him from turning. The ball sprung loose as James fell to the ground and Detroit recovered it.

Caldwell-Pope received a screen from Harris that put Thompson on him, then cut from the left elbow across a Morris brush screen to the boundary above the right break, where he sank his third three-pointer over a trailing Thompson, closing the deficit to 97-96.

Irving drew a foul driving into the lane, so the Cavs inbounded from the right side with 53 seconds left. Irving dribbled there above the right break, well beyond the boundary, took a rhythm dribble, pulled up, and sank a big three that was eerily similar to an even larger one he'd hit almost two months hence.

That made it 100-96. Jackson beat Thompson with a hesitation dribble going down Main Street for the slam as help arrived too late. On the next possession Irving's dribbling derring-do went nowhere, resulting in a terrible fallaway three from the corner, which he airballed, and the Pistons recovered with 10 seconds left.

Detroit didn't have a timeout so Jackson advanced the ball. He went behind his back to the right while crossing halfcourt, and back again to his right before pulling up at the arc for the straightaway three. As he shot, Jackson leaned into Irving, who was on his left but slinking away from contact. Jackson's airballed his shot, and complained loudly about the no call while the Cavs celebrated the 100-98 win.

"I knew he was going to try to lean into me so I just tried to get out of the way and live with the results after that," Irving told TNT's Craig Sager afterward. "He's been doing a great job all game of getting downhill, so I just wanted to make it tough on him."

The Pistons played their best second half of the series, shooting 50 percent and holding the Cavaliers to 41 percent, including 7-of-21 from three. But the Cavaliers had just a little bit more every time, rising to the occasion as needed.

"To hold this team under a hundred three times to 90, 91, and then 98 tonight, I thought our defense was good outside the shooting percentage," said Lue. "Overall our guys did a great job. It was a physical series. It was a great series for us and they tested us."

Lue noted how the team leaned on each other, and needed each other, a theme of togetherness that he threaded through many comments since taking over. It was all about prioritizing the "we" over the "I."

"Kevin didn't shoot well, so Kyrie took it upon himself to score the basketball. LeBron did the same thing," Lue said. "Delly came in and scored 11 straight points for us. J. R. made some big shots—four threes—and then that big shot at the end of the shot clock. I thought it was a total team effort. Our guys withstood their runs and weathered the storm."

11
CAVS' LONG-RANGE MISSILES DOWN HAWKS

I T WAS HARD to escape the sense at times that the Cavaliers' locker room wasn't all candy canes and mistletoe. From the rumblings about Blatt and his eventual ouster to Griffin's comments about their lack of joy to the ever-present on-court angst, the atmosphere around the Cavaliers stood in stark contrast to their Western Conference counterparts, the Golden State Warriors.

While the Warriors' fast-paced, freewheeling style was all unbridled id, the Cavaliers could feel like an overactive super-ego, never quiet or satisfied, always demanding more and better effort. If one came off significantly more dour, that wasn't necessarily an indictment of the approach.

Indeed, as the season went on, despite the in-house frustration with their inconsistent play, there were indications that the early-season issues were slowly being resolved. The Cavaliers hadn't been together as long as the Warriors, who used the time to clearly define their roles and build bonds. That's something that Cleveland had to do on the run, and it often wasn't any more fun than watching legislators make sausage.

"We're family," explained Thompson. "Even though we might get on each other and you might think it's unfair and it is, it's about tough love and we're just trying to help each other get better."

The first major indication that things might have begun to turn came after Channing Frye's arrival. As you may recall, Frye transformed from an anxious worrier to a mindful happy person after his heart scare in Phoenix.

He had practically become Bobby McFerrin since, and perhaps the perfect person for the Cavaliers' locker room.

"I'm excited every day," the comic book-loving Frye enthused in March. "I get excited because of the selection of soaps in the hotels we stay at. I'm easygoing."

In his conversation with Adrian Wojnarowski after the season, Griffin singled Frye out for the positive impact of his personality and how it bridged the team's different cliques. For his part, Frye has known Jefferson since high school. They became friends at University of Arizona, and Jefferson mentored Frye during his first two years when they played in New York together for the Nets and Knicks, respectively.

"Channing Frye was an enormous piece of the puzzle in terms of what he did for our spirit. I think Channing and RJ together sort of brought the group together. I think all teams tend to have cliques," said Griffin. "It's not that there's animosity between them, but there's never a bridging that takes place where all 15 guys are always together."

Enter the fun-loving Frye, the olive in the Cavs' martini.

"Channing's that new kid in school that doesn't know that there's cliques and he just sits at the table with everyone," Jefferson said. "He puts random people on text chains. All of a sudden I was just on a text chain with Bron, Kev, and Champ. You're just like, 'Why did you…?' He's like, 'I don't know, you guys are the ones I wanted to talk to.' All of a sudden the four of us are texting through a game."

By season's end Frye was telling reporters that tales of the Cavs' dysfunctional locker room were "overblown," calling it "one of the best I've ever been in." He went on to crack on the media's coverage.

"I just literally stopped watching ESPN and all that other kind of stuff," he said. "It's like I'm in the locker room and you guys are making up stuff that doesn't even exist. It's kind of crazy. For us, it just makes us meld together. We laugh about it at times; it brings us together."

Frye's arrival helped his co-conspirator, Jefferson, step further out of his shell. A true professional in all his dealings with the game and the media, Jefferson is more of a goofball in his free time, a product of his Arizona upbringing.

"I'm very silly off the court. I'm always joking around," he said. "I'm a Phoenix, Arizona, kid. I'm not this Chicago tough guy. I'm not this New

York gritty kid. I'm not this New Jersey guy. Those places are synonymous with toughness. That's not me. I'm from Phoenix. It's sunny all the time and it's beautiful."

With Frye's undoubted encouragement, Jefferson started posting on Snapchat candid, humorous windows into life behind the scenes with the Cavs, and it was a lot closer to *Weekend at Bernie's* than *The Great Santini* or *Silence of the Lambs*. The nutty thing is that Jefferson had heretofore sworn off social media.

"I'm not on Facebook. I've no Instagram. I'm not on Twitter. Some of my teammates and I were joking around with Snapchat," Jefferson explained. "I've had it for about a year, a year and a half, I would use it to look at other people, kind of how people are about Twitter, and just recently I started doing it and having some fun with it."

Jefferson's playoff Snapchat moments are worthy of their own show— landing between Conan O'Brien and Mad TV. The ten-second segments featured Jefferson kidding LeBron about actually driving home in his Kia after they returned from Atlanta (echoing one of James' commercials), suggesting LeBron's really a vampire in his oxygen-enriched casket pregame, or just capturing the crew hanging out, singing along and dancing to popular hip-hop tracks.

However, his most memorable bit involved turning Kevin Love into Charlie McCarthy via a Tommy Bahamas ad featuring his alleged doppelganger, Will Chalker. The 36-year-old British model bears a resemblance to this year's leaner, bearded, *300*-inspired Love. So after giving Kevin grief about it, Jefferson cut out the picture and had it enlarged and laminated.

After that "Lil Kev," as Jefferson dubbed him, appeared *Zelig*-like Photoshopped onto the bench during games or in shots of practice. Players wore Lil Kev masks in the locker room, and Lil Kev sat beside Jefferson during TV interviews. Channing Frye had to sit in the backseat to accommodate Lil Kev, who had already called shotgun. He was the Cavaliers' traveling gnome, and the irreverence caught the team in a different light.

"I started to hear stuff from different people like, 'Wow, you guys actually do hang out. You guys actually do like each other. I'm like, 'Yeah, we're like siblings.' We hate each other. We get pissed off at each other, but there is no bad blood here. There are not fights in the locker room. There are no cliques such that guys don't hang out,'" Jefferson said. "Even with just the Snapchat, it's given people more of an insight to see, hey, we do have fun. We are enjoying the process."

E. C. Semifinals, Game 1. Monday, May 2, 2016, Cleveland. (Even)

Atlanta came into Cleveland after outlasting the Boston Celtics in seven games. They won just 48 games a year after taking the top seed with 60 wins. They boasted the league's second best defensive efficiency rating (101.4) behind San Antonio (99.0), but also the ninth-worst offensive efficiency (105.1). It went beyond the loss of DeMarre Carroll to free-agency and inability of the smaller, quicker Kent Bazemore to replace him. They just weren't as sharp as the year before when they caught the league a little by surprise.

Despite the eight-day layoff, it was the Cavaliers who looked sharper to start the game. Irving and James had layups in the opening minutes and J. R. Smith launched the three-point pipe bomb over Kyle Korver's outstretched hand.

Kent Bazemore scored the Hawks' first eight points in large part because Smith and James were switching any screens featuring three-point *Übermensch* Korver (particularly those baseline double picks once used by Ray Allen). Korver had an off year, shooting just 40 percent from three, after leading the league the prior two seasons and shooting above 47 percent.

Those switches opened up a couple good looks for Bazemore, and the Cavaliers were willing to live with that. Cleveland planned to take away Korver, Al Horford, and Paul Millsap, letting anyone else beat them. During the year Millsap and Horford combined for 32.3 points, 16.3 rebounds, 6.4 assists, 2 threes, 2.6 steals, and 3.2 blocks a game. (The trio ended the first a collective 1-of-9.)

The Cavs were very physical with Atlanta and taking them out of their game. "We had a great game of being physical early," Lue said later. "We were on bodies. I liked the physicality."

The Cavaliers jumped out to a 16-8 lead thanks to four threes—one each by Smith and James followed by a pair from Irving, one in transition, the other a last-second prayer from four feet past the line.

"One of our main objectives tonight is to get off to a good start. After seven-eight days off that's something we want to come out and do," Love said at morning shoot-around. "It's pace of play and making sure we're getting the right shots. We drilled that this week; watched a lot of film."

Then the Cavs endured a mid-quarter offensive lull. During that six-minute first quarter siesta the two teams shot a combined 6-of-24 and played sloppily, taking hurried shots without much passing.

LeBron checked out early, with 4:16 left in the first and the Cavs up 22-15. James had received a foul for apparently tossing Millsap to the ground defending the post. Thirty seconds later Dellavedova checked in for Irving when refs whistled his second foul.

Oddly, things didn't turn around for the Cavaliers until the final member of the Big Three came off the floor, when Love checked out with 97 seconds left in favor of Channing Frye. First Smith came off a Frye screen and drove down the heart of the lane, Bazemore chasing. As Horford came over to challenge at the rim, J. R. lofted a perfect alley-oop to Horford's man, Tristan Thompson, for the jam.

After Dennis Schroder beat Dellavedova badly to his left for a layup, the Cavs ran Smith through a couple screens as Tristan Thompson ran a dribble handoff for Smith. Instead of curling around Thompson, Smith stepped back and stuck the three. Then Delly led a fastbreak with six seconds on the clock, driving the lane and dishing to a trailing Frye for a three above the left wing, giving them a 30-19 lead going into the second.

Irving had 10 points, including two of the team's six first quarter three-pointers. More importantly, the Cavs had nine assists on 11 baskets, evidence that they were finding each other, not just going one-on-one.

"They shot it extremely well," Hawks coach Mike Budenholzer told TNT at the end of the quarter. "They made some tough threes and then in transition they were getting some threes. We have to do better in transition to stay more connected. We always want to play with passes and more ball movement.... We make a few more shots and we'll be in good shape."

The Hawks shot 33 percent in the first quarter, and continued to struggle in the second. A Schroder three was their only bucket in nine shots (with five free throws) the first five minutes. Love's three out of a pick-and-pop on the left wing made it 38-27 Cavaliers with 7:22 left. It was Kevin's only bucket in 10 shots during the first half.

Jefferson added another three a moment later—the Cavaliers' ninth of the first half—and caught a beautiful James fastbreak bounce pass from halfcourt to the free throw line, where Jefferson caught it in stride and slammed it home for a 43-31 lead. Atlanta hit a string of three consecutive shots but James answered with a couple jump shots, and the Cavs took a 51-41 lead into halftime despite scoring but twice in the final four minutes.

The Hawks finished the half shooting under 30 percent. Millsap was 2-of-10 from the field, Horford 0-of-6. Korver missed his only shot. Millsap had seven offensive boards, but only one resulted in a bucket.

While the Cavs were only shooting 44 percent from the field themselves, they were 9-of-21 (41 percent) from three. Even more impressive, 16 of their 20 shots were assisted. The Hawks were crowding the paint to prevent penetration, but the kick-outs to the perimeter were producing high yields.

The second half got off to a sluggish start, as each team managed only a couple baskets almost four minutes into the third quarter. A flagrant foul call on J. R. Smith for an elbow to the head of Millsap slowed the action.

Upon review it seemed ticky-tack for a flagrant (especially considering the four or five uncalled elbows to James' noggin the previous series). Millsap tried to come around Smith as he put his arms up, receiving an inadvertent elbow to the jaw. Millsap missed both free throws, and Atlanta failed to convert on the possession.

The stoppage of play didn't help the Cavaliers' rhythm. They proceeded to make only their second and third turnovers of the night sandwiched around a LeBron ISO layup over Millsap. The ball movement wasn't great as the team indulged in fruitless pick-and-rolls, and the offensive execution wasn't especially crisp.

Love set a couple screens for Kyrie before receiving the pick-and-pop pass on to the left wing. He head-faked, sending a leaping Horford past, and after a rhythm dribble stepped in and banked it off the glass from 15 feet making it 58-45, with eight to go. It was just his second bucket in 12 attempts, most on the team to that point. Despite his struggles the team didn't go away from him.

"The first half was tough. I kept coming to the bench and talking to [Channing Frye] and he says, 'Just keep being aggressive.' Same thing with RJ," Love reported. "I was getting great shots—they just weren't falling— but in the second half I kept my aggression. Bron was finding me quite a bit. A lot of great looks, and I was able to convert."

With seven minutes left, Irving missed a midrange pull-up, but Thompson grabbed his fourth offensive board over two Hawks and put it back. Not to be outdone, Millsap tipped in his own miss—his eighth and last offensive board of the evening—cutting the lead to 60-51.

That's when the Cavaliers hit the turbo. James hit a catch-and-shoot three. (He was 2-of-11 on such threes in the first series, but made his only two that night.) Then Thompson resuscitated another possession featuring a LeBron miss at the rim, feeding Kyrie out top.

Irving beat the trap, drove the lane, and passed to LeBron chugging baseline from the corner. James leapt at the rim. As the Hawks rose up, he found Love on the opposite wing for Cleveland's 12th three of the night. A minute later Love hit another three from the left corner, again off a James penetration drive.

On the other end Love tipped a Schroder pass. LeBron snagged it and raced up court. He fed Irving on the wing, who tossed it back to the King for the royal flush. It was 72-54 with less than four minutes to go. Everyone thought it was over except for the Hawks, who kept playing.

"Whenever you get a team down 15 points they are almost dead," said Jefferson. "When you get them to 18, all you have to do is lift the shovel up and pour dirt on them. Especially if you want to be a high-level team. We didn't do that tonight and it almost cost us."

A Channing Frye jumper was the sole Cavalier score in a 16-2 blitz by Atlanta to close the quarter. The Hawks got hot from international waters, draining four threes, including two by Schroder (eight during the run) as he repeatedly abused Love on the switch and sank threes when the Cavs tried going under the screen.

"They made some shots. Mike Scott made a three in front of Kevin, and Schroder made a three," Lue said. "That got their confidence up."

The Cavaliers regrouped to begin the third. Shumpert snaked inside for a layup and Frye got Horford in the air late in the clock to draw the foul on a three-pointer. He hit all his fouls shots, pushing the lead back to 79-70. But the reenergized Hawks came back.

Schroder hit a straightaway three when Dellavedova went under a Horford screen, and Millsap tapped away a James pass to ignite a fastbreak that he finished with a dunk. After LeBron missed up-close off a Shumpert drive-and-dish, the Hawks drew a foul on a three-pointer in which Shumpert ran into a Millsap screen, "knocking" him into Korver as the latter took a three. Korver converted them all to close the deficit to 79-78.

"Schroder made five threes," Lue said in the postgame presser. "The gameplan we came in with we adjusted the final six or seven minutes of the fourth quarter and we were able to get stops."

"Whenever Kyrie does this," Lue elaborated the next day, rubbing his head with both hands, "it means something is wrong. He looks at me and he's like, 'Are we going to keep going under with Schroder?' I was like, 'Let's give it one more try.' And then we adjusted."

After several empty back-and-forth possessions Schroder hit Horford for an alley-oop out of the pick-and-roll for the Hawks' first lead, 80-79. Lue called a timeout.

"We as a group have to do a little better job of maintaining during those runs," said Jefferson. "We did not do a good job, and as you go along, each game and each series, it only gets more difficult."

Schroder and Irving engaged in a *mano-a-mano* duel for the next 90 seconds. Irving hit a three, a pull-up, and a layup. Schroder answered with two layups sandwiched around a dish to Millsap for three, tying the score at 86.

The Cavaliers wilted a tad. J. R. Smith missed two free throws and Horford snuffed a LeBron layup attempt, but the Hawks couldn't capitalize. When Bazemore fouled Tristan Thompson with 5:23 left, Lue called a timeout and preached composure.

"I had a couple turnovers that led to some of their runs, and I just had to make some plays for my team," James said. "Coach Lue stayed on us. He was, 'It's okay. They're making shots. Let's jut try to execute and stop turning the ball over, get back in the game and finish it off the right way.'"

That's precisely what they did. Thompson hit one of two from the stripe. Horford retook the lead, 88-87, beating Love off the bounce with a floating half hook. The Cavaliers answered holding Atlanta scoreless the next three minutes during a 10-0 run fueled by charity.

Smith hit a three from the right break after coming off a series of baseline screens. Love drew a foul at the three line, then converted two of the free throws. James stole the ball from Schroder. After two offensive rebounds saved the possession, James cut to the basket, caught the ball, head faked, and scored through the Millsap foul. He hit the freebie, his only trip to the line all night. That made it 95-88 with just over two left and the Hawks didn't get any closer, losing 104-93.

"Defensively we had some possessions where we gave ourselves a chance and just couldn't quite come up with a couple big rebounds late," Hawks coach Mike Budenholzer said. "We had a couple good open looks and I know we had two turnovers. I think our spacing wasn't as good as it needs to be and the execution in the last two to four minutes needs to be better."

The Cavaliers finished with balanced scoring. James had 25, Irving 21, Love 17, and Smith 12. They shot only 45 percent from the field but went 15-of-31 (48 percent) from three and had 27 assists on 37 buckets. Cleveland also had a 12-5 edge on loose balls, a sign of the better energy they brought for much of the evening.

Unable to establish an inside game—the Hawks were just 18-of-41 in the paint—Atlanta took even more threes than the Cavs while hitting four less (11-of-34). The Hawks had made it close, but were outplayed most of the game and the only substantive contributions they received were Schroder with 27 and Bazemore with 16. Starters Teague, Horford, Millsap, and Korver finished 12-of-42 (29 percent).

James wasn't complaining despite surrendering an 18-point lead. "A win is a win in the postseason," he said. "We're going to get better as the series goes on."

E. C. Semifinals, Game 2. Wednesday, May 4, 2016, Cleveland. (1-0 Cavs)

Between games reporters asked Lue and Budenholzer about strategy and tactics. Teams generally have a gameplan that they've worked out based on the other team's weaknesses. This would be strategy. Meanwhile, most people get bivouacked in tactics—how they carry out the strategy. Tactics change; strategies are more durable.

"You always come in with a gameplan but if it doesn't work you have to adjust, and our coaching staff does a great job of being able to adjust in games, not when you watch the film the next day and say we should've done that," Lue said. "We do a great job of understanding what a team might do next game so you can always be one step ahead."

But while it's often portrayed as a chess match, it's a bit more like a pachinko machine.

"There's more talked about it than there is in reality, whether it be within the game or from game to game," said Budenholzer during the pregame presser. "Coaches and teams and amazingly players oftentimes will make adjustments in a game and between games, but it seems to be a big talking point every playoff series. I think the adjustments are very subtle. But subtle's important."

The Hawks recognized the Cavaliers as a drive-and-dish team. The ability of Kyrie Irving and LeBron James to get by their men using pick-and-rolls (or just in the open floor) forced the Hawks to make some kind of concession, just as the Cavs did in daring Schroder to beat them from three in Game 1. Like the Pistons, the Hawks chose to seal the lane, hoping to coax James, Irving, and their mates into settling for midrange jump shots. The Hawks lacked a shot-blocker like Andre Drummond, which made that more complicated. Atlanta was forced to make help rotations that good passing could exploit. That's just what the Cavaliers did in Game 2, showing the same willingness to move the ball as in Game 1.

The Cavaliers got off to a slow start, missing four of their first five shots and making two turnovers. The Hawks, meanwhile, got Korver two shots in the first 60 seconds—twice his output in Game 1—and he converted one. Atlanta took an 11-8 lead on a Millsap putback of his own point-blank miss with four minutes gone, before momentum shifted to the Cavs, who staged an 8-0 run.

Irving drew a shooting foul on Teague, and cashed both. (It took 47 minutes to get his first free throw in Game 1.) Thompson poked the ball away from Millsap on a post spin move and James grabbed it, firing to Irving at halfcourt. Kyrie then found Love in the right corner for three.

After Millsap forced a three, James pushed in transition, finding Irving open in the right corner for another three after catching Teague ball watching for a 16-11 lead. Budenholzer called a timeout. The Hawks answered with a couple of Millsap free throws and a Thabo Sefolosha three to tied it back up at 16, then all hell broke loose.

Kevin Love rebounded Kent Bazemore's long missed three and threw a two-handed overhead pass to LeBron at the opposite free throw line. James outleapt Bazemore for it, spun toward the lane, and finished between two other Hawks. Then Atlanta left LeBron unattended at the arc following an Irving pick-and-pop, and he made them pay.

On the other end Irving poked the ball away from Schroeder and raced upcourt, receiving the pass from LeBron and zipping it to Love in the corner for three. After a missed Horford three, James pushed it again in transition, finding Smith above the left break. Korver probably thought he was covering Smith, but that foot or two of space might as well have been the Atlantic: He couldn't bridge it before J. R. popped that piñata.

After an Atlanta timeout, Lue sat Thompson and James for Shumpert and Jefferson. Shumpert secured a Horford miss and pushed the pace. He drove the left lane and hit Jefferson in the right corner, who touch-passed it to an even wider open Smith, who drilled his third three of the quarter, capping the 14-0 run.

"We need to be a lot better starting with our transition defense," Budenholzer said after. "We need greater urgency, greater understanding getting to all their shooters. I think it starts there."

During the run the Hawks missed five shots and made three turnovers. The Cavs missed five shots as well, but grabbed three offensive rebounds, extending possessions and putting further pressure on the Hawks' help defense.

"Our activity in making sure every field goal attempt they take is difficult sometimes requires some help, and if you help they're active on the boards," explained the Hawks coach after Game 1. "I know it's more important we make them miss first. That's our priority and then have all five guys competing and getting in there."

Smith would hit another three just before the buzzer as he ran left over a Thompson screen near the top of the key, took one dribble, and launched while still drifting a little right to left. Nothing but net. That made it 35 points in the quarter thanks to eight Cavs threes (half by Smith) in 12 attempts. Indeed, they were only 3-of-13 on closer shots!

Even Itchy & Scratchy would find the Cavs' second quarter highlights cruel and gratuitously graphic. The Cavaliers apparently digested Jefferson's dictum on how to handle when you have a team down 15 points: Don't wait to throw dirt on them. The Cavaliers made two more threes to open the second quarter, by Frye and James, who also finished a nice reverse layup in traffic.

The score was 43-25 with nine minutes left when Lue took a timeout.

The Hawks would only make one more basket the entire rest of the quarter, getting the balance of their points (11) at the line.

If the Hawks' first issue was transition defense, inability to stop penetration followed closely behind. James and Shumpert both drove the lane like it was their driveway and found Dellavedova and Richard Jefferson alone on the left wing for threes. James followed the next time down with a dribble pull-up three out of a pick-and-roll screen with Frye. A minute later Frye rebounded a missed James three from the corner and hit the putback for a 54-28 lead with 6:39 left.

Millsap drove to the rim for a bucket and made a couple free throws during a 7-2 run over the next 90 seconds. But the Cavaliers weren't about to let Atlanta back in it. Irving dropped a right-corner three on a seven-pass possession and Smith got a screen from Love as he sank another three over a strong Horford contest.

Ninety seconds later Smith came off a Frye screen, received the ball at the arc straightaway, head faked, watched Korver fly past, dribbled the ball behind his back to the right, and lined up the inevitable three, his sixth of the night.

After a couple Love free throws, Dellavedova found Jefferson in the right corner in transition for his second three. Then Frye stole the ball from Millsap, who was trying to go behind his back in the lane, and rifled a pass up the court. The ball swung and finally found Love for a wide-open three. It was the Cavaliers' 18th three-pointer in 27 attempts, and gave them a 74-38 lead.

Besides their troubles in transition, the Hawks were unable to compensate for the Cavs' crisp, generous passing.

"In the halfcourt I think they're probably in the paint a lot," said Budenholzer. "We collapse when they get to the paint. People help. They're moving the ball. They're making the extra pass. They're making shots, and then the third piece [is] several of them, including J. R. Smith, are hitting extremely difficult threes."

Necessarily, there wasn't much of a game after that; in Little League it would've fallen under the mercy rule. Atlanta did play better offensively, putting up 32 points in the second quarter, but didn't have much more success stopping the Cavs, who also scored 32.

James and Irving put the boot to the neck or maybe the pedal to the metal, scoring 11 apiece in the third, while the team made four more threes and just one turnover. Cleveland made three more in the fourth quarter (25 for the game), including the 24th by little-used reserve Dahntay Jones to break the NBA record of 23 (set by two teams). They also broke the playoff record of 21 set by Golden State a week earlier in their first round series against Houston. The Cavs' 18 halftime threes shattered the old mark of 12.

"Our guys have a lot of trust. They trust each other on the defensive end and they trust each other on the offensive end," Lue said. "Outside of the threes I thought our defense was great. That was our best defensive effort in a long time. If we compete and we play great defensively, we can get out and run and get almost anything we want."

Ironically, the Hawks' plan had worked to some extent. The Cavaliers were only 9-of-33 in shots at the rim for the game, though there was a lot of uncalled contact. Obviously there are limits to any "successful" strategy. The Cavaliers were quick to say their three-point explosion was the natural outgrowth of the way Atlanta defended them. It didn't make them a three-point shooting team.

"Obviously we got guys that can knock down shots from the perimeter, and it's been key to our success, but we need to continue to understand that we have to be very balanced offensively. Tonight was just a byproduct," James said.

"If you look at a lot of the threes that were made and that were taken, the ball was getting into the paint first and then it was spraying out," he continued. "We're not a three-point shooting team and we don't want to be labeled that. We're a well-balanced team that's capable of making threes.... I always look at the football analogy. When you have a well-balanced offense running and passing, it can free up a lot of things. That's what our team is about."

12
FEARSOME THREESOME RULE HAWKS' ROOST

DEPENDING ON YOUR predilections, you might wonder what happened to D. B. Cooper, Amelia Earhart, or Anastasia Romanov. If you're a Cavaliers fan, you wondered what happened to the whistles. In one of the greatest heists in NBA history, somebody stole LeBron James' rep with the refs.

Since time immemorial James and his supporters have complained about the imbalance between the amount of contact he receives and the number of calls. Many invoke the man-among-boys narrative, comparing James to the equally exotic, large, lithe, and frequently mugged Shaquille O'Neal. (Maybe he didn't complain as loudly because he couldn't make free throws.)

"He's the Shaq of guards," said Tyronn Lue after James earned but one foul shot in Game 1. "When he goes to the basket guys are bouncing off of him. Those are still fouls, but he doesn't get those calls because he's so big, so strong, and so physical."

Since coming to Cleveland, James' long-standing beef about not getting enough love from the zebras has taken a dramatic turn for the worse. Maybe all those years in his prime whining about calls in Miami beside co-complainant Dwyane Wade finally soured officials on him. Who can say? But there's no good explanation for why he's lost the NBA's judicial benefit of the doubt, leaving only conspiracy theories.

	Drives/Gm	Percentage shots <3'	FTA/Drive	FTA/FGA
'13-'14	7.6	39.9	.34	.43
Playoffs	7.4	37.6	.324	.47
'14-'15	9.8	33.2	.327	.41
Playoffs	17.0	30.3	.22	.31
'15-'16	9.2	45.9	.25	.35
Playoffs	10.0	46.0	.20	.30

The first thing some might suggest is that James has aged with the implicit subtext that he's lost some of his athleticism. That hardly passes the eye test. But even if it did, wouldn't the fact that he's not just driving more but getting to the rim more suggest a commensurate increase in contact and foul calls?

While the aging Michael Jordan started to eschew inside contact and hone his midrange jumper game, James' career has gone in the opposite direction. He's taking fewer jump shots than anytime in his career. How does that also correlate with his lowest rate of foul shots per field goal attempt since his rookie season?

"I don't get involved in it too much. I just play the game [and] whatever the referees decide the call may be, just move on," James said. "I can't let my focus go somewhere else. I can't allow my energy to be somewhere it shouldn't be."

Indeed, during the Pistons series James noted that it's an ever-present challenge to keep up the attack and not backslide into bad habits and lazy threes that quite honestly aren't his game. (James shot 31 percent from three during the regular season, but shot over 37 percent after the first round of the playoffs.) James' game is taking it at the defense and either beating his man or creating adjustments that open up shots for others, based upon how the defense reacts.

"When you got guys making shots it's a conscious effort by me not to fall into it. I have to be the one to say, 'Okay, you need to get to the rim, you need to continue to put pressure on the defense,'" said James. "I don't want to add to the burden of us just casting three-point shots. I want to be a guy that continues to put pressure on the rim…. They are deadly snipers and that's what we got 'em for. I'm not one of them. I'm more like a tank."

The Hawks' downplayed the the deficit and the fact the Cavaliers had beaten them nine straight times in the postseason. In the end, they said, it was just two home games. The series shifted to Atlanta, where they hoped to hold serve. Kent Bazemore suggested that Atlanta need only get Cleveland down a few points to change their demeanor.

"Everyone knows how they play," he said after Game 2. "They get out in front and they're a totally different team. It is what it is. We'll see them again. That wasn't Game 4."

E. C. Semifinals, Game 3. Friday, May 6, 2016, Atlanta. (2-0 Cavs)

After watching the Cavaliers shut down Korver the first two games (10 points, one three), the Hawks benched Korver for Thabo Sefolosha. That freed their one truly dangerous piece of artillery from Smith's smothering coverage and hopefully matched him to less attentive second-stringers.

Sefolosha was the Hawks' best wing defender and had guarded LeBron James well in the past. (The Atlanta small forward missed the 2015 playoffs when New York City cops allegedly used too much force making an arrest and broke his leg. The lawsuit's still pending.) The move also freed Bazemore to chase J. R. more vigorously than Korver could. Atlanta wasn't about to let Smith make seven threes again.

The Hawks also chose to blitz the Irving/Thompson pick-and-roll, much as the Cavaliers had Detroit's Reggie Jackson/Andre Drummond pick-and-roll. Atlanta forced the ball out of Irving's hands deep in the frontcourt, leaving Thompson to make a play in the open floor—not exactly his forte.

Atlanta came out of the gates with good pace, quickly putting Cleveland on its heels. First Teague beat Irving off the bounce for two. Love answered with a three, but Horford came right back at him. Twice the 6-foot-10 Hawk dribbled from the arc into the post, backing Kevin into the lane and scoring over him with a little half hook. When Sefolosha stole a Thompson pass to the corner and got it back on the break for a dunk to make it 8-3, Lue called timeout.

"The first possession that we had, we had a play we wanted to run. I see that they're blitzing me and I'm coming to the bench kind of looking for answers for myself because they were up a certain number of points and they took me out of a rhythm," Irving said.

The Cavaliers adjusted by screening for Irving with Love instead of Thompson, so when the Hawks trapped with the screener it left Love uncovered. That's how Big Kev got his second three in the game's first three minutes.

"They're tying to double-team the basketball," Lue told ESPN sideline reporter Lisa Salters between quarters. "So if Kevin [pick-and-] pops, he can get any shot he wants."

On another occasion Cleveland moved the Irving/Thompson pick to the middle of the floor, so when Thompson rolled open he could catch the ball and immediately shoot it. This drew Horford's second foul, bringing on Kris Humphries to replace him.

Thompson missed both free throws, but Love tipped in the second, tying the score at eight. Humphries paid immediate dividends, hitting an open wing three when Love and Smith attempted to trap Teague in the right corner. Love followed his own missed three with the offensive board, drawing a foul by Bazemore on the putback and cashing both free throws.

If Love's offense was going to hurt the Hawks, they seemed intent on extracting a similar payment on the other end. They isolated him on Teague, who took Kevin into the lane and drew a foul. Undaunted, Love popped out to the left wing after screening for J. R. Smith and made a wide-open three, his 13th point and all the Cavaliers' scoring.

It also kicked off a 10-0 run, capped when Tristan Thompson made a beautiful post-up move. Thompson took the ball on the left block, drove hard middle, then left Millsap there like the tip, spinning baseline for a lefty hook. That made it 20-13 Cavs with five and a half left.

Atlanta recaptured the momentum with an 11-3 run, featuring threes by Sefolosha and Schroder, as well as a technical foul on Smith for arguing a call. Meanwhile, Cleveland went cold, missing six straight shots to allow the Hawks to retake the lead 24-23 with 99 seconds left in the quarter.

Channing Frye and Matthew Dellavedova answered with threes in transition/early offense, and a reinserted James converted a layup on the final play of the quarter, giving the Cavs a 31-28 lead.

"Defensively, the Hawks had to make a choice. Every game they chose somebody different to leave open, and...I knew they weren't gonna leave

FEARSOME THREESOME RULE HAWKS' ROOST

J. R.," wrote Frye in an August online article for The Players' Tribune. "Al Horford was on me, and he's a center. It was Horford's job to sag off the center some in order to help defend the lane from LeBron's drives. That was just their defensive scheme. So I let it fly. The first one went in, and I said to myself, *It's your time*."

Budenholzer brought back starters Horford, Millsap, and Bazemore to match up with the LeBron-led Cavs second team, planning to rest them mid-quarter.

Channing Frye outleapt Horford for the second of two Shumpert missed free throws, tipping it out to LeBron deep in the frontcourt. He whipped it cross-court to Jefferson in the right corner. Jefferson attacked the closing Hawks, getting into the lane and airborne when he found Frye at the arc for the straightaway three.

"I just tried to be aggressive when they put two people on the ball," Frye said. "In the first half I saw that they were going to pull-rotate to me and there was some space. I figured I was 7-foot so they're not going to block it."

Right away Delly pressured the ball on the inbounds and Jefferson picked up the Hawks' other outlet player at halfcourt. Bazemore threw it away trying to thread the ball into tight coverage. Running the pick-and-roll on the left wing, Shumpert spotted James cutting backdoor through the lane and fed him for the layup.

A moment later Shumpert stole the ball. James took the pass from him and posted Millsap, taking a six-foot fallaway that was long. However, Shumpert grabbed the rebound high above the rim and, with his right hand, flushed it back through in one motion, igniting the Cavaliers' bench and making it 38-30 Cleveland.

Both teams' offenses started clicking, and for a stretch of four minutes battled toe-to-toe. Frye and Shumpert's long-distance dialing answered Korver and Teague threes; Irving and Jefferson layups met with Horford post-ups.

With just over six left, Budenholzer called a timeout and came back with a small lineup featuring Humphries, Millsap, Sefolosha, Korver, and Teague. Over the next five minutes the Hawks shot 9-of-11 and outscored the Cavaliers 23-5.

Mainly the Hawks got stops. The aggressive defense frustrated Irving. Cleveland was 2-of-10 and committed three turnovers. Korver got loose

165

for three triples (12 points in the quarter), while Humphries, Horford, and Bazemore each contributed a couple baskets. The Hawks outscored the Cavs 35-24 in the second and took a 63-55 lead at half.

"For the most part it was just us relaxing and not being aware," Lue said of Korver's outburst. "Our awareness wasn't up and he showed us in the first half when he had two threes where we weren't on his body. We were relaxed."

The Cavaliers continued their hot shooting from three, making 9-of-19, but the Hawks were even better at 10-of-17, thanks to Korver's 4-of-6. Atlanta committed just six turnovers and turned the Cavs' 11 turnovers into 15 points. The Cavaliers had as many offensive boards as the Hawks did defensive ones (12), powered by Thompson's seven offensive rebounds, but Cleveland only shot 3-of-9 on second-chance opportunities.

Like the first quarter, the Cavaliers opened the third going to Love while the Hawks set out to attack him. Millsap's driving dunk drew an and-one blocking foul on Love, though replays showed his feet were planted and outside the restricted circle. Love answered with a post-up score over Sefolosha and a corner three, but with nine minutes left Love picked up an offensive foul, his fourth, for lowering his shoulder into Millsap while posting up, forcing him to the bench.

During a timeout James implored Irving to get it together. The Hawks' traps had taken him out of his game. Up until that point he had four points on 2-of-8 shooting with one assist and one turnover. "I said I don't care what happened up to this point—just hit the reset button," James recalled. "We need you to lead us."

Sure enough the Cavaliers mounted a comeback. Frye, Smith, and Irving hit threes—the first two on James drive-and-dishes, the latter on a Thompson kick-out—and Frye stepped in and hit a wing bank shot after head-faking Millsap past him in the corner. With their lead cut to 77-73, the Hawks called a timeout.

Millsap put together a personal 6-0 run while the only Cavs points were a free throw split by Thompson on a Hawks intentional foul. That gave Millsap 13 of the Hawks 20 so far in the quarter. The lead was back to 83-74. Irving kept working, setting up in the left corner for a quick transition three, and answering a Sefolosha triple by splitting a double-team and pulling up for a 16-foot jumper.

"From the four-minute mark in the third quarter to all the way through the fourth he just did what Kyrie does," said James. "He hit big shots for us."

The Cavaliers cut it to four when James tipped in Thompson's miss with 45 seconds left in the third, but Atlanta hit Horford with an alley-oop from Schroder out of the high pick-and-roll, for a 91-85 lead. Both teams entered the fourth shooting an identical 14-of-27 from three.

"We made some things up in the first three quarters. We didn't do a very good job of helping each other," said Jefferson. "We made a couple uncharacteristic mistakes. What happens is five or six guys make one or two mistakes. Just a simple mistake, nobody having a bad game, nobody getting killed, but ultimately what that leads to is 12 mistakes and that combination of things puts you down eight. Everybody just needed to raise their level of intensity."

Lue sat Irving after he picked up his third foul with about two and a half minutes left in the third, and let LeBron finish the quarter, so Irving came back with the second squad, including Love, Frye, Dellavedova, and Jefferson, arguably their best three-point shooting lineup, especially with Irving back to his old tricks.

(During the season, Irving shot a career-low 32 percent from three, far off his 38 percent lifetime rate. His long-range touch was the last thing to return from his knee injury. It began to recover after the All-Star break (34 percent), and he shot 42 percent in five April games, but nobody expected Irving to shoot 44 percent during the playoffs.)

"We stuck with it the first three quarters, knowing the way the game was going that if we could get to the fourth quarter in striking distance we'd be able to adjust, and we did," Lue said. "We tried to do some different things defensively so they couldn't adjust on the fly. We held it down for the first three quarters and kept it close, then were able to adjust."

The Frye/Love paring apparently caught the Hawks by surprise. "We didn't prepare for that," Horford said. "They took advantage." That coach Budenholzer could intentionally foul Tristan and not expect Lue might replace him with Frye, especially in the fourth quarter, seems strange. (They were expecting maybe Mozgov?)

The Hawks were a little bit stuck because with all the shooters on the floor, they really couldn't afford to trap Irving, but by not pressuring him, they let him get cooking.

"Maybe we could've or should've stayed more aggressive. But they had an awful lot of shooting on the court for most of the fourth quarter. Sometimes that dictates, and you have to do something different," Budenholzer said. "Obviously Frye had a heckuva night. They played Frye and Love together some, er, a lot in the fourth quarter."

Irving hit a three off the dribble and Schroder answered with his own. After Love missed a three, Teague replaced Schroder and beat Delly and a helping Love for a short floater that gave the Hawks a 101-93 lead with 9:14 left.

Over the next six minutes, the Cavs crushed the Hawks 20-3. Cleveland went 8-of-11, including four threes, while Atlanta went 1-of-7 and committed three turnovers. After making 18 turnovers the first three quarters, the Cavaliers were flawless during the final stanza.

"To start that fourth quarter I told Kyrie, 'I want you to be aggressive and look to play fast and early and try to play without the screen at times [to avoid the trap] if you can get to the basket,'" Lue said. "He did a great job of carrying us offensively the first half of the fourth quarter until we brought LeBron back."

Indeed, the next time down the court after the Teague layup, Irving pulled up and head-faked Bazemore past him, then calmly sank the open three from the right wing. When Irving pushed after the next Hawks miss, three players surrounded him in transition. Kyrie threw back to the middle of the floor, finding a trailing Frye, who sank his sixth three to cut the lead to 101-99 with 8:39 left.

LeBron returned a minute later. He got Korver isolated on the right wing, with Love and Frye in the corners keeping the Hawks' bigs honest. James took the ball to the center of the lane and swooped in like the Angel of Death with a thunderous two-handed jam.

After Korver stopped a James one-man break with a foul on the floor, Atlanta left him alone at the arc, and he took his time, set his feet, and sank it, his first three in four attempts. The next possession Cleveland deflected the ball several times before J. R. Smith intercepted a Millsap pass. He threw a baseball pass to Frye, who had started upcourt a moment earlier on a near steal and as a consequence was all alone for the jam, making it 106-103 Cavs with just under six to go.

The Hawks called a timeout, but looked demoralized. They failed to convert on two opportunities, and then James hit a fallaway 20-footer over Sefolosha with three seconds on the shot clock. It was a stake through the heart. After Millsap airballed a three, Irving pushed it into the frontcourt. He crossed over Bazemore, leaving him like a bad habit, cutting to the middle of the lane for the layup and a 110-103 lead.

Kyrie picked up his fifth foul, but hung tough and never got the next one. A moment later James found Love in the corner for his fifth three to make it 116-106, which became a 120-108 victory.

The Cavs outscored Atlanta 36-17 in the quarter and held them to 35 percent shooting while shooting over 50 percent themselves. Frye, Irving, and James all scored in double figures in the fourth alone.

Frye had a game-high 27, Irving and James had 24, and Love finished with 21. The team made more than 20 three-pointers (21-of-39) for the second game in a row, outrebounded the Hawks 55-28, and made 16 free throws, including seven by LeBron, who got to the line nine times for the second game in a row.

"We had some uncharacteristic turnovers, 20 for 27 points, which is not what we've been doing in the playoffs so far," James said. "But we were able to get 26 assists. We have some great shooters, and the reason we have great shooters is the ball is popping and the ball has great energy behind it."

It was another challenging game that tested the Cavs yet never truly imperiled them. James Jones agreed it was their most challenging game of the playoffs, and that these games were helping to hone the team's execution, spirit, and intensity.

"Every situation you need to get better, develop better habits, grow, and you gotta take a step back. They're pushing us, they're stretching us, and we're responding," said Jones. "They're forcing us to make adjustments. They're forcing us to stick to our gameplan and do it better, to be more efficient. But also to be decisive in making the right play and not try to force things to make things happen."

E. C. Semifinals, Game 4. Sunday, May 8, 2016, Atlanta. (3-0 Cavs)

Things were looking bleak for the Hawks. Nothing they'd done had been effective enough to stop the Cavaliers juggernaut. They couldn't afford to let Irving and James go one-on-one without a rim protector, meaning help rotations and an effort to close off the lane. But you can't take everything away; Atlanta had to decide again what to give up. In Game 4 it'd be Kevin Love, and the crazy thing is it almost worked.

The Hawks were well coached and opened with good energy, but the Cavs were ready for it, and matched their intensity. Love, Irving, and Smith all hit threes, and James added a layup and a step-back jumper as the Cavaliers sprinted out to a 13-8 lead. Then Thompson was called for a loose ball foul on a missed Horford three, his second foul.

Losing Thompson discombobulated the Cavaliers' defense and let Millsap cut loose. Now guarded by Love, Millsap went to work, scoring half of the Hawks' points in a 12-4 run that gave Atlanta a 20-17 advantage. A pair of Irving free throws, a Frye corner three in transition off a James drive-and-dish, and a Jefferson corner three off a crosscourt pass by Frye helped the Cavaliers tie it up at 25 with three minutes left.

But the Hawks closed the first frame on an 11-2 run, six of them by Millsap, as well as the second three-pointer of the quarter by Kim Kardashian's ex-husband, Kris Humphries, giving them a nine-point lead, 36-27. Millsap finished the quarter with 15, 11 of them after Thompson left the game.

The Cavaliers were 5-of-7 from beyond the boundary and only 5-of-15 inside it in the first, committing five turnovers that the Hawks turned into seven points. The Hawks shot 59 percent, including 6-of-11 from three. They'd go 4-of-21 the rest of the way.

"The guys that shot the ball, we wanted to shoot the [three] ball. We just tried to do a good job on Korver. He didn't have any threes tonight so that was big for us, just trying to contain him," Lue said. "They came out early and made some shots. Sefolosha made some shots and Bazemore. You have to give credit to those guys for playing well."

When Bazemore and Schroder scored to start the second, the Hawks held a 40-28 lead with 90 seconds gone in the quarter. Atlanta would be outscored 30-16 the rest of the quarter, while committing six turnovers.

The key was shutting down Atlanta's first quarter offensive engine, Paul Millsap. He sat to start the second, and when he returned a well-rested Thompson was waiting. The Hawks forward scored only four more points, all at the line, going 0-for-6 with four rebounds, an assist, and two turnovers.

"We had to sit Tristan, and Millsap kind of hurt us in that first quarter," said Lue. "We had to go small, and put [Richard Jefferson] on him. We didn't guard him as good as we wanted to but our guys fought and it's a tough matchup. Then in the second half I was able to play Tristan like 18 minutes straight to cool Millsap off."

The turnaround began with Kevin Love as Budenholzer revealed his answer to the Love/Frye conundrum. He was going to let Love shoot the ball. The next two times down, when Kyrie ran the pick-and-roll with Kevin, Horford trapped Kyrie. When Irving passed to Love, nobody rotated over.

Perhaps cowed at first by the coverage, Love airballed the first wide-open three from the right wing. But they ran it again on the left side. Love screened and flared all the way to the corner, where he dropped it. Horford and Schroder answered with buckets, but the Cavaliers kept coming.

The Cavaliers ran it again with the same result, another three, as Love head-faked the recently inserted Mike Scott, made an escape dribble to the right, and sank the three from the break. Atlanta put Kevin in the pick-and-roll, with Schroder feeding Scott an alley-oop over the late-returning/no-help-receiving Love.

Undaunted, the Cavaliers ran the same pick-and-roll, only in the middle of the floor. As Irving was about to go over Love's screen and Schroder cheated to the left side, Irving went behind his back to his right, leaving both defenders on the wrong side of the pick and taking it to the rim unimpeded. Atlanta called a timeout.

Down 48-41 after a couple Millsap free throws, the Cavaliers ran the Love/Irving pick-and-roll again, and Love drained another three, cutting the lead to four, and the Cavs would cut it to 58-56 at the half. The Hawks shot 56 percent from the field to Cleveland's 48 percent, but the Cavaliers were 10-of-16 from beyond the arc. After being doubled up on the boards in Game 3, the Hawks had a 21-16 edge.

"Kevin just stayed with it. He missed his first four or five shots, then he hit two big threes in a row—that's how he's been. He's been staying with it," said Lue. "Usually when you miss shots early on, you might get frustrated, but he stayed the course and he had a big third quarter that got us over the hump."

Atlanta opened the quarter with five points but ran into a problem defensive wrinkle that the Cavaliers exploited for four straight threes. First James screened for Irving and got an unescorted three. Then Love screened for Irving and James on separate occasions, both culminating in left-corner threes for Kevin. The third Love three came when he suddenly popped out to the arc from the baseline and James spotted him from across the court.

"The pace slowly started to pick up in the third quarter. We were getting downhill, myself and LeBron, and our aggressiveness was there," said Irving. "We just started to see something that kind of unraveled with their defense. I came down and it kinda was spur of the moment I ran double drag with Kev. I don't think they prepared for something like that, where I'm screening and he's screening and he's popping and I'm rolling. We came to a timeout and discussed it and kept going to it, and it worked."

After Atlanta called a timeout while behind 68-66, Love stepped inside the arc as Sefolosha flew by on his contest, making a 21-foot jumper from the left wing. That was Love's first basket *inside* the arc in eight attempts, while he'd made 7-of-9 from beyond the boundary.

"We tried to take away significant parts of their team and significant parts of their offense," Budenholzer said. "At some point, Kevin Love may be an option that they have to get to and he has to make enough shots for four quarters."

The Hawks weren't beaten yet. There were still 20 minutes of basketball. Sefolosha and Humphries blocked James shots at the rim, and both grabbed key rebounds followed by Sefolosha baskets (a three-pointer and a putback) to retake the lead 73-72.

Again Irving showcased that Samsonite handle, beating the double and entering the lane with Millsap on his hip, drawing the foul while scooping it in with his left and converting the and-one. After James missed two free throws, Schroder evened it at 75 on a 19-foot pull-up.

Love gave the Cavaliers back the lead, hitting a three and drawing a foul on Sefolosha for slapping his off-arm, which he converted for the rare four-point play. Cleveland carried that four-point lead into the fourth, up 81-77.

The Hawks trapped Irving, forcing a turnover that afforded Schroder a fastbreak layup. On their next possession Schroder lined up a three when Delly went under a Horford high screen, giving Atlanta back the lead, 82-81. Schroder had 13 points, and the rest of the game turned into a slugfest between the German point guard and the Cavs.

A Delly drive, a Frye block of Schroder at the rim, and a long Shumpert pull-up jumper gave the Cavaliers a three-point lead, but the Hawks came back with a Schroder drive and Horford three-pointer out of the pick-and-pop. A floater by Frye knotted it at 87.

"[Schroder] is great attacking the basket, and we were trying to take that away as much as we could by going under the screens. But he knocked down shots," said Delly.

The lead changed hands more than a pedicure before Cleveland strung together an Irving baseline drive and pull-up bank shot in the lane, a James layup in transition, and a Frye three-pointer on an early-offense cross-court James pass for a 96-91 lead. Atlanta answered with a floater by Horford, rolling after setting Schroder a screen, and then consecutive Schroder layups to give the Hawks a 97-96 lead with 90 seconds left.

"It became a two-minute game for us," said Love. "It came down to a couple possessions where we made plays and got stops when we needed to."

Coming out of the timeout, LeBron ran a give-and-go with Love, as an Irving backscreen opened James' path to the rim. But Horford blocked it, and three consecutive tips failed to go down, before Horford knocked the ball out of bounds. Delly substituted in and threw the inbounds, which featured a quick break by James from the free throw line down the lane. James got the ball and laid it off the backboard. Millsap blocked it from behind but was called for goaltending.

Coming out of a timeout, Atlanta ran a pick-and-roll for Schroder, isolating him on Thompson. Tristan hung with the skittering Hawks as he cut across the lane left to right and timed his leap perfectly to knock away Schroder's shot. Irving rebounded the ball.

With their next possession James isolated Millsap at the elbow, facing him up. He jabbed his right foot forward and dipped his shoulder as if to drive, then rocked back for the 20-foot fallaway jumper. It fell through and the Cavaliers had a 100-97 lead. Schroder beat Dellavedova to his right without a screen to pull the Hawks within one, 100-99, with 34 seconds left.

"[Schroder] is a shifty guy that puts a lot of pressure on the defense by getting downhill," said Lue. "He was able to get to the basket a lot tonight, and we didn't want to help too much and give them open threes because they were hot early."

LeBron ran down much of the clock before tossing up the almost obligatory dribble pull-up brick from three (*see*, Pistons Game 4). On some level he has to know every team in the league heaves a sigh of relief and crosses themselves every time he pulls up for three rather than taking it to the rack, regardless of his recent foul-drawing issues.

"I went for the dagger three to put us up four and I missed," said James in an on-court interview. "I knew they had no timeouts so they had to come full court, and Schroder did a great job of getting into the paint like he did all season."

Schroder received a screen from Horford and took Thompson to the hole similarly to the play before, only from right to left. This time as Schroder got to the left side of the lane, James was there and grabbed the ball just as he brought it up to shoot. The officials called a jump ball with two seconds left. James tipped it toward the corner. By the time Millsap recovered it and hoisted a shot, the buzzer had sounded.

Budenholzer all but acknowledged that the Cavaliers had better talent. "I'll just say they are playing at a high level," Budenholzer said. "Our players executed everything we asked of them, I would say at a very high level…. It's really on me at the end of the day. Our players did everything I asked them to do."

It's easy to miss the fact that the Hawks were pretty successful at what they did. Over the four games, the Hawks held the Cavs to 48 percent shooting in the restricted area (12.5-26.3) and 22 percent on non-restricted area paint shots (1.5-6.8). Meanwhile, the Hawks shot 61 percent in the restricted area (16.5-27.3). But that's not enough when your opponent shoots 51 percent from three and makes more than 19 a game.

"We just took what the defense gave us," Lue said. "If the three-point shot was open, we wanted to take it. If not we wanted to drive it to the basket. I thought we did a great job of mixing that up."

The Big Three all passed 20 points, led by Love with 27 points on 8-of-15 shooting from beyond the line, 1-of-10 within it. Love added 13 rebounds, and James had a near triple-double with 21 points, 10 boards, nine assists, and six turnovers. Irving had 21 points and eight assists, while Shumpert chipped in 10 big points off the bench and two steals.

"We're growing. We still have a lot of work and a lot of growth. We have a long way to go. We're still chasing that elusive 48 minutes of basketball where we control and dominate every facet of the game," said elder statesman James Jones. "Guys are starting to see their sacrifice pay off. The habits that are formed, the continuity, the chemistry, it's going to another level because guys have accepted their roles and their responsibility within this team framework."

13
JUST ROPE, THROW, AND BRAND 'EM

B Y THE BEGINNING of the Eastern Conference Finals, reporters had begun to ask about James' scoring fall-off. That is, when not trying to reframe the hundredth question about the team's outside/perimeter/three-point shooting or the long lay-off, rest, and rust. (As monotonous as the days of practice were without an opponent, we imagined the daily onslaught of similar questions to be twice as numbing.)

What the reporters had seized upon was a very real effect: For the first time in James' career, he was not his team's leading playoff scorer. Kyrie Irving was averaging 24.4 to James' 23.5 points per game. Indeed, that was the lowest playoff scoring average of James' career. Let's be clear, James was still taking half a shot more than Irving, and two and a half more than Love; nonetheless, there was an undeniable passing of the crown.

It was more apparent because James had taken on so much the year before in ferrying the full load. Sure, he tallied 30 points, 11 rebounds, and 8.5 assists a game during the playoffs. He also took 27 shots to do so. He was the team's entire offense, and couldn't be as efficient as he would have liked carrying so much offensive burden. There simply had been nobody left to share it with once Irving went down the last time.

"He's the best player on our team. The best player in the league. We understand that he understands that when he needs to take over a game, he's going to be ready and willing," Lue said. "But he also understands that in order for us to win, we need everybody. It's not just going to be him about him. He needs to get other guys involved. Keep up other guys with their confidence, and that's what he's been doing during the playoffs."

By comparison, the 2016 playoffs were night and day. Love was averaging 19 points on 44 percent shooting from three—just 36 percent from the field—and 12.5 rebounds a game. Irving was scoring 24 points and dishing out 5.5 assists a game, while shooting an absurd 54 percent from three, 48 percent overall. Add J. R. Smith's 12 points a game on 51 percent from beyond arc, and you could see where James must've felt like he were sitting in the lap of luxury compared to the year before.

"LeBron is letting the game come to him. When he wants to be aggressive when he sees fit to be aggressive, when teams have a good run or whatever, he just takes over a game," Lue said. "I don't think he's been in this position before, to just sit back and see the flow of the game and see when he needs to take over the game."

Lue suggested that James had invested that extra focus on the defensive side of the ball. Even during the year he expended more energy than before on the defensive end. Yet James wasn't selected to either first or second All-NBA Defensive Teams for 2015-16 for the second straight year after six consecutive choices.

It seemed a grievous oversight given that James led all players (with at least eight shots defensed a game) in defensive field goal percentage, reducing opponents' shooting percentage by 7.3 points. That's more than a point better than the next highest, Kevin Durant (-6.3 percent) and Draymond Green (-6.1 percent). While that's hardly the only metric, it's one of the best. (It measures opponents' expected field goal percentage from that area of the floor versus how opponents shot when guarded by that player.)

"I've never really trusted the individual shooting percentage because it's a five-man game, and sometimes if you're guarding the ball, there's supposed to be a guy behind you helping, and if he's not there and the player scores, the stat goes against you. So those can be tricky," Kerr said during the finals. "I had no idea LeBron didn't make an All-Defensive Team. He's a tremendous defender… I'm surprised to hear he wasn't on there."

In the playoffs, James turned it up another level to -9.9 percent, and nearly doubled his defense inside of 10 feet. In the regular season James reduced opponents' shooting -11.3 percent within six feet and -8.9 percent within 10 feet; through the first two series' those numbers shrunk to -21.7 percent and -16 percent.

James suggested it was natural to defer to mates who were making their shots. "When you have guys that can go out and command the court on their own, it allows me to focus on other facets of the game to help better our team to help still make an impact," he said. "My approach hasn't changed with regard to coming in and dominating a game. I just feel out the game and see what is going. If we got a guy going, we'll continue to go to them and I'm able to pull back a little bit offensively."

Greater deference by James to his mates played into how he was being defended. Both Detroit and Atlanta had loaded up the lane to stop him. By getting by his man and into the heart of the defense, James caused opponents to contract around him, opening up the perimeter for his shooters.

E. C. Finals, Game 1. Tuesday, May 17, 2016, Cleveland. (Even)

To face the Cavaliers, Toronto had to survive two seven-game series in which they lost Games 1, 4, and 6. Just two days earlier, the Raptors had beaten the Miami Heat 116-89 to advance. During the series they'd lost their center, Jonas Valanciunas, to a sprained right ankle, and the Raptors ruled him out for the first two games in Cleveland.

Toronto had beaten the Cavaliers two out of three in the regular season, and Kyle Lowry really bedeviled them. Lowry averaged 31 points in their three meetings, shooting 66 percent from the field and 44 percent from three, with 8.3 assists, 3.3 steals, and just 0.7 turnovers.

The Cavs had played only four games in the 23 days since sweeping the Pistons. For all the brave talk about coming out with good energy, they failed the first couple minutes of Game 1 at Quicken Loans.

Irving had an open three rim out. James made two beautiful feeds only to have the timid recipients choose to pass instead of shoot, leading to a turnover. Twice rotations to the screener, Patrick Patterson, on pick-and-pop with Lowry were slow, leaving him open threes. He made the first and missed the second only for Valanciunas' replacement, Bismack Biyombo, to tip it in.

Though Toronto went up 7-0, Lue didn't call a timeout. Cleveland got the ball to LeBron in the post against DeMarre Carroll. The King backed the former Hawk down, pushed him into the lane, and spun back right to the baseline for a layup.

Carroll came to the Raptors as a free agent after a breakout year in Atlanta (49 percent field goal, 40 percent three, 12.6 points per game), but by his own estimation was only 70-75 percent healthy after suffering a sprained left wrist against the Heat, after coming back from in-season knee surgery. He struggled all series, shooting 30 percent from the field and 19 percent from three, while taking the second-most three-point attempts on the team with 4.3 a game.

A minute later, James rebounded a Carroll three and threw it three-quarters of the court to Smith, who'd gotten ahead of the pack and was fouled on his layup attempt. Smith returned the favor the next possession, stealing a Lowry pass and feeding upcourt to James for the transition hoop, cutting the Raptors' lead to 9-7.

DeMar DeRozan got free for a driving layup and consecutive pull-up jumpers sandwiched around an Irving end-to-end drive and layup off a made basket. Toronto had led the Eastern Conference during the regular season in free throw attempts a game (26.7), and one of Lue's principles for the defense was not to leave the ground on DeRozan's pump-fakes. While he hit his first couple shots, Lue was proud of how his team didn't fall for the fake.

With the score 17-11, the Cavaliers made a run to even the game. With Love triggering from above the top of the arc, James broke backdoor on Carroll and Love fed him perfectly for the slam. Next time down, Love ran a pick-and-pop at the arc with J. R. Smith, sinking the three from the right wing. He sank a couple free throws and then dropped another three in another pick-and-pop this time with Irving.

The score was tied when James blocked DeRozan's drive, sparking a fastbreak. Kyrie grabbed the ball and went the length of the floor, finishing with Carroll in his chest yet failing to get the call. The Raptors' Terrence Ross drained a three and DeRozan scored his 12th point of the quarter on another midrange jumper to reclaim the lead, 26-25, with a little over two minutes left.

"DeRozan came out and had a great first quarter. He made some shots and some in-between twos. We wanted to get a late contest on those and we'll live with those shots," said Lue. "But we did a great job of keeping him and Kyle [Lowry] off the free throw line, and the guys followed the gameplan perfectly."

The Cavaliers ended the quarter on an Irving-centric 8-2 run, featuring two Irving transition layups (one after robbing Lowry of the ball), a pair of free throws, and a thunderous Shumpert dunk off an Irving feed. The Cavaliers led 33-28 at the end of one.

"We were able to get downhill and get to the basket and get a lot of layups. They didn't collapse as much as previous teams had," said Lue. "We're just taking what the defense gives us. If they open up the paint we're going to drive and attack the basket; if not we need to be able to step up and hit the threes."

Both teams made 13 buckets in the quarter, but it took Toronto 25 shots and the Cavs just 19. Toronto had to be worried how easily the Cavaliers were getting inside. Cleveland was 10-of-12 in the paint for 20 first quarter points, while the Raptors were 6-of-9 for 12. Meanwhile, the Cavaliers' Big Three had accounted for 28 of the team's 33 points.

"We knew that they're an attacking type of team, but one thing we want to be sure we do was take away the three," Raptor head coach Dwane Casey told ESPN sideline reporter Doris Burke between quarters. "We can do a better job of that, but the number one thing is to contain the ball where it doesn't break down [and end in layups]."

The Cavaliers started the second with the same lineup they used the last two games against Atlanta, featuring Frye, James, Jefferson, Shumpert, and Dellavedova. They brought a different intensity than the starters, which derailed the Raptors. In the first 60 seconds Ross threw a ball out of bounds and Biyombo was called for an offensive foul.

Delly cut into the lane and then swung the ball to his left, where Frye nailed the three from the wing. Then he grabbed a loose rebound and pushed ball up the court. Four passes later the ball found its way back to Dellavedova for a wide-open three from the top of the arc. That was 12 straight Cavaliers points going back to the first and made it 39-28. Casey called a timeout.

"They're going a hundred miles an hour and we're folding," Casey could be heard saying in his miked huddle. "You've got to cut hard, run the floor hard. All right? You've got to pick it up."

Toronto got back out on the Cavaliers' shooters, but it worked against them as Dellavedova noted the overplay and cut backdoor. Frye spotted him and Delly made the shot despite a Lowry push, and converted the and-one. On their next possession Delly ran the pick-and-roll with James, hitting him for an uncovered alley-oop slam.

Ninety seconds later, Jefferson tried to find James with a back-to-basket no-look pass in the paint, but it eluded James. He chased it down in the corner, went past the closing Carroll like he wanted to borrow money, and finished at the rim with a tomahawk jam that brought the arena to its feet. James backpedaled up the court, head back, mouth open, like a wolf baying at the stars. He even drew the and-one, though he didn't convert.

On the next possession James screened for Shumpert, forcing the switch and giving Iman a shot at Carroll. Shump must've been salivating as he quickly crossed to his left, leaving Carroll to his thoughts while Iman threw down. Toronto called a timeout already down 49-30. They'd been outscored 20-2 over the past six minutes.

"Our bench came in and defensively they were great—they were active, they were physical—and then we also got out in transition and made shots," said Lue. "We just knew we had to pick our physicality up, and once we did that and once the second unit came in, we had a chance to pick our defense and our physicality up."

Toronto hit five straight shots in the middle of the quarter to cut the lead to 54-42 with just under three minutes left. Lue responded with a timeout, and the Cavaliers closed out the half on a 12-2 run. It started with six free throws and concluded with a trio of magnificent plays.

Advancing on the lane in transition, Irving went left and back to his right hand behind his back, leaving Cory Joseph spinning on the merry-go-round as Irving laid it in. On the next time down Kyrie knocked the ball out of Joseph's hands and into Love's mitts. He threw it to a streaking James at halfcourt, and LeBron took it to the hole with his left over Lowry. The Cavs concluded the half with a pick-and-roll alley-oop to Tristan Thompson for the 66-44 halftime lead.

"They were trying to take a lot of our perimeter shooting away. That opened up the lane for [Kyrie and LeBron] to go to work, and those guys are tough to stop," Love said. "When they play downhill and get their shots, especially in rhythm, we're tough to beat."

The Cavaliers were only 4-of-8 from three, but were 20-of-28 (71 percent) inside the arc and 17-of-21 in the paint. James had hit all seven of his shots while Irving was 8-of-11, for 14 and 18 points respectively. The Cavaliers outrebounded the Raptors 21-11 in the first half and outscored Toronto's bench 15-7.

During halftime Casey (heard via ESPN's locker room mic) told his team that they hadn't given up all year, and they came out to start the half with moxie. Biyombo got two quick dunks. Then Love was called for a flagrant foul on offense when he elbowed Patterson in the noggin while holding the ball above his head and twisting his torso. After Patterson split the free throws, the Cavaliers put an end to that.

James put back a J. R. Smith miss and drew a foul on Carroll. James found Irving in the right corner for three, and Smith found a cutting LeBron for another layup. Smith stole the ball and fed James, who was fouled on the fastbreak and then split the pair. A moment later James stole the ball and took it to the house, tipping in his own missed layup to push the lead back to 24 with eight minutes let. The Raptors wouldn't seriously compete the rest of the way.

Defensively, Cleveland succeeded in keeping the Raptors off the charity stripe, holding them to 20 attempts while taking 33. DeRozan and Lowry failed to shoot a free throw between them, the first time that had happened in their four years together.

Irving finished with 27 points, five assists, two steals, and two blocks. James scored 24 on 11-of-13 shooting and Love added 14. The bench scored 39 points and Cleveland annihilated the Raptors on the boards, 45-23, outscoring them in the paint 56-36. The lone Cavalier bugaboo was 16 turnovers, though Lue was also concerned about the slow starts to each half.

"Sixteen turnovers is too much for us. If we can get it to around 10 that would be great, and we could be better defensively starting the first and third quarters," said Lue, looking for gray in clouds raining gold doubloons. "We got down 7-0 to start the game, then in the third quarter they went on a quick 6-0 run to start the third quarter. So taking care of the basketball, in that first stretch we had two turnovers that led to easy baskets, and in the third quarter just starting slow and being stagnant coming out."

The Raptors tried something different than the Pistons or Hawks, but they didn't fare any better chasing the Cavaliers off the three line than prior opponents shutting off the paint.

"Once you run them off, the rotations, the discipline, you have to have to…[also] take away the roll guy, because I thought that hurt us, especially in the second quarter. You want to take away one thing but you don't want to open a whole can of worms," Casey said. "You take away the three, but if you're not careful you're giving up layups. We have to get that balance."

E. C. Finals, Game 2. Thursday, May 19, 2016, Cleveland. (1-0 Cavs)

Toronto had a certain confidence going in to Game 2, having lost the first game in each of the previous two series. They'd yet to lose two straight games in the playoffs. Lue told his team to expect Toronto to be physical "and do whatever they can to win."

In his locker room [thanks to ESPN's coverage], Casey said, "It's going to be a boxing match for 48 minutes.... One or two guys are not going to carry us. It's going to take all 15 of us. If we go in, it's going to take that mentality of toughness and togetherness when you're on the court."

Toronto made an adjustment in Game 2, starting Luis Scola for Patrick Patterson at power forward. That moved Patterson back to the bench, where he'd had his greatest success, and put Scola on Love, a player he would seemingly be able to guard, while providing a better all-around game (if not better three-point shooting) than Patterson.

The Cavaliers had shaken off any first-game rust, coming out for Game 2 more like the team that had won 16 straight Eastern Conference playoff games.

J. R. Smith curled around a Love pick on the block and James fed him perfectly for a dunk. A minute later Irving found James in the lane for a dunk. On the next possession James drove and there was a miscommunication on the Raptors help, which LeBron exploited by finding Love for a wide-open three.

When the Cavs trapped Lowry on the baseline, he found Scola open at the arc for an answering three. James responded by isolating Carroll on the right block and drawing the foul, then cashing both freebies. After a Raptors turnover, James beat Carroll baseline and passed to J. R. Smith in the opposite corner for another three and a 14-7 lead with just under eight left in the first.

Benches cleared midway through the first when going into a timeout, Biyombo bumped Kyrie as he walked to the bench. The wiry-strong 6-foot-9 Congolese center put a hand on Irving's chest, presumably to stop him to complain how hard Kyrie had run into his screen. Irving knocked the hand away and teammates rushed in, and then were sent to the bench. The pair received double technicals, which don't result in foul shots.

The Cavs led 22-14 with 5:20 left when Smith received his second foul with a stupid reach on Patterson, bringing on Shumpert. To that point James had scored or assisted on all but two of Cleveland's points, racking up six assists and making four free throws and the only field goal he'd taken. It was just another example of how James was deferring his offense to get other players going.

"With him distributing and getting guys involved early, it opens up a lot for him in the post," said Thompson. "They were trying to double-team him and paint him in the post with Carroll and Biyombo guarding the rim behind him, but once he started finding guys, kicking out for threes, they had to change up their gameplan. When a great player like LeBron is doing everything, it's tough to stop that freight train."

"I've got great teammates that are getting me open. I'm trying to be aggressive and see what the defense is giving me," James said. "They opened the game trying to make me pass the ball and keep me out of the paint, so I got six assists in the first quarter and that opened things up."

The Raptors came back and hit their next four shots, three of them by DeRozan, the final one a three by Terrence Ross to cap the 9-0 run and give Toronto a one-point lead. It went back and forth over the final three minutes of the quarter, but Irving sank a couple pull-up jumpers to close out the first, and give the Cavaliers a 30-28 lead.

"They did a good job of kind of coming out and being aggressive especially in that first quarter," said Jefferson. "I don't know if it was fatigue or we just got going. But we kept our foot on the pedal."

Ross hit three jumpers to open the second as Toronto took a 35-34 lead with 10 to go. Again James went into takeover mode. He found Frye in the corner for a three, picked Lowry's pocket pass to Biyombo from the baseline, and raced up the court ahead of everyone for the reverse slam. After blowing an alley-oop feed from Delly, on the next possession he pushed a Shumpert rebound and again got to the rack for a rim-rattler.

But too much prosperity tended to dull the Cavaliers' senses. James missed three out of four from the charity stripe, Dellavedova committed a turnover, and the team missed four consecutive threes, as the Raptors retook the lead, 43-42, on a DeRozan pull-up 12-foot jumper, his 14th point.

Irving followed by backing Lowry down and shooting a short baseline fallaway over him, then found a trailing Thompson after getting bogged down in the paint, feeding Double-T for the slam. Patterson's three tied it at 46, but the Cavaliers had found their groove.

"We changed our defense and got a little bit more physical. We were able to get out in transition and get some easy buckets. That run was a big spark to our win," Lue said. "Guys came in—RJ came in gave us a great lift. Shumpert came in defensively, Delly before he got hurt, and LeBron and Channing were great. So that second unit came in and gave us a great burst to end the first half."

Over the next five and a half minutes, the Cavaliers made 6-of-7 from the field and 8-of-9 from the line, while holding Toronto to 1-of-11 from the field and just two free throws. The Cavs outscored the Raptors 20-5 down the stretch. Four different players made buckets, and another four had free throws as the team continued to get into the paint, move the ball, and find the open man.

"Tonight we played harder but again we hit that area, that lull where we made some uncharacteristic mistakes, fouling too much, backdoors, offensive rebounds, things you have to do to beat a very good team in Cleveland," said Casey.

For the second consecutive second stanza, the Cavaliers had put a hurt on the Raptors. This wasn't such a surprise to those who followed the team. The Cavaliers had the fourth-best overall point differential in the league, and the second-best in the second quarter.

Cleveland also had the best differential in the second quarter after the All-Star break as Lue's lessons took hold, and they improved during the playoffs, from +13.4 pCp to +21 pCp to that point. While James' addition to the second squad made a definite difference, it was icing on a well-baked cake.

All of the Big Three finished the half in double figures, led by LeBron with 17 points (including 9-of-13 from the line), Love with 15 (only one three), and Kyrie with 12. The Cavs shot 53 percent in the first half while holding Toronto to 42 percent. Cleveland was 16-of-21 from the line in the first half; the Raptors just 7-of-7.

Casey suggested afterward that Lowry's offensive struggles (1-of-6 in the first half) may have impacted his defense. The 30-year-old point guard actually left the floor before the half was over to compose himself in the locker room before returning again, so great was his frustration.

"He's missed some great looks and he's taken some of those looks down to the defensive end," the Raptors coach said. "He is an impactful player, but he can't let that go to that end. None of our guys can."

Cleveland opened the second half sloppy, with Carroll snuffing a Thompson dunk, two turnovers, and three missed free throws (another pair by James and a technical foul shot by Irving). But the Raptors couldn't take advantage. For two minutes neither team scored.

Early in the third, James scored on a drive to pass Shaquille O'Neal on the playoff scoring list with 5,250 points. It took Shaq 216 playoff games to accumulate those totals. James had done it in 188. His next target was Bryant (third all time) with 5,640 playoff points in 220 games, though he wouldn't catch him this year. Michael Jordan ranks first at 5,987.

"It always takes me back to my childhood and watching so many greats play the game of basketball and saying that I wish I could be a part of that. Or at times saying there was no way I could be a part of such a great league," James explained in the postgame. "To be in this position today where I see my name linked to a lot of the greats that play this game and paved the way for myself, Kyrie, and Kev, it means a lot. It is very humbling."

The Raptors got threes from Lowry and Carroll to cut the lead to 69-57 with a little over seven minutes to go in the third, prompting a Cavaliers timeout. A moment later a couple DeRozan free throws cut the lead to 10, 71-61, with 5:23 to go in the half, but just as in the second quarter, that seemed to be when the Raptors ran out of gas.

"They challenged us the first half and we picked it up the second half and got it done," said Thompson. "We have another level we can tap into, especially on the defensive end. We need to get multiple stops and multiple efforts. If teams swing it a few times with the pick-and-roll, you have to stay with it and limit them to one shot."

The team continued to stymie the Raptors after James went to the bench. He left with 4:11 on the clock up 15, 76-61. Irving drained a couple pull-up jumpers and a couple free throws (10 points in the quarter) while Love went 4-of-5 from the line to take an 86-69 lead into the fourth. In spending so much energy getting his mates going, they were that much better without him around.

"He understands the bigger picture. The more the team plays, the more the team performs, the easier it is for him and for us," Lue said. "The style we're playing, he understands if we're getting everybody else involved and everyone is playing well and everyone has the confidence. When we get to the next step we're trying to take, then everybody will be okay and ready to play."

When Frye opened the fourth quarter with a layup (James' 10th assist) and a three to push the lead to 22, you sensed the Raptors had lost the will to compete. They got no closer than 16 the rest of the way and lost 108-89.

Irving finished with a game-high 26 points. James had a triple-double with 23 points, 11 boards, 11 assists, and three steals. Love had 19, and Frye contributed 10 off the bench. The Cavs were only 7-of-21 from the arc, but held the deed on the line, going 25-of-37 from the stripe and holding the Raptors to just 18 free throws. Again Cleveland crushed Toronto in the paint, 50-28. Their lone bright spot was DeRozan with 22 points.

"We want to protect the paint. That's why we start early in the game going under a lot [of screens] to try to keep DeRozan and Kyle and those guys out of the paint," said Lue. "DeRozan had another great first half. But only having six points in the second half, we stayed true to our gameplan and we adjusted in the second half by going over the top of the screen.... We're just trying to keep them out of the paint and keep them off the free throw line—that's our biggest thing."

Casey singled out his team's defensive focus and shot selection. "We're losing some of our zing by missing some shots, missing some good looks," said Casey. "We got 33 three attempts. Probably too many. There were some alleys to get to the paint and *then* kick it out for threes, but we're settling a little too much."

Lowry sounded frustrated after the game. Still, he denied that going to the locker room during the game was at all strange, and he said he'd done it before to clear his head. He tipped his hat to the Cavaliers for his 4-of-14 shooting and mere 10 points.

"Give credit to the defense. They're showing hard and being active, but I'm getting some good looks that I've missed," he said. "I don't think I'll be missing many more of those."

Jefferson seemed to agree. "He's the heart and soul of their team, the guy that really makes them go," he said. "We've been trying to key in on him, but eventually he's going to knock them down and we just need to be ready."

14

CAVS GET LOST ON WAY TO LAND TIME FORGOT

IN BEATING TORONTO, Tyronn Lue earned his first bit of personal coaching history, passing Pat Riley for the most playoff wins to open a career with 10 straight. Riley had led the 1982 Los Angeles Lakers to nine straight wins his freshman year at the helm.

The Cavaliers were one away from tying the best playoff start ever at 11-0, which the Lakers had achieved in 1989 and again in 2001, when Lue was on the team. That year Los Angeles finished 15-1, losing only in Game 1 of the Finals to Philadelphia. (The '89 team lost to the Pistons in the Finals.)

Contrary to initial reports, Lue did not sign a new contract when he became coach, and instead kept working under his (generous) associate coach contract. He could have locked in the security of a three-year contract worth—if those faulty reports were to be believed—$9.5 million. Instead he bet on himself and his team. The reward would be a five-year, $35 million contract—not a bad return on a five-month investment, whatever the risk.

Lue was nearly universally respected around the game, with friends on every team. He comes off as humble, genuine, earnest, and passionate, but with a firm grip on his emotions. This was apparent from his attitude toward officials and personal fouls, where he chose to remain above it, as part of a larger, worthier goal than working the refs.

"When you're calm, you're not complaining, not rattled. It carries over to the team," said Lue, citing Phil Jackson as his inspiration. "If you react to every single call, every single shot, or every single turnover, it doesn't give your team confidence. Just being even-keel, poised, and staying with it, being positive with the guys, is the best approach. Just playing the game over the years, I've seen how guys react to certain situations and I think it's the best way to coach guys."

Lue's approach echoes the humanistic approach first employed by coaches like John Wooden. It makes the team's success a partnership between the coach and the players. If the league was once dictatorial and heavily micromanaged by coaches who called every play of the game, the amount of money that's poured into the league has changed that. Nobody pays good money to see someone coach, they say. Nowadays, a coach often must first win the players' trust and respect to get authority and accountability. It doesn't come with the title.

"I've played this game before and I understand if you treat them like men and tell them the truth and are up front with the guys, they can respect you," Lue said. "It's nothing different than I learned from Doc Rivers, Phil Jackson, or other guys I've coach or played under: If you deal with the players like men, they will respect you more."

This same quiet confidence reigned in the huddles and the locker room. Seeing their unflappable leader reminded them of the task at hand, not the emotions of the moment.

"He's always preaching 'next play.' We come to a timeout, no matter what's going on with a play, he seems to breed confidence in us," James said. "He's always talking about the next possession: Let's not worry about what happened the previous possession or a couple possessions before, and figure out how we can get better. He keeps us calm in those moments."

Beyond bringing serenity to tense moments, Lue's presence hedges the emotional states of his players. To reach this level a professional athlete must be competitive to a fault and compulsive to the point of obsession. They don't need Gipper-style rah-rah. Just the opposite.

"At times we can get frantic," Jefferson said. "LeBron is emotional. Kev is emotional. Kyrie is emotional. We have a lot of emotional guys that want to win, and so [it's good] to have a coach that's kind of that counterbalance of 'Hey everything is going to be all right. Everything's *fine.*'"

E. C. Finals, Game 3. Saturday, May 21, 2016, Toronto. (2-0 Cavs)

Though the team promised after the Game 2 victory that having Canadian native Tristan Thompson in tow would smooth the waters crossing into the Great White North, that wasn't the case. Jefferson took to social media to grouse, sitting with LeBron, Tristan, and J. R. on the deplaning stairs of their jet lamenting their boredom after waiting more than an hour for customs. Jefferson wondered in another snap to Dellavedova if this might be related to the Cavs' 2-0 series lead.

Dellavedova twisted his ankle late in Game 2, but after testing it in shoot-around he deemed it ready to go. However, his effectiveness dropped substantially going forward. In the 10 prior games, Delly played 15 minutes, shooting 42 percent from the field and 35 percent from three, and was +20 in net efficiency per hundred possessions.

In the 11 games after injury, Dellavedova shot 24 percent from the field and nine percent from three, didn't make a single steal, and had a net efficiency of -26 per hundred possessions. The media hardly noticed Delly's post-injury struggles, but it was a huge loss for the Cavaliers. Up until that point, the Aussie guard had the team's highest usage outside the Big Three.

After Game 2, Jefferson mentioned how frenzied Toronto's fans can be during the playoffs, but it's safe to say after 10 straight Cavaliers wins the team didn't take the Raptors' homecourt advantage seriously enough. Air Canada Centre's diverse crowds might suggest a Benetton ad before the games start, but after the horn sounds it quickly escalates to "church revival" pitch, just a couple notches short of Heaven's Gate.

"They brought that physicality. We expected that. It's unfortunate we weren't able to match it," said Thompson. "They were definitely trying to push us off our spots, make it tough for us. Tough for our catches—try and make us uncomfortable."

The Raptors hit their first two shots—a Carroll three off a DeRozan kickout and a Lowry transition three—and DeRozan added a pull-up 16-footer and a layup, but the Cavaliers hung with them thanks in part to two J. R. Smith threes, the latter of which prompted a Casey timeout with 7:40 left and the Cavaliers up 12-11.

The Raptors nearly overpowered the Cavaliers coming out of that timeout. DeRozan converted an old-fashioned three-point play, drawing the foul on Irving while sinking a turnaround jumper at the free throw line.

Lowry stepped behind a Biyombo screen at the top of the arc, and the Cavs went under allowing the Raptor point a clean look he didn't miss. A moment later, Lowry went right by Smith in transition for the layup to give Toronto a 19-14 lead.

"We weren't as physical as we should've been coming into a building where we knew we had to be a little more physical, understanding that they were going to play with a lot of speed and a lot of force," said James. "We didn't start the game as physical as we should've at the point of attack."

On the next Cleveland possession Smith initiated the offense and wound up taking it to the rim and drawing a foul on Lowry, his second. Backup point guard Cory Joseph—who had played with Thompson on the Grassroots Elite AAU team as a teen—came on to replace Lowry. This discombobulated the Raptors' offense for the rest of the quarter, as they went 4-of-12 from the field over the final 5:30, with one assist and no free throws.

Love threw a long outlet pass to James for a dunk while Carroll complained to the refs about contact on the previous play. J. R. followed by drilling his third triple of the quarter to tie it at 21 with 3:23 left. Two missed Irving layups and two missed Love fallaways later, Toronto was ahead 25-21. The pair missed all nine of their shots in the first but tried to make an impact in other ways. For instance, Love's block of a Terrence Ross layup turned into a Shumpert transition three.

DeRozan ended the quarter with a 15-foot fallaway for a 27-24 lead at the end of one. It was DeMar's fifth basket of the quarter for 12 points while Lowry added eight before leaving with foul trouble. The Raptors kept up the pressure in the second, making three triples by Ross, Lowry, and James Johnson, which were followed by a Joseph driving layup that began at halfcourt.

"They made the plays they needed to. There was one mistake I made where I got Delly to switch and Terrence Ross hit a three," Jefferson noted the next day. "Our second unit has a very small room for error. When I talk about making the play they needed to, when they needed to, that was the one shot Terrence Ross hit."

Channing Frye made a nice cut for a layup and hit a three sandwiched around a James putback, then a few minutes later Frye landed a second long-range missile to close the lead to 38-35.

It was preceded a moment earlier by the departure of Lowry with his third foul. However, this time Joseph did a better job leading the team than in the first. Toronto went on a 16-2 run over the next four minutes. That's nearly half the 33 points they scored in the quarter.

"I thought Cory, once Kyle got in foul trouble, did a good job of handling their defensive pressure and switching, making sure he had the right person involved in the pick-and-roll," Casey said. "Most of all I thought he did a terrific job with his defensive presence in the pick-and-roll situations."

The Cavaliers were 1-of-8 during this stretch, and their offensive futility fed into the defensive struggle as the Raptors pushed the ball and Cleveland didn't get back. Joseph hit a dribble pull-up, then DeRozan passed to Patrick Patterson behind the arc on the left wing in the last gasps of the shot clock for a contested three.

"They put it on us good in the second quarter," said James. "Kyle hit some huge shots in that second quarter. DeRozan hit some big shots.... Obviously [being outscored] 30-17 is not a good ingredient for a win."

Every misstep seemed to go the other way. A missed James step-back three resulted in a DeRozan reverse layup. When Irving pushed the ball off a made basket, it led to a Biyombo block and Joseph fastbreak. Carroll drove through the lane and dished; two passes later the ball found its way back to Joseph, who rattled home the three. A missed Love three similarly resulted in a quick pass upcourt and a Carroll three. DeRozan capped the run with two free throws, giving him 17 points.

"We just have to do a better job of closing out to shooters, making them put it on the floor and activating our weakside defense," Irving said, helping to explain the simple fact that after making less than 40 percent of their open shots in the first two games, the Raptors made half their uncontested shots in Game 3.

DeRozan and Irving would trade buckets the next two times down, as Kyrie's only three buckets of the game came in the second quarter. James capped the first half scoring with a dribble pull-up three to cut the lead to 60-47.

The Raptors made nearly half their shots (23-of-47) and half their threes (9-of-18) and outrebounded the Cavaliers 28-19 thanks to Bismack Biyombo, who had 16 rebounds at half, four of them offensive. He'd helped give the Raptors a 9-2 advantage on second-chance points and 16-8 on points in the paint. Biyombo finished with 26 rebounds.

"As a rebounder and a guy who plays hard with a high motor, it kind of disrupts you when there's a guy doing the same thing," Thompson said. "So I have to pick up my energy to give our team an extra boost."

Love opened the third with his only bucket of the night, a transition three created by a James steal. The Cavs cut it to 62-56 with a J. R. Smith three-pointer and a James three-point play after hacking Scola's dribble, and scoring on an underhand fling, despite having his right arm pulled so hard by DeRozan that James couldn't leave the ground. (He switched to his left to toss it in.)

DeRozan refused to back down, scoring 10 of the Raptors' next dozen points with a series of floaters, step-backs, and free throws. Just like the first quarter, James and Smith singlehandedly kept Cleveland in the game. J. R. dropped two threes while LeBron got a couple putbacks while working the offensive boards, cutting the lead to 72-67 with 3:36 left in the third. Smith and James accounted for 17 of the Cavs' 23 points in the quarter

"Even though we were shooting in the 30s, it was a five-point game in the third quarter," James said. "J. R. did a great job of trying to pick up the slack for Kyrie and Kev. Channing tried and I did as well."

However, the Raptors closed the quarter strong like the previous two, on an 8-3 run, highlighted by Joseph's long three to beat the buzzer, staking Toronto to an 80-70 lead.

"I honestly didn't think it got away until we came out for the fourth," said Smith. "Whatever the deficit I think we have the ability to come back. We have the pieces and the weapons—it's just a matter of staying focused mentally and locking in."

It wasn't so much that either team ran away with it in the fourth; it was more like no one claimed it. The Raptors scored on a Patterson three and a Lowry layup in the first 60 seconds of the fourth frame. It would be over five and a half minutes until they scored again. Richard Jefferson was the only Cavs to score during that same stretch—also five points—on a three-point play and a slick reverse layup in transition through two Raptors.

Toronto missed nine straight shots and committed two turnovers, opening the door for the Cavaliers. James pulled them close as 85-77 when (with his back to the basket) he spotted Smith breaking backdoor and threw a perfect no-look bounce pass for the layup.

Toronto answered by exploiting the Cavaliers' small lineup with

Biyombo in the pick-and-roll three consecutive times—his only baskets of the game. It was 91-77 with 3:38 left, making the game close to over. Frustration with the tough physical play boiled over in a flagrant foul call on Biyombo for pushing James as emotions reached a flashpoint.

James hit the free throws, but Irving couldn't make the three on the accompanying possession, and the Cavaliers went down to their first 2016 playoff defeat, 99-84. The Raptors shot 46 percent to the Cavaliers' 35 percent and held Cleveland to just 16 free throws after allowing 70 in the first two games.

After scoring 50 points in the paint in Game 2, Cleveland had just 20 to the Raptors' 36. Several players pointed out that the Cavaliers' defense tightened, allowing 39 points in the second half after allowing 33 in the second quarter. What they neglected to mention was that Toronto held Cleveland to 37 points in the second half.

"We kept them to 20 [points in the paint] tonight, which is what we needed to do in those first two games, but we didn't get it done," said Casey. "We played with force on the offensive end and with confidence. They're a good defensive team. They do a lot of switching, and I thought our spacing was much better."

For Cleveland it was more about what they didn't do than what the Raptors did. The Cavaliers failed to make at least half their uncontested shots for the first time in the series, and Kyrie had unusual trouble finishing in traffic.

Toronto blitzed the pick-and-roll, sending guys at Irving all night long, and Biyombo met him at the rim, blocking two of his shots. Sixteen of Irving's 19 shots were contested/closely contested, and he made two of them. (For the year, Kyrie shot 48 percent on closely contested shots—probably mostly at the rim—and 43 percent on contested shots.)

"They did a great job on penetration, collapsing, and getting out to our shooters," said Lue. "We weren't able to knock down shots tonight, but I thought we got the shots we wanted."

"We could've moved the ball better," Lue continued. "We could've moved the ball side to side a little better. They switched some pick-and-rolls, which made us stagnant. They went under a few times."

Casey claimed there weren't any tweaks or changes, just better execution and greater energy and physicality. DeRozan led the team with 32. Lowry scored a couple buckets down the stretch and finished with 20 despite playing just 32 minutes because of fouls. Joseph stepped in with 14 points and three assists; Patterson added 10.

"We just did a better job of things," Casey said. "We did a better job of being up, being into the ball, making them feel us. [Kyrie] is a tough guy to play against because every time he pushes off, that off-arm is coming off, so that's tough to play against."

The comment about Irving's off-arm was one of several in which Casey lambasted the referees after sucking up to them in the pregame presser. Casey would later assert that Biyombo was fouled "on every play," which obviously sucked for him, if true.

The NBA fined Casey $25,000 for his comments, but he'd gladly pay the money if it helped win the charity stripe. To Casey's point, the refs called only 10 fouls on the Cavaliers all game, the second fewest ever in a playoff game, compared to 17 on Toronto. (The Raptors only trailed in free throw attempts 16-13.)

Love, who finished 1-of-9 with just four rebounds in just under 30 minutes of play, copped to backsliding into the tentative player he was at times before the playoffs.

"I need to match that [physicality] and be just as aggressive as them. Tonight I felt I wasn't," Love admitted. "I was a little bit passive. I need to come out Monday and have that kind of mentality and do better at that end."

He reasoned the loss might be for the best in the end. "Sometimes it's good to be kicked in the teeth," he opined, without regard for his modeling career. "Toronto did that do us tonight. For Game 4 we need to have better intensity and more sense of purpose."

Speaking the next day, Lue felt that not only had the team lacked the physicality they needed to compete, but let their offensive struggles bleed into their defensive play, a bad habit from the regular season he hadn't seen in the playoffs. Lue also took the blame for not returning to James earlier when things weren't working offensively.

"We went away from posting LeBron where they had the double-team and had easy three-point shots. That's on me," Lue said. "We continued to run the plays that had been effective during the series knowing that Kevin or Kyrie could get going at any time. I should've put the ball in Bron's hands a little more to let him create and draw double-teams."

E. C. Finals, Game 4. Monday, May 23, 2016, Toronto. (2-1 Cavs)

In his locker room comments before Game 4 [miked again by ESPN], Lue focused on playing with pace and poise, being aggressive and initiating physicality, not reacting to it. The Cavaliers responded with better energy than Game 3, but seemed to get a little discouraged in the sloppy early going. Both teams missed four of their first six shots, stalking each other warily like the first round of a title fight.

The Cavaliers started the game with James on DeRozan, while the Raptors tried playing Biyombo on James in the post—that is until the Cavs screened for James with J. R. Smith. This left Biyombo on the remorseless cold-blooded shooter known as "Swish"—who toasted the Raptor with a right-corner three.

Toronto responded by making its next four shots beginning with a three by Carroll in transition, followed by a DeRozan floater and pull-up jumper, and finally a Lowry alley-oop to Biyombo out of an early-offense pick-and-roll, taking advantage of Cleveland's still-scrambling transition defense for the 13-5 lead. Lue responded with a timeout.

Both teams attacked the many cross-matches (players guarded by a different player than they defend on defense, which can cause issues in transition) when they could, isolating the defender and beating them one-on-one when the opportunity presented itself.

The Cavs pulled Thompson during the timeout, returning with Channing Frye to help space the floor and pull Biyombo away from the basket. On the next possession the ball went to James in the post. He found J. R. Smith weakside, who swung it to Kyrie, who attacked his close-out, got into the paint, and, when a Raptor rotated to defend the rim, tossed a high pass to James, who slammed it home.

Irving converted a couple drives through the lane, and Love stuck a corner three off a rebound-kickout. After blocking DeRozan at the rim, James took a feed from a penetrating Irving while cutting baseline for an acrobatic finger roll around Biyombo's leaping body/help defense. That cut Toronto's lead to 18-17 with four and a half minutes left. A minute later Frye's three deadlocked it at 20.

Toronto closed out the quarter with a Patterson catch-and-shoot three and Joseph layup to give the Raptors a 27-24 lead at the end of one. Toronto shot 52 percent in the first, including 3-of-8 from beyond the arc. The Cavs finished 9-of-23 including 3-of-14 from three. While 14 is obviously a lot of threes for a single quarter, Lue protested that it was what the defense was giving them.

"By getting Channing in there early in the first quarter to spread them out, we were able to get some open threes that we would normally knock down but we just didn't make," Lue said. "If we had made those threes it would've been a different game."

The same dolor that struck the Cavs in the first quarter undermined them to begin the second. In Game 3 the Raptors made their run in the last six minutes of the quarter; they made the move earlier in Game 4.

Toronto put together a 12-4 run featuring three layups and two uncontested threes by Ross and Lowry, thanks to good ball movement in the first case and the Cavs' decision to pass under Lowry's screens, giving him good looks all half. The latter fired-up rapper Drake, who rose from his sideline seat to talk smack to no one in particular.

Toronto didn't let up. They put together a 12-5 run over the next three minutes, pushing the lead to 16. Lowry scored eight points in the run on a couple threes and another driving layup to make it 51-35 with four minutes to go until half. Irving scored on a pull-up and James scored in transition off a Thompson steal, but Cleveland didn't score again for three minutes. A couple James free throws at the end of the half left Cleveland behind 57-41.

The Raptors shot 56 percent in the first half, and Cleveland shot under 40 percent. Toronto controlled the boards 22-16 and had 13 assists against just four turnovers. The Cavs had eight assists and five turnovers. Their only advantage was 7-0 on free throws.

Toronto's switching defense had caused timidity and hesitation, limiting the Cavs' ability to put pressure on the Raptor's D. When Cleveland missed shots, Toronto got out in transition and early offense where the Cavaliers were weakest defensively.

"I feel like we slowed them down the second half and made them a little bit more tentative. But obviously guys got it going," Irving said. "What it boils down to is we need to lock in on that weakside when they're doubling myself and Bron and getting guys shots. We just all need to be ready to shoot and to make that extra pass."

Lue told his players at halftime that the Raptors needed to feel them.

They weren't being physical enough preventing Lowry and DeRozan from getting to their favorite spots on the floor.

"In the first two games Toronto made a conscious effort of taking us off the three-point line so we were able to get 106 paint points in those first two games," said Lue. "Now they're clogging the paint and giving us open three-point shots and we need to knock them down." (In the second the Cavs were 0-of-8 from three, and 3-of-22 for the half.)

The Cavaliers finally brought some energy to open the second half. After DeRozan hit a floater, Irving made three straight buckets, including a pair of threes, then drove the lane and bounce passed to J. R. Smith in the right corner for another three, cutting the lead to 59-52 with three minutes gone.

The Cavs were still having trouble getting consistent offense, as they tried working through Love in the post. Lowry, on the other hand, was just getting warmed up. He scored three straight times, beating the switch in the pick-and-roll (Thompson twice, Love once) for two uncontested layups and a pull-up jumper, giving him 26 on the night. Lue called another timeout while trailing 71-56 and made a change.

"We've got to man up and guard one-one-one," Lue told his players during the huddle, challenging them to stay with their man.

The Cavaliers started trapping Lowry's pick-and-rolls, forcing him to give it up, forcing someone else make a play. As it was, DeRozan and Lowry were killing them. They'd had success trapping Reggie Jackson in the Pistons series and went back to that. They forced a 24-second violation on the next possession as the Raptors struggled to adapt.

"Late in the third quarter we got aggressive and started blitzing the pick-and-roll," said Lue. "[We were] having trouble guarding the point of entry, them attacking us one-on-one and just having to sit down and take on the challenge one-on-one."

Finally, the Cavaliers' three-balls began to fall. James, Love, and Smith all hit threes in a two-minute span, cutting the Raptors' lead to 73-65. The Cavs were 6-of-9 from three in the quarter as their cold touch warmed, and Cleveland entered the fourth down 78-69.

Having played the starters the entire third quarter, Lue went to the James-led second squad for the first five minutes of the fourth. They really brought it, wrestling back control of the game from the Raptors. Cleveland made their first nine shots of the quarter to stake the Cavaliers to their first lead, 90-89.

Interestingly, James didn't dominate the ball or even particularly figure in the first few minutes. Dellavedova ran the offense, James screened for him, and the shots came from ball movement. Jefferson started it off by beating Patterson (the center in a small lineup) off the dribble from the top of the key for a reverse layup.

Frye then proceeded to hit three straight triples—in transition, after his man helped defend a rolling James who'd just screened for Delly, and (after a Casey timeout) on a drive and kick-out right over the arm of a leaping Biyombo, who'd just entered the game.

"We started being a lot more aggressive, started picking up the pace of the game. The ball started moving and we started getting really good shots, executing with a sense of urgency," said Frye.

Next time down they ran a different variation of the same play with Dellavedova taking a dribble handoff and James rolling, unguarded, for an alley-oop, because the help man was too concerned about Channing Frye. On the next time down, James went by his man to the right like they were stopped at a light, laying it in.

Cleveland ran Dellavedova off a Jefferson screen before moving toward James. Meanwhile, Jefferson rolled to the basket with Delly's smaller defender on him, catching the alley-oop from James and posterizing Joseph. It was the same screen next time, but Delly took the dribble handoff and, as the defenders went with the rolling James, dribbled up and hit a seven-foot floater.

"We executed well to start the fourth quarter, but we didn't get enough stops to separate," Dellavedova said.

Usually scoring 23 points over the first six minutes is a recipe for success, but it's important to play defense as well. When Casey came back after the timeout with Biyombo and Lowry, the Raptors went on their own run, making six of seven baskets against stout Cavs defense.

"I thought the beginning of the fourth quarter, the group that went in there, we lost our composure," said Casey. "When we put the starters back in they kind of regained their foothold and got it back under control. That was huge for us."

When DeRozan ducked inside of Shumpert for a layup on an

up-and-under move, Lue called a timeout. While typically noted for his defense, Shumpert did not have a good postseason on either side of the ball. But his weakness on defense was glaring at times. Shumpert frequently matched up on the opponent's best perimeter player, whose scoring rate immediately went up.

We mean no disrespect, but the numbers tell a story and it's PG-13. Anyone taking a two-pointer on Shumpert during the playoffs saw a 16-point jump in their field goal percentage. He held three-point shots more or less even, exactly how he'd fared on two-pointers during the season. So it's fair to wonder if by the playoffs Shump's injuries had thoroughly compromised his efficiency. He saw modest improvement from round to round, suggesting the post-sweep rest might have helped his convalescence.

After the timeout, Irving returned for Shumpert while Love remained on the bench. He'd left the court at the end of the fourth with a limp, but after the game said he was fine. Lue said he liked how well Frye had been playing. "Channing gave us a great lift off the bench and we just kind of rolled with it," he said.

The Cavs ran the same play they'd been running all quarter out of the timeout. This time Delly went to Frye at the arc, who threw inside to a doubled James. LeBron drove under the basket and threw behind him to a cutting Jefferson for a demonstrative two-handed jam.

On the other end the Cavs trapped Lowy deep in the frontcourt. Patterson ran back and took the handoff and tried to throw it back to Lowry, having resuscitated his dribble, but James knocked the ball away and was fouled on his fastbreak opportunity. He sank both free throws to give the Cavaliers an improbable three-point lead with six minutes left in a game they'd played pretty poorly for 30 minutes.

The Cavs stayed with the set like a running gag on a treadmill. James slipped the Dellavedova screen and cut backdoor, receiving the pass for a right-handed jam with Carroll trailing behind. LeBron took the elbow again, and found Jefferson cutting backdoor from the other elbow with a bounce pass for another uncontested slam. Cleveland made its first 11 shots of the fourth, and six of the last seven were dunks or layups.

But the Cavaliers couldn't stop the Raptors either. DeRozan kept making dribble pull-ups, floaters, and layins. His next-to-last basket was over a late-contesting LeBron for his 28th point, tying the score at 96 with 4:37 left.

"We had some cross-matches where DeMar had different people guarding him," said Casey. "Luckily DeMar had it going in that stretch because we were scoring on them and they were scoring on us. It was kind of tit for tat."

Bored with running the same successful play over and over, James went one-on-one trying to break down his man off the dribble before feeding Frye for a missed contested three. They didn't return to it either, trying a couple fruitless high screens by Irving on James.

"It's something they fell into, and when you have LeBron James as your point guard and they execute pretty well…," Casey said. "They fell into a play that we had trouble with. We found a way on the last possession after the timeout to kind of talk about it, and we got a stop and they went away from it."

The Cavs posted James next possession, but Delly and Frye missed threes and Cleveland fouled Biyombo on the rebound. He split the pair, giving Toronto a 101-96 lead. Kyrie hit a straightaway three from four feet beyond the arc with the shot clock's last ticks to cut Toronto's lead to two. DeRozan missed a baseline jumper with 97 seconds left, but Patterson grabbed the board, feeding a cutting DeRozan, who banked it over Smith and Thompson's outstretched arms.

"I felt we came back and took control of the game, was up three points, and they just made some defensive mistakes that you can't do down that stretch, and they cost us," Lue said. "Each time we made a mistake they made us pay."

On the next possession Smith had the ball at the left arc above the break, but with six seconds on the clock couldn't create separation with the lithe, long Biyombo, who blocked J. R.'s attempt. James bothered a Lowry fallaway in the lane, but Biyombo grabbed the offensive board. After a timeout, Lowry beat Smith to his right for the layup with 22 seconds left and a 105-99 victory.

"We were fortunate enough to get the switch we wanted, and Kyle Lowry executed it," said Casey.

The Raptors beat the Cavaliers in the paint again, 44-36, and enjoyed a 19-2 edge at the foul line in the second half, after finishing the first half without a free throw. Toronto shot 54 percent, the Cavaliers 49 percent.

While Cleveland took a lot of threes (13-of-41, 32 percent), it's almost moot considering that as badly as they had played they still almost won.

"We felt we had an opportunity to not play well and still win that game," Lue lamented. "And we came up short."

The Raptors stepped up, hitting tough shot after tough shot. Two-thirds of their shots were contested and they made 63 percent of them, but, oddly, just 37 percent of the uncontested ones. DeRozan and Lowry were a big part of this, shooting 21-of-30 on contested shots.

"We kept going back and forth [at the end]," said Frye. "Give them credit. We were making dunks and layups and wide-open corner threes and they're making floaters and hard-contested twos. They established their pace and continued to do what they wanted to do. We finally got a little bit of mojo, and then we had to be perfect. They hit some big shots had some balls that went their way. It is what it is."

1 5

CAVS CRUSH RAPTORS, LEAVE OIL SLICK

LIKE ANY TACTICAL engagement, basketball strategy is based on overplaying the opponent's strength to force them to their weakness. Individual defenders often overplay a ballhandler's strong hand, shading their stance so the ballhandler has more of an open lane to his weak hand.

Similarly, defenses scheme to take something away and force opponents toward what they perceive as a weakness. In the first two series, coaches Stan Van Gundy and Mike Budenholzer attempted to take away the lane from the Cavs, forcing Irving and James to settle for midrange jumpers or pass out to the perimeter, and make someone else beat them. That strategy went 0-8, and produced a playoff record number of threes. Twice.

Naturally, Toronto's first instinct was to do something different, and in the first two games of the series the Raptors helped on Irving and James less, staying with their man to force the two Cavs to beat them one-on-one, instead of drowning beneath a deluge of threes.

After allowing 106 paint points the first two games—while being held below 100 points in both—Toronto switched things up and began collapsing more. They also started blitzing Irving on pick-and-rolls and doubling James in the post. This put the onus back on the Cavaliers' role players. Suddenly, after shooting better than 45 percent from long distance in the first two rounds, Cleveland made only a third of their 82 threes against the Raptors.

This kind of stylistic counterpunching is built into the individual matchups as well. How well players develop depends on their ability to continually build, prune, and adapt their repertoire each year. As soon as players arrive in the league they must find a niche to fill within their team's ecosystem.

Playing with Jason Kidd on consecutive Eastern Conference champ New Jersey Nets teams, Jefferson found his niche on the defensive side to help him earn time as a rookie. "We had a defensive-minded team," Jefferson said. "That was kind of my calling card, and it allowed me to get on the court as my offense started to develop. So I always tell people, defense is the key to getting out on the court."

Over the years he worked on his shot. As a youngster he got by on athleticism, but he continued to work on the other parts of his game.

"If you get five to 10 years and you actually take the game seriously, it's easy to work on things and get better," he said. "I've gone from a guy that was left open that could not shoot a 16-footer to now a guy that teams don't want to leave. And I still look back on my career and think I could've done more. You always look back on things and evaluate yourself rather harshly, but you can improve on so much over a period of time."

It takes young players time because they have to develop an identity, and for other than the first few picks, probably have to change from what it was in college, just as they did coming out of high school.

"When you're younger you have to establish your tendencies and your strengths," James Jones said. "As a player you have to build a body of work. You have to be effective at some things long enough to put people on their heels where they can't take away your signature strength."

As that body of work develops, strategies develop to limit what you want to do, and you must necessarily develop counters. But it doesn't start that way. In the beginning you have to know what you're good at.

"It's about developing a bona fide strength," Jones said. "You can work on it off the court, you can work on it in practice, but until you get it into the game and it becomes fluid, you're constantly searching for what your strength is. So you'll try three or four things until you find two that stick, and those two may work hand-in-hand or they may need combos. Or they may be two totally distinct skills."

Once you start to understand who you are as a player, you also start to see how teams want to stop you, and it all starts to come more quickly.

Ideally, you're acting before the defense because you're anticipating what they'll do rather than responding to it.

"You see the way they cover you, you know the spacing, you've seen the rotations, and so you're no longer trying to process and make a move. You'll process simultaneously to making the move because you've seen it before," he said. "You try to be as efficient as possible. Teams start to show their hand. They know you're a great right-hand driver, so they start shading you to your right and you start straight-line driving to the left—moves and counters."

But it's not only about how you can beat the man across from you. It's also how your strengths and skills mesh with teammates and what you can do to improve that situation.

"Once you get into the NBA and see what teams try to take away from you, you work on those. You work on that aspect of the game a lot in the off-season," said James. "Also from a team aspect you see where you need to be out on the floor to help the team as much as possible, so you start to work on that as well. From a basketball aspect as well as a cerebral mindset of the game as well, you just try to hone in on a few of those skills a little at a time, and for the most part, if you put in enough work, it will come."

Of course, strategy and tactics can only do so much to disguise and leverage strengths and weaknesses. Having strong execution is great, but most coaches would prefer better talent. In the Cavaliers' case it wasn't about the talent; it was about motivating them to play their hardest every moment of the game. Those games in Toronto reminded/taught them what that was about.

"I had to take a step back," Irving said. "It was just really, really loud, and I can say those two games in Toronto were the first legitimate road games I've experienced in my playoff career in which our communication—everything—needed to be a lot sharper. We took a lot that we had to learn from that game... and I know wasn't the only guy that thought that way."

E. C. Finals, Game 5. Wednesday, May 25, 2016, Cleveland. (Even)

Returning home offered a chance to try these new lessons out in an environment that felt safe and comfortable. Inevitably, the Raptors felt the opposite—from the opening tap.

The Cavaliers took the tap and Irving missed a two, but Thompson crashed the boards and cleared the ball to J. R., who threw back to Love, posting on the left block. Kevin backed down Scola, then turned right toward the middle of the lane for a short hook and the first lead.

"His first touch was in the paint, a right-handed jump hook, and we knew from that point," James said, "and we continued to go to him."

Indeed, in playoff games to that point, when Love hit his first shot of the game he made 54 percent of subsequent shots. If he missed his first one (nine games) he shot 31 percent. After two of his lowest-scoring games of the playoffs (three and 10 points, respectively, without a free throw in either game), Love came out looking to score, though it would be a moment before he'd really get his chance.

James missed a driving bank shot, a pull-up, and a last-second three while Irving made only one of three to start off. Were it not for Tristan Thompson's two offensive rebounds and a steal and putback underneath their own basket, the Cavaliers might have started the game in a more frustrating way than up 8-7.

They'd put pressure on DeRozan and Lowry in particular, but other Raptors hit three of their first four shots. That wouldn't last. Toronto made two turnovers and missed three shots. Meanwhile, Love was just getting warmed up. He scored seven of the game's next nine points and assisted on the other, starting with a transition three, and followed with a feed to LeBron for a bucket. Love hit all four of his first quarter shots for 12 of his game-high 25 points (on 8-of-10 shooting).

"Even though he didn't shoot the ball well those two games, he came out and wanted to be aggressive early, which we need him to be," said J. R. Smith. "You could tell he wanted the ball. So as much as I got it, I tried to look for him—post-ups, threes—whenever I could. He got it going. Once one or two start falling for Kevin, his shot starts falling."

Love's outburst gave the Cavaliers a 17-7 lead. With Love at the stripe for a couple free throws with six minutes left in the first, Casey went to his ace in the hole, 7-footer Jonas Valanciunas. The 24-year-old Lithuanian was sidelined for a week with an ankle injury in the prior series, but was available to Casey for the two games in Toronto. However, with his team performing so well, Casey let Valanciunas recuperate before unveiling him in Game 5 as a new wrinkle.

It helped Toronto go on a 9-3 run, scoring on a Patterson three, Carroll steal, and DeRozan fastbreak layup. Valanciunas got going with a layup out of a pick-and-roll where Love was left defending him at the rim, and another bucket as the trailer on a Lowry transition drive, when he casually dropped the free throw line jumper. Suddenly, the Raptors were within four.

That's when Kyrie Irving took control, showing Lowry who was the true Eastern Conference All-Star. Then again, it's much easier when the best player in the league is screening for you. Twice James received the ball on the baseline and threw back to Irving for a midrange jumper. Then after recovering an errant Irving pass, James drove baseline and found Love in the left corner for three to make it 27-16.

The Raptors were having trouble getting free from the fierce defense. Thompson's quick feet and lateral speed made it tough for Lowry to get around him, and then there's the fact that he's 6-foot-9.

"We blitzed a lot with Tristan. He's one of the best blitz guys in the league. Just having him on the defensive end helped us out," Lue said afterward. "But I also thought moving [his location] around—we posted LeBron, we posted Kevin. I thought moving him around keeping him high, keeping him low, and just continuing to move him around gave those guys problems," since Thompson's positioning off the ball dictated how Toronto sent help.

Lue suggested the Cavs' strategy of going under screens/picks for DeRozan had invited passivity, helping DeRozan to get comfortable early. DeRozan averaged 10 points in the first quarter alone, so it was important not to let him find his groove so readily. That meant bumping him, getting into his body, and letting him feel the defense. DeRozan scored only four points in the first on 1-of-3 shooting.

"When you tempt teams by going under screens your aggressiveness lacks, and I think we were getting off the body a little too much at times," Lue said in the pregame. "We said we were going to go under the picks on DeRozan...but J. R.'s more of a physical kind of guy fighting through screens staying on the body. We changed that up a little bit so hopefully he can be more effective."

James took a seat while DeRozan shot his free throws, but Irving didn't let up as the Cavaliers hit their next seven shots in a 17-3 run. First Kyrie ran a pick-and-roll with Thompson, which resulted in Valanciunas guarding him and Lowry chasing from behind. Going left to right from above the left elbow, Irving jabbed his right foot and then crossed over left with slight hesitation that had Valanciunas looking like a deer in halogen lamps, as Irving lofted the eight-foot floater with his left hand.

Smith stole a sloppy Joseph pass and took it to the house. Irving grabbed the rebound of a missed Patterson three and drained a pull-up transition three for the 34-18 lead. James came back for the last possession. After faking a screen for Kyrie, LeBron rolled to the basket. Irving threaded a pass between two defenders and James sliced through two more defenders with a single step to finish at the rim, for a 37-19 lead at the end of one.

Any hope of a second quarter run like the Raptors enjoyed in Toronto ended when the Cavs returned to the same Dellavedova/James pick-and-roll set they'd used to slice them up for 11 straight baskets in the fourth quarter of Game 4. While Casey might've *said* they had an answer, they clearly didn't run it by *Jeopardy*'s Alex Trebek.

Cleveland happily ran that same play with its Kama Sutra of variations over and over again. Frye drained a right-corner jumper (that proved upon review to only be a two). James got an alley-oop dunk; Jefferson got an alley-oop. James drove by James Johnson for the layup and-one. (He missed.)

On the next possession Jefferson grabbed a long rebound and, while racing up the court, showed his still great athleticism, picking up his dribble just before the free throw line. He reached the rack in two steps with a Eurostep sort of finish (bringing the ball high and from the right side to the left while crossing in front of the defender). That made it 47-22 and Toronto wouldn't get any closer.

Cleveland's 65-34 halftime lead was the largest ever in a Conference Finals game, and the Cavs parlayed it into a 116-78 rout. Love had 25 points in 23 minutes, Irving and James each had 23, and Jefferson added 11 off the bench. Thompson had 10 rebounds and nine points, and, more importantly, held Biyombo to just four rebounds. Lowry and DeRozan combined for 27 on 7-of-20 shooting. No other Raptor made it into double figures.

"Our defense dictated what we did on the offensive end tonight. When we play like that we're tough to beat," said Love. He credited Channing Frye with helping him stay focused after a couple bad games.

"I talked to Channing last night and he told me nobody's immune to the NBA playoffs. These types of things happen, and you have to keep fighting through it," Kevin continued. "He said in order for us to win, I needed to be aggressive. I give him a lot of credit for staying on me and staying vocal."

Jefferson piped in from the next door locker: "I wasn't nearly as positive." Stilll, Love dug the ex-Wildcat duo's good cop/bad cop act.

"RJ talked to me after the game and said, 'That's why we're hard on you, big fella,'" Love offered a moment later. "I know my teammates expect a lot out of me and I expect a lot out of them as well, and I love these guys."

Frye was typically humble. "We just tell him we believe in him and constantly reinforce it," Channing said. "He puts a lot of pressure on himself to be exactly what he wants to be, and we want him to just be regular old Kevin. 'I Love Nuggets' Kevin. He just needs to have fun out there, stay in the moment, and know that we believe in him."

For Lue it goes back to an off-day comment about initiating contact, not responding to it. "[It's about] hitting first and not retaliating," he suggested. "When you come out and play aggressive and play physical, you tend to get more calls." Referees only tend to see the response, plus the physicality usually puts the recipient on their heels.

"In Toronto they were the aggressors and we were the reactors. They attacked us early and it was hard for us to get back. Here at home we came out early. We had it in our minds to be aggressive, to be physical and to jump on those guys early, and we were able to do it."

Cascy seemed to agree with Lue's overall assessment, saying, "We knew they were going to come out like a freight train, and we didn't meet that level of physicality on either end of the floor. We turned the ball over 19 times and were outrebounded—which had been one of our strong points—by 21. We got outworked."

E. C. Finals, Game 6. Friday, May 27, 2016, Toronto. (3-2 Cavs)

The Cavaliers wanted to take care of business up north and not leave anything to chance, not to mention seizing the opportunity for a couple extra days of rest. To do this, they talked about bringing the same intensity as the Raptors, and behaving as if *their* back were against the wall.

"This is it for them, but we have the same mentality. This is our Game 7. That's how we're approaching it," James said at the shoot-around. "We haven't played to our capabilities in two games here. That's what my focus is."

Of course, the Cavaliers had the trump card in James. As Lue noted earlier in the series, "When the occasion arises and he needs to be great, he's always been great."

To counter the traps on Lowry and DeRozan, the Raptors dispensed with the pick-and-roll. They spaced the floor and relied on one-on-one moves, allowing the Raptor pair to try to beat their man instead of double-teams brought by screeners. It worked initially as DeRozan and Lowry opened the game with three hoops and Biyombo added a free throw for an early 8-5 lead.

At that point, LeBron decided to stop fracking around and get to work like a ruthless global multinational, manufacturing a 15-2 Cavaliers run. It began in an unlikely way with a James dribble pull-up three. (To that point, James was 4-of-15 from three in the series.) There was a highlight reel alley-oop from Irving to James. LeBron assisted or scored all the points in the four-minute run besides two Irving free throws, and capped it with a second, catch-and-shoot three to make it 20-10. The only Raptors bucket came on a miscommunication between Kyrie and J. R. that yielded a Lowry layup.

"I knew this was going to be a tough game, coming into this building, and I just had to bring my game," said James. "I had to be in attack mode from the beginning, trust my shot, and I knew once my shot started going I could start getting my teammates involved, and they were able to carry me down the stretch."

The Raptors clawed back, and had success screening for Lowry with DeRozan. They scored three straight buckets, prompting a Lue timeout. Carroll deflected a James pass and Toronto gained possession, but Biyombo immediately traveled, giving the ball back.

He made up for it by blocking Kyrie's subsequent drive to the basket, but Cleveland retained possession and Smith caught and sank a three off an inbound pass pretty much in the same motion, as is his wont. On the other end Carroll took a three and Biyombo grabbed the offensive rebound. But going up with the ball, he popped Love solidly in the jaw, drawing the Flagrant One call.

Love hit the two flagrant free throws, then drew a foul on the retained-possession play for another pair of freebies, pushing the lead to 27-16. The Raptors finished the quarter strong, making four of their last five shots, including a pair of midrange jumpers by Valanciunas to cut that first quarter deficit to 31-25.

"[They're] getting out in transition. We've got to get back and find our matchups," Lue told ESPN sideline reporter Doris Burke between quarters. "I thought we're doing a great job of playing with pace, getting the ball up fast, getting out early in transition, but we have to get stops to do that."

Frustrated at being fouled on an offensive rebound, Valanciunas swung his ball arm around after the whistle blew and caught Jefferson in the chest. RJ gave up four inches and 50 pounds to the Lithuanian big man, but got up in his face with his finger saying something about "right now." Perhaps it was when he was ready to throw down as Dellavedova pulled him away by his midsection.

Though a thoughtful, unassuming guy, Jefferson won't back down to anybody. While playing basketball with kids from tougher circumstances when he was younger, Jefferson wouldn't allow himself to be cowed or intimidated.

"It's funny," he continued. "Once I got my chip on my shoulder—and I had this at a young age—people stopped trying me. People never talked to me. People didn't try to elbow me; people didn't try to do anything dirty. I think it goes to show that you don't have to be this loud in-your-face tough guy. If you can just hold your own and won't back down, people will leave you alone."

Well, Valanciunas woke that tough guy and Jefferson was hot. The incident seemed to focus the Cavaliers. After a Lowry fastbreak layup off a Patterson steal a minute later, the defense clamped down. Unfortunately for the Cavaliers, Toronto's defense joined them.

The next seven minutes Toronto shot 1-of-9 with five free throws and the Cavs were 3-of-11 with three turnovers and no free throws. James missed a short shot over Biyombo and Toronto turned it into a two-on-one break, ending in a Patterson slam that cut the lead to 44-36.

It was an evenly fought battle by and large until a Cavaliers flurry over the final 75 seconds of the half. First, LeBron rebounded a missed Smith three and hit Love at the arc above the break. Kevin swung the ball to J. R. in the corner, who sank a three. Then James blocked a Lowry drive from behind. Love grabbed the loose ball and quickly outleted to Irving, who took it to the rim for the basket and-one.

A Lowry three trimmed the deficit to 11, and a moment later the bulldog point was again racing up the court on a fastbreak when Irving poked the ball away from behind. James scooped it up and pushed it up the hardwood and into the lane. When he got near the rim he passed to Smith in the corner, who returned the favor to Love for Kevin's second three and a 55-41 lead at half.

The Cavaliers had forced the Raptors into a lot of one-on-one. Toronto had just five assists and seven turnovers at halftime. The Cavaliers assisted 13 of their 18 buckets, which included 10-of-15 from deep. The Raptors were just 2-of-12 from three. Both teams had 11 free throws, but the Cavs made two more. James led Cleveland with 21 points. Love had 10, Smith and Irving nine. Lowry had 12 points and DeRozan had 10 on a collective 9-of-21 shooting.

The Cavaliers pushed the lead to 20 points on Irving's fourth bucket of the third quarter, 75-55 with just under five remaining. Toronto wasn't going quietly, though. They made six straight, going on a 12-3 run over the last 95 seconds of the quarter, all the points scored by Lowry, who finished with 18 in the quarter. The Cavaliers scored 31 in the quarter, but Toronto scored 33 to trim the deficit to 12.

The Cavs led 94-81 after Lowry sank a three with 8:21 in the fourth. James would take a breather a minute later, while the Cavaliers went on a 19-6 run to close the game. Irving scored seven and Smith and Jefferson each hit threes. The Cavaliers won 113-87, to take the Eastern Conference crown and advance to the NBA Finals.

James finished with 33 points, his first 30+ game of the playoffs, as well as 11 boards and six assists. Irving finished with 30 points, nine assists, and three steals, while Love added 20 points, 12 rebounds, and four assists. Cleveland's Big Three combined for 83 points, their highest total in the postseason and third-highest combined total in two years.

Lowry had 35, DeRozan 20, and the rest of the Raptors 32. Yet as they left the floor the fans chanted, "Let's Go Raptors!"—a sign of their fans' respect, an experience for which James admitted he could find no equal in his 13-year playing career.

"LeBron really set the tone for us in the first quarter offensively and defensively, but we had to keep staying with our other guys, Kyrie and

Kevin, knowing there was going to be an opportunity for those guys to step up and take over also when LeBron was tired," Lue said.

"At the end of the first half, LeBron was dead. I think we played him 23 minutes in the first half. And he didn't want to come out. Even the 30 seconds I took him out he got mad about it," chuckled Lue. "But I said we're going to need other guys. We had to keep the ball in Kyrie's hands, keep trying to post Kevin. Give him a feel for the basketball. When LeBron came out, Kyrie and Kevin really took over down the stretch and really brought us home."

Because there was no champagne in the locker room, they splashed each other with cups of water. Spirits were high. While holding the trophy for the Eastern Conference title, J. R. promised to bring back her sister in a couple weeks. There was much celebrating, perhaps more than when the Cavaliers swept Atlanta the year before, because Lue had made enjoying the moment a part of the process.

"I don't think last year I appreciated it enough," James told ESPN's Doris Burke. "Getting back to the Finals this year I'm going to appreciate this, these guys tonight and for the next couple days before we lock back in."

It was great to win. But it was even better, and necessary given their coming opponent, that they did it together, as a family. "The biggest thing," Lue said, "is we came together and we trusted. You could see it on the floor, and it's beautiful to watch."

THE FINALS

16

RECORDS ARE BROKEN, CHAMPIONSHIPS GO ON THE WALL

SPORTS—UNLIKE LIFE—HAVE UNDISPUTED champions. They might never give you respect, but no one can take away the title. Having won the latter, the Golden State Warriors sought the former, and earned it with a regular season for the ages. If people scoffed at their 2015 championship, achieved with series wins over badly injured teams, it was difficult to disparage their record-setting play the ensuing season. Yet in hindsight it's easy to see ways the Warriors' vanity and/or insecurity hurt them.

The most obvious is physical and/or emotional exhaustion. Not only were the Warriors competing against opponents bringing their A game every night, but against the 72-win 1995-96 Bulls team's legacy, a record once believed unassailable as DiMaggio's 56-game hit streak. The pursuit demanded concentration and effort that any team would find difficult to maintain for long stretches.

Golden State head coach Steve Kerr—who was a reserve on the Cavaliers when Michael Jordan hit The Shot over Craig Ehlo—also played for that record-setting 1995-'96 Bulls club alongside Scotty Pippen, Dennis Rodman, Toni Kukoc, and Ron Harper. Indeed, after winning three rings in a row with the Bulls, Kerr took a fourth consecutive ring as a member of the Spurs, and then four years later won again with the Spurs, his fifth championship as a player.

If he were perfectly honest, Steve Kerr would've preferred the team not set this goal. But their coach believed in partnership, and in March acknowledged this was something that the players wanted, even if it meant playing starters more minutes at the end of the season than Kerr would have probably liked.

"I know they want to get it. So we'll act accordingly," Kerr said. "It's the players who are setting a record. It's not the organization. It's the players who are doing it... So they will absolutely have some say in matters down the stretch."

The players could only see the glory and the recognition a record like this represented. The 1995-'96 Chicago Bulls are possibly the greatest team in history. Never mind that only six NBA champs have ever repeated; this was a one-of-a-kind record. Asked what it would mean to win 73 games, Draymond Green said, "That I'm a part of the best team ever."

For them, it was worth it. "If we are a 70-win team and champions versus a 73-win team and depleted energy and banged up going into the playoffs, we're trying to avoid that," said Stephen Curry. "But at the same token, it's a tough balance. How many times are you going to have this opportunity?"

Kerr missed the beginning of the season due to back surgery and complications that included leaking spinal fluid. Kerr suffered blinding headaches, nausea, and dizziness that prevented him from coaching the first half of the season. Associate coach Luke Walton held the reins for the first 43 games, leading the Warriors to a 39-4 record. Kerr returned after a road trip that featured a victory over the Cavaliers. Indeed, he coached his first game of the year the day Cleveland fired David Blatt.

In the beginning of April, Kerr reiterated his focus on the Finals, not the regular season record. "I think it'd be cool, but we all know what our focus is. We want to win a championship," he said. "The championship goes up on the wall. Records are broken...championships last forever."

Toward the end, the grind seemed to get to the Warriors. They lost four times in the first 52 games, then lost five of the next 30. In the final two weeks of the season they lost two home games, putting the team on alert. The last one was an overtime loss to the Minnesota Timberwolves, giving them their ninth and final loss. The Warriors overcame San Antonio and Memphis in a pair of home-and-away sets to finish the season with 73 wins.

Kerr cited the constant media attention as an unnecessary distraction, whether the players recognized it or not.

"All that stuff does take its toll, whether the players know it or not, whether it's a conscious thing or not, and it probably has taken a little bit away from our process," Kerr said, relating it back to the end of that record-setting Bulls year. "If you look back at that season, we lost two home games in the last week, 10 days of the season, both by a basket or one point.... When we did break the record, in Milwaukee, I still remember it. It was a horrendous basketball game...same kind of thing. Constant scrutiny, little slippage in our execution, eking out wins, so it does feel the same way."

Besides their 24-game win streak to start the season, the Warriors put together an 11-game streak and three seven-game streaks. They were also the only team to go the season without losing twice in a row or twice to the same opponent. They posted a record number of road wins (34) and the longest home win streak (54, going back to 2014-2015).

The Warriors endured their first serious hardship in two years when Stephen Curry turned his right ankle in Game 1 of their first round playoff series with the Houston Rockets. He missed the next two games, which Golden State split. Curry came back for Game 4 only to sprain his knee and leave before halftime, though they ran away with a 27-point win. Curry would sit four more games before returning for Game 4 in Portland, with the Warriors up 2-1. He wasn't feeling perfect, but well enough to set an NBA record with 17 overtime points in a 132-125 victory.

Golden State won the next game at home to advance to the Western Conference Finals against the Oklahoma City Thunder. The Thunder's length and athleticism posed problems for them. Oklahoma City was quick enough to switch everything, forcing the Warriors into one-on-one situations just as they did on defense. The Thunder also weren't afraid to play "big," crushing Golden State on the boards and in the paint with Serge Ibaka and Steve Adams. (The Warriors were 25th in allowing paint points; ironically; Oklahoma City was 26th.)

Golden State lost the opening game of the series at home 108-102 and both games in Oklahoma City (by 28 and 24 points) to return home down 3-1, on the brink of elimination. Only nine times in NBA playoff history had the trailing team come back from a 3-1 deficit, out of 232 series, a 3.8

percent chance. That suited Golden State just fine. "We're a special team," said Curry. "This isn't how we're going to go out."

The Warriors held serve at Oracle, but were down seven with five minutes remaining in Game 6 before closing on a 19-5 run for a 108-101 victory. It and Game 1 were the only ones in the series where the lead changed hands more than a handful of times. Golden State set a record for three-pointers in a seven-game series with 90 (the Cavs set the record in Atlanta in a four-game series with 77, for perspective), and Curry set the individual record with 32. (Backcourt mate Klay Thompson had 30, including 11 in Game 6.)

In beating the Thunder, the Warriors felt they had survived their trial by lightning. They'd been down in a series 2-1 against Memphis and Cleveland the year before, but never on the brink of elimination. They felt winning that series proved something not just to the haters, but to themselves.

Some of the Warriors even allegedly felt the Cavaliers were a formality. Having beaten them their last five meetings, Golden State was confident they had the Cavs' number. "You know what they were whispering this year," Brian Windhorst shared during a podcast with fellow ESPN writer Zach Lowe after Game 2. "They knew they had won the [Finals] when they beat the Thunder; that their tough series was over."

NBA Finals, Game 1. Thursday, June 2, 2016, Oakland. (Even)

The Cavaliers had warmed up for Curry and Thompson with a succession of playoff opponents that featured quick lead guards and sharp-shooting wings. Similarly, the plan was to blitz Curry or Thompson pick-and-rolls, forcing someone else to beat them. The Cavaliers' offensive gameplan remained drive-and-kick. The Warriors were switching liberally and doubling James or Love when in the post and recovering to three-point shooters. The results were a combination of open outside shots and a lot of one-on-one play, by virtue of the switching.

The Warriors opened Game 1 of the Finals with three straight buckets from Harrison Barnes, as the Warriors' supporting players stepped up. First the long-limbed wing beat LeBron backdoor as James readied for a Curry pick, then Barnes lost James on a transition screen for another layup, and finally he beat a mismatched J. R. Smith with a left-handed drive to the front of the basket, where he switched back to his right to lay it in. Love answered with a nine-foot turnaround fallaway from the middle of the lane, tying it at nine.

"They're going to make life tough for Steph and Klay. That's their focus. So everybody else has to be able to step up and be aggressive," Barnes said. "Whether that means putting the ball in the basket, whether it's driving and kicking, whatever it may be, we know they're not going to just let those guys spot up and get wide-open threes."

Twice in the early going James beat Barnes to the rim off the bounce from the wing. When he got a mismatch, he exploited it, taking Andrew Bogut to the hole on a switch. He missed the shot, but Thompson grabbed the offensive board and put it back in on the other side of the rim, closing the deficit to 16-15 midway through the quarter.

The Warriors sandwiched a pair of threes around another hard James finish at the rim, as he spun baseline around Festus Ezeli. Green sank a straightaway three that the Cavs appeared to be goading him into taking (much as they did Schroder and Carroll in the prior series), and Curry perpetrated a three from the left wing when he shook loose of Irving on a pin-down action.

Pin-downs are screens that occur off the ball along the baseline or post area, allowing the offensive player to pop up or out to the elbow, wing, or corner with a step on his man who has to negotiate the screen. The Cavaliers were switching a lot of this, much like a zone defense in football, passing responsibility with a glance, the same way James and Smith collaborated to keep Korver blanketed in the Atlanta series.

Golden State was getting back in transition, rotating quickly and getting two men at the rim for drives as well as doubling post-ups, leaving Cleveland few easy ways to score. Indeed, two of their next three buckets—James and Irving layups—came in transition without being fastbreaks, showcasing the difficulty handling the Cavaliers pair in the open court without help. Shaun Livingston added a pair of pull-up jumpers for the Warriors, who had a 28-24 lead at the end of one.

"[We're] just paying attention to Klay and Steph," Lue told ABC's Doris Burke. "The other guys are getting open but we're fine with that. We came back, cut the lead to four, so we're in good shape."

The Warriors' bench derailed that plan by starting the second *el fuego*, hitting their first four shots, three of them with a difficulty rating of "semi-ridiculous." Onetime "Brazilian Blur" Leandro Barbosa hit a left baseline floater (switching hands in midair) while going out of bounds, Livingston sank a turnaround over a strong Shumpert contest, and Barbosa beat Dellavedova with a behind-the-back crossover before finishing high off the glass over Shumpert's weakside help contest. It pushed the lead to 36-28, and Lue called a timeout with nine minutes left in the second.

It would be over three minutes before Cleveland made another basket—following two missed free throws, five missed layups or putbacks, two turnovers, and some slow transition defense that afforded the Warriors a 4-on-3 break that resulted in a Barbosa right-corner three-pointer, which brought the crowd to their feet.

"He's still very fast. Maybe not as fast as he was five years ago, but he's still a guy who loves to get up and down the floor," said Kerr. "He came in and gave us a huge lift. Got a couple layups to go early, tough layups, and then made that three in the corner."

Andre Iguodala divorced both James and Irving from the ball on consecutive finishes at the rim during this stretch by swiping down as they brought the ball up. One led to a Klay Thompson fastbreak bucket that gave the Warriors a 43-29 lead midway through the second, leading to another Lue timeout.

"I caught myself last game talking to LeBron about kind of holding the ball above his head," Irving said. "They have athletic guys with length. But [they need to be] meeting us up at the top of the rim rather than bringing it down low and us trying to bring it up. It didn't work in our favor. I remember going baseline a few times on Iggy, and he got his hand on the ball a few times. I'm thinking I have an open reverse, and he's not even contesting me at the top of my shot but rather at the bottom. Going forward, I've definitely taken note of it."

Coming out of the timeout Irving was able to take Klay Thompson baseline and draw his third foul, sending the Warriors guard to the bench for the rest of the half with just four points. Irving continued to enforce his will offensively. He scored seven points and assisted on the other two buckets during a 12-6 run over the next three and a half minutes. After a couple James free throws, Green finished the scoring with an uncontested three-pointer for a 52-43 halftime lead.

The Cavaliers shot 36 percent for the half while allowing Golden State to shoot 52 percent. Golden State did much better in the paint, going 14-of-23 while the Cavs shot 9-of-24, including 3-of-9 on second-chance points. Poor ballhandling hurt them. Cleveland's nine turnovers led to 15 Warriors points. Golden State had just four turnovers.

In keeping with their "Strength in Numbers" motto, six players on the Warriors had at least six points, while the Cavs' Big Three accounted for 34 of their 43 points. On a positive note, their aggressive defense held Thompson and Curry to 10 points on 4-of-13 shooting.

The second half got off to a ragged start, with each team hitting but two of their first six shots, and the Cavaliers added a couple more turnovers. Finally with eight and a half left in the third, Irving advanced a James rebound and beat Barnes to his left in transition, then finished the and-one. On the next possession Irving picked off a pass intended for Barnes and Tristan Thompson put back a missed Love fallaway, cutting the deficit to 56-52. Kerr called timeout.

As the Cavaliers made a run during the last half of the third, Iggy kept making plays for his teammates, hitting a three and assisting on the Warriors' next three hoops amidst a 16-8 Cavaliers run following his three-pointer.

"Andre is not only a phenomenal athlete with long arms and great quickness and strength, but he's incredibly smart. He's one of the smartest players I've ever been around at both ends of the floor," Kerr said. "He anticipates plays; he anticipates moves from individual players. He studies his opponents and he's smart. He doesn't reach very often. He only reaches when he feels like he's got a chance to make a steal."

After Irving and Green traded pairs of free throws to make it 63-57 Golden State, the Cavaliers scored the next seven points to take their first lead since the opening minutes. James received a double-high screen (aka "Horns") and drove down the right side of the lane, while Double-T rolled down the middle, receiving a perfect alley-oop lofted over Draymond Green's arms that Tristan snagged and slammed home.

Cleveland smothered Curry with a trap above the right break and Love recovered his deflected his pass. Irving wasn't able to create anything in transition and the ball went to James out top, who caught the pass with his right hand and in one motion whipped it to Love in the left corner just ahead of Iggy's passing lane swipe. Love drove baseline and scored, drawing contact from Ezeli for the and-one. A moment later Kevin tipped in Tristan's tip of his own missed hook to give the Cavaliers a 64-63 lead.

"In the first half we struggled a little bit offensively. I just thought in the second half we came back in that third quarter, really got physical, really got aggressive...you saw when we were able to get stops and get out in transition," said Lue. "That really opened the game up for us and we were able to go from a nine-point deficit to going up [one point] by playing faster and being more aggressive in transition."

The teams swapped the lead several times before the Cavs took their final lead, 68-67, with two minutes left. James airballed a contested three—his worst shot of the night—but the Cavaliers retained possession. LeBron drove on Ezeli from the arc, finishing with a sweet lefty scoop around Green's weakside help contest. This would've been the perfect time to pull James and rest him for the fourth, but Lue didn't for another 90 seconds and the Warriors finished the quarter on a 7-0 run anyway to recapture the lead, 74-68.

Lue tried unsuccessfully to rest James the beginning of the fourth. Irving wasn't as effective running the second squad (unsurprising given he'd hardly done so the past two months). "We took LeBron out towards the end of that third quarter, and a couple minutes in the fourth quarter, and the game kind of got away from us," Lue confessed.

Kerr told Burke between quarters that the team lacked intensity in the third quarter. "It felt like a November game, not a June game." Golden State responded by opening the fourth with a reserves-led 8-0 run. Shumpert got punked by a Varejao flop, earning an offensive foul, and Livingston followed with an elbow jumper in Tristan's face.

Love made a nice post spin on Iguodala but blew the layup, and Barbosa scored on the other end, hitting a nine-foot runner. Suddenly it was 82-68 Warriors. Irving stopped the run with a layup, but Livingston came back and stuck a jumper in Irving's face, his 14th point.

"Just his length, being 6-foot-7, and no matter who you try to put in front of him, he's always going to be bigger at the point guard position. So we try to keep a bigger defender on him," said Lue. "But he got to his spots, to the free throw line, 12 feet in on the baseline, and got to his shot, and he hurt us with that tonight."

James came back in with the score 84-70 and just over two minutes gone, but the Cavaliers couldn't get much closer, losing 104-89. At that point Cleveland's Big Three were 20-of-53 (38 percent), and their role players an even worse 7-of-20 (35 percent).

"We got lucky a couple times in the first half in particular; we had some breakdowns," said Kerr. "But over the course of the game, to hold that team to 38 percent shooting, we did a lot of good things."

Irving finished with 26 points and four assists, and James totaled 23 points, 12 rebounds, nine assists, and four turnovers. Love added 17 and 13 boards, and Tristan also had a double-double with 10 points and 12 rebounds, six of them offensive. Klay and Steph were 8-of-27, but the rest of Golden State's players were 35-of-60 (58 percent), including 13-of-15 between Barbosa and Livingston, as the Warriors showed their depth. Seven Warriors hit double figures in scoring, led by Livingston with 20 points and Green with 16.

"When you get outscored 45-10 on the bench and give up 25 points off 17 turnovers, no matter what someone does or doesn't do, it's going to be hard to win," said James. "Especially on the road. And that's what it was. Obviously the game ball goes to Shaun Livingston. Came in, gave them a huge spark."

For the Cavaliers the evening was a partial success in that they had successfully stopped the Warriors' high-scoring backcourt and made other people beat them, which they did.

"We rely on a lot of people," Kerr continued. "We play a lot of people, and we feel like we have a lot of talent on the bench that can come in and score when we need it. So, it's a great sign, obviously, that we can win in the Finals without Steph and Klay having big games. But it's not really that surprising to us. This has been our team the last couple of years."

Similarly, the Cavaliers were getting shots they wanted; they just weren't making them. They had two more shots in the paint (49-47) but made six less than Golden State (27-21), and trailed on second-chance points 15-13 despite seven more opportunities. Green was a particular issue at the rim; Cleveland was 4-of-17 on shots he contested there. They were 7-of-12 over Bogut or Ezeli and 7-of-11 over Barnes.

"We got stripped five or six times with LeBron and Kyrie getting to the basket. We missed nine point-blank layups when no one was around," said Lue. "We've got to be able to finish those shots around the basket. When

Bogut goes to the bench, they don't have any shot-blocking. So we were able to get the shots we wanted to in the paint, and we've just got to make them."

In the end Lue felt the Cavaliers just needed to play quicker and maintain a better pace. "We went to the matchups we had where they switched and they had a disadvantage. We posted the ball with LeBron and Kevin, and now we have to make them pay for when they come and double-team," Lue continued. "We want Kyrie to be aggressive, but it has to be sharp, quick attacks. You can't dribble for eight or nine seconds. We had that discussion, and he understands that."

Kyrie went 1-of-9 on possessions when he didn't pass after crossing halfcourt. That couldn't persist, and he knew that.

"Rather than settling for mid-range jump shots where I'm coming off pick-and-rolls in the last few series and bigs are dropping all the way back, now it's the one-on-one challenge of just beating your guy. So you've got to find that balance," Kyrie said. "Because when you're going one-on-one, guys are still watching you, and the offense kind of becomes stagnant. So finding that balance where we can have continuity and getting the ball moving and finding guys in their ISO areas where they're most effective."

NBA Finals, Game 2. Sunday, June 5, 2016 Oakland. (1-0 GSW)

Going into the game, much was made of the fact that LeBron was 9-0 after Game 1 playoff losses. He had also won a road game in a record 25 straight playoff series after their victory over Toronto in Game 6 of the Western Conference Finals, breaking a tie with Michael Jordan.

Golden State got off to a slow start in Game 2, missing its first four shots (all threes) and—after Bogut and Green hoops—committing consecutive turnovers. Meanwhile, the Cavs were reprising their Game 1 troubles at the rim. Each of the Big Three missed a point-blank shot in the first four minutes. J. R. Smith capped the run of futility by missing two free throws. Still, Cleveland held a 10-6 lead after Tristan Thompson recovered a lost James dribble under the basket and scored.

The Warriors shook out of their lethargy, mounting an 11-3 run fueled by boards. Golden State grabbed seven offensive rebounds in four minutes, outrebounding Cleveland 13-2. Bogut had three offensive boards and three blocks in the run (four in the quarter), including a rejection of a Smith layup that turned into a Curry transition three.

"Yeah, they were crashing," said Tristan Thompson. "That's on the bigs so we have to limit the offensive rebounds. [Festus] Ezeli got one on me and a putback. We have to limit that. It's on the bigs to secure those rebounds and box people out."

Curry finished the run by pushing a missed Smith three and beating both Irving and Jefferson with a little hesitation dribble drive to his left, getting Irving airborne before laying it in. That gave the Warriors a 17-13 lead with three minutes left in the first.

Lue was more strategic with James' rest in Game 2, sitting him at the four-minute mark and bringing him back with 90 seconds left in the first, score tied at 19. James rebounded a Livingston miss with 35 seconds left and floated a rim-running Double-T the perfect transition alley-oop from six feet beyond the arc, giving the Cavs a 21-19 lead going into the second quarter.

"I thought early we did hit first," said Lue, referring to the team's physicality. "We had a great first quarter, but they were still making the tougher plays. I thought they got to all the 50-50 balls. They were tougher than us and more aggressive. I mean, holding them to 19 points in the first quarter was really good for us, but I just thought over the course of the night they just continued to make the tougher plays."

Draymond opened the second with a three over Channing Frye, who was having trouble getting floor time because he didn't match up well with Golden State. Frye wasn't quick enough to stay with most Warriors, Green in particular. When the series began, Kerr had sat less-athletic Marreese Speights (an easier matchup for Frye), bringing Green back with his second squad.

The Cavaliers reclaimed the lead with a 7-0 run. Shumpert screened for Thompson near the free throw line before popping out to the arc, receiving James' pass, and sinking the triple. James stole the ball from Barnes, posted up Green, and spun around him baseline for the layup, his first bucket. On the next possession as Delly drove the lane, James shadowed behind, receiving the backward pass and ascending for the right-hand slam to give them a 28-22 lead.

A series of mental mistakes and bad plays slowed the Cavaliers' roll, almost all of them occurring with Curry on the bench. First Shumpert got stuck on a pin-down, giving Klay Thompson enough time to open a checking account before sinking a three—his first basket of the game. Then Green knocked away James' pass to a rolling Jefferson, leading to an uncontested Livingston dunk thanks to Shump's transition defense lapse.

"The game kind of broke open when we had two straight turnovers," said James. "I think the game was at 28-22, I turned the ball over. Draymond got it and was able to hit I think Livingston for a dunk. And then we had another turnover and Klay hit a three, and that kind of slowed us down."

Barnes caught Frye watching the ball and beat him backdoor with the help of an Iguodala pass, putting the Warriors back in the lead, 29-28. Klay hit an elbow jumper over James, who answered by taking Livingston to the hole with a crossover, drawing the foul and converting both freebies. Green came right back with consecutive three-pointers over late contests by James and Love.

"The way they're playing defense against our guards, Draymond's going to be open all day," said Kerr. "He's a good three-point shooter. We like it when he gets that shot in rhythm, and he knocked them down tonight."

Then after Curry made a jumper, Barnes came over Love's back, grabbing an errant Klay three and pummeling his elbow into the back of Big Kev's skull. He collapsed in a heap. Draymond received the ball on the left wing and took Tristan to the hole over Love's still prone body, drawing a foul when Tristan stopped short. That made it 42-30.

When Love responded with a left-corner three off a Smith drive-and-dish, it was the Cavs' first basket in nine shots and almost six minutes. James added a transition layup pushing a Jefferson rebound to cut the lead back to seven. However, after a Kerr timeout, Steph and Klay got loose for consecutive threes (step-back and transition, respectively), then after a pair of James free throws (Curry's third foul), Curry and Iggy converted back-to-back transition layups for a 52-37 lead with just over two minutes left.

The Cavs closed the quarter strong with a 7-0 run to cut the lead nearly in half, 52-44. James had four of those points on two layups, and he finished the half with 14 points, seven assists, four steals, and four turnovers. Tristan was the next leading scorer with eight. Cleveland's backcourt was struggling; Smith and Irving were a combined 3-of-13 for seven points. Green led the Warriors with 18 points followed by Curry with 12.

Love started the second half, but checked out after two minutes in favor of Jefferson because of concussion symptoms that surfaced suddenly after halftime. "[Love] showed no symptoms. He didn't talk about it," said Lue. "When we came back out in the third, I could see in the timeout he looked kind of woozy."

Jefferson gave the team a spark. He picked off a crosscourt Curry pass and drew Steph's fourth foul on the ensuing fastbreak, sending the Warriors star to the bench. Jefferson's defense forced Green to dribble the ball out of bounds, and on the next possession J. R. spun around Iggy for a lefty layup.

After Green stuck his fourth three over another late (James) contest, Irving scored, breaking to the basket and receiving a great crosscourt pass from Smith after a long offensive rebound. On the other end Irving knocked the ball away from Klay on a drive, but Shumpert fumbled the ball out of bounds in transition. Barbosa scored a layup when he recovered the ball after being stripped. Jefferson followed by beating the Warriors baseline in transition for the slam, cutting the lead to 62-53 with just under seven left.

That's as close as it got as Golden State closed the third on a 20-9 run, nine of them by Klay Thompson, to take an 82-62 lead. The Cavs didn't even score during the first three and a half minutes of the fourth, until the reserves were in and Mozgov made a putback dunk. Green finished with 28, while Steph and Klay combined for 35. James had 19 points and Jefferson was next with 12.

The Cavaliers shot 35 percent to Golden State's 54 percent, while making 18 turnovers (eight by LeBron) that the Warriors turned into 26 points. Golden State actually committed three more turnovers (21) but the Cavs scored six less points than them. The Warriors also outrebounded Cleveland 46-32 in the 110-77 pasting.

"We didn't win anything. [At] no point in the game did we beat them in anything. Even when we had an early lead, they beat us to 50-50 balls. They got extra possessions. They got extra tip-ins," said James. "Obviously not much is working, especially offensively. Defensively we've been good at times and then at times we just looked like we're a step slow. We messed up on the coverage. We don't get back or we're just one step behind where we should be."

The Cavaliers were down 0-2, like much of the press predicted, and the media saluted themselves in the aftermath while Cleveland circled the wagons.

17

WHEN HYPERBOLE ATTACKS

T HE WARRIORS WEREN'T the only ones confident the Cavaliers would lose the Finals; most of the press was in the bag for Golden State before they left California. There had been two convincing wins by a total of 48 points, including a 33-point victory in Game 2. Then again the Thunder beat the Warriors by a combined 52 points in Games 3 and 4 at home, which didn't prove all that predictive.

One reporter posed this "question" of Channing Frye during the Saturday practice in Oakland after Game 2: "It's probably different back in Cleveland, but driving in today listening to the radio, there was a lot of talk of whether the Cavaliers can win *a game* in this series. Obviously, we're moving pretty fast with that assumption. Does that amuse you, bother you? How do you feel about it?"

Or put another way: "A lot of us don't feel you have a chance in hell. How does that feel? Does it amuse you?"

"Y'all are bored. That's it. Ain't got nothing else to talk about," replied Frye. "If you're talking about that, y'all are crazy."

Nobody gave the Cavaliers much of a chance. Four of ESPN's five experts had the Warriors in five. "As much as I think they are fully capable of sweeping the series (in resounding fashion, no less), I just have a gut feeling they'll drop one out of pure carelessness," offered expert Amin Elhassan, who once worked under Kerr.

"There may be a way for the Cleveland Cavaliers to get back in this series against the Golden State Warriors…but if there is, I can't even begin to imagine what that might be," wrote *USA Today*'s Nate Scott.

Those who believed the Cavaliers were a better team than they showed those first two games were apparently delusional. "To the extent anyone talked themselves into picking the Cavaliers to take home the title, it was because they beat up on some truly underwhelming competition…while the Warriors had to fight back heroically against the extremely talented Oklahoma City Thunder," scoffed Jesse Singal of *New York Magazine*'s Daily Intelligencer section. "The true talent differential between these teams, in other words, wasn't fully on display until they were occupying the same court."

Meanwhile, ESPN's big-data crew at FiveThirtyEight.com followed blown predictions on Donald Trump, and Bernie Sanders in Michigan (where Hilary Clinton was 99 percent assured of victory), by pegging the chances of the Cavaliers beating the Warriors at 11 percent. Though 538 writer Benjamin Morris suggested the odds were likely longer, perhaps "along the lines of 99.7 percent, around a 1-in-300 proposition for the Cavs," noting the Warriors "have only lost three of five once, against the Thunder in the Western Conference Finals." (*That was just the week before, right?*)

For his part, Steph Curry remained bullish. "The crazy thing is we can all play better."

Of course, the same held doubly true for the team in the other locker room. And if we're simply talking about regression to the mean, you have to wonder whether the Warriors had been flying awfully close to the sun for a bit too long.

Cavaliers' followers had the opposite issue. They'd spent seven months watching their team hang back until the last minute before turning it on. Nobody had seen the team play a full 48 minutes all year because even one half of sustained effort had almost always been enough and usually a tightly focused fourth quarter was sufficient.

"We were not a front-running team all year; we were quite the opposite," Griffin told Adrian Wojnarowski. "We were better when our backs were against the wall."

The Cavs got a tongue-lashing from assistant and player development coach Phil Handy after Game 2. The former Lakers coach/trainer took great exception to the Cavaliers' lack of intensity.

"We looked like a deer in headlights," Handy told ESPN Magazine's The

Undefeated. "They were acting like we were weak. I just told all of them that 'this was some shit.' That the Warriors are 'just out there punking y'all and ya'll ain't doing shit.'"

NBA Finals, Game 3. Sunday, June 8, 2016, Cleveland. (2-0 GSW)

The Cavaliers would play Game 3 without Kevin Love, who was still smarting from Harrison Barnes' elbow. Love had to go through the league's concussion protocol, which required 24 hours of rest and then a battery of tests. The results were compared to Love's preseason baselines; he didn't pass.

"Kevin wanted to be on the court. I saw how pissed off he was when he wasn't able to be cleared in time," said Jefferson, who started in his stead. "We're in this together. We've all picked each other up. You have to go with the next-man-up mentality."

Jefferson was really more of a small forward, bumping James to power forward, his favored position in Miami. It not only made the Cavs quicker, but naturally put James on Green and matched Thompson on much smaller players in Golden State's quick lineups.

Jefferson tied the NBA record for longest time between Finals appearances (13 years), a record also held by Elden Campbell (1991 Lakers and 2004 Pistons) and Sam Cassell (1995 Rockets and 2008 Celtics), but it wasn't any kind of honorarium. He'd shot well all postseason (at that point 53 percent field goal, 10-of-23 from three), and had more rebounds than any other reserve, including Frye. Perhaps most importantly, RJ had only six turnovers over 252 playoff minutes.

The Cavaliers not only came out with better energy, but a few new wrinkles. When not in a pick-and-roll during Games 1 and 2, Warriors defenders on Tristan Thompson would cheat toward the lane to load it for James and Irving penetrations. So Cleveland stationed Tristan out high, where no big would follow, and used him to screen for J. R. Smith on an open left-wing three (he missed) and for Kyrie Irving on a pull-up jumper after a dribble hand-off (made).

On the next possession LeBron caught Curry overplaying Kyrie's pin-down screen toward the three-line and fed Irving perfectly on his backdoor cut for an easy layup. Going back to a pick-and-roll between Irving and Tristan, Barnes pinched toward the lane to cut off Kyrie's penetration leaving,

Jefferson open in the right corner for three, making it 9-0 with nine and a half left in the first.

"I had a couple of lapses where I didn't follow the gameplan, and Kyrie gets an easy layup, gets his confidence going," Curry said. "I take the blame for that."

Kerr called a timeout, which helped stop the run. James blanketed Green once he picked up his dribble, but Draymond still managed a perfectly timed pass to Bogut beneath the hoop after he popped free from a weave of weakside screens like a lottery ping-pong ball. Next time down Bogut hit a long lefty hook from nearly the elbow against a good Thompson contest. It'd be four minutes before they'd score again.

Four of Cleveland's next five buckets came at the rim. Jefferson's penetration forced Bogut to rotate, leaving Thompson alone on the boards for the rebound and putback. James scored three times in a row—dunking off a Curry turnover, and making layups to each side, beating Iggy one-on-one to the right and elevating for the score, then coming off a great Smith screen to the left and accelerating to the bucket to beat Bogut's rim protection. That made it 19-4 with five minutes left in the first.

"I started off the game going in the interior and just trying to fan out their defense a little bit. We did a great job of spacing out with RJ, Ky, and also with Swish, so it gave me a little bit more room to work down in the post," James said. "I missed a ton of chippies, but I was loving the space that I was getting and my teammates created for me."

James sat down a couple minutes later, handing the keys to Irving. He scored 12 of the Cavaliers' next 14 points as he held the Warriors at bay (12 points over the rest of the quarter) by himself. He sank two pull-up jumpers, a layup, and a couple of threes, in that order. Mostly Kyrie just attacked off the dribble, putting Curry into pick-and-rolls with James. Steph had trouble keeping up.

"He was able to attack in transition. And even versus the switches he really attacked quicker so they couldn't load up on him," Lue said. "He really attacked quick, and got downhill and got into the paint. No one can stop Kyrie one-on-one when he has the basketball. We just have to attack quicker and keep them on their heels."

In the last couple minutes they ran an interesting set with Mozgov and Frye on the floor with Kyrie. Steph wound up on Frye and picked up his second foul in 30 seconds. He left having failed to score. Cleveland followed with a 10-2 run. Mozgov was an unsung cog, offering three beefy screens that gave Irving the space for three of those buckets.

One Mozgov screen sent Klay Thompson to the locker room. He inadvertently kneed the Warrior guard in the thigh as he fought over Mozgov's moving screen. Klay beefed afterward: "I rewatched it. I'm just confused why he's trying to set a screen in the middle of the key when we're both running full speed downhill," he said. "It seemed kind of dirty to me. He stuck his knee out too, but, you know what? That's basketball."

"Timo was running in to set a high pick-and-roll, and at the same time the ballhandler was going forward, so he just tried to stop and they ended up running into each other," explained Lue. "But I wouldn't say it was a dirty play."

The Cavs made 15-of-21 (71 percent) in the first and committed just three turnovers. The Warriors were just 7-of-20 including 1-of-10 from international waters and 1-of-4 from the line. Kyrie finished the first with 16 while Steph and Klay did not score, going 0-of-8 from the field.

Harrison Barnes scored Golden State's last three points of the first quarter and five of their first seven in the second as the Warriors scored 10 unanswered points before an Irving three with nine minutes left in the second pushed the lead back to 36-23.

The Cavaliers didn't have the same intensity, and neither team could get very much going. J. R. Smith's second bucket and first three, with under five remaining, pushed the lead to 43-31.

However, the off the ball movement and screening that went on in the first quarter began to dissipate. The team's pace had also dropped along with the defensive intensity. Smith and Jefferson both made steals, the latter resulting in another Smith corner three that pushed the lead to 48-33 with three and a half left.

"The offense comes very free to him and very easy, but the defensive side is what's making him so great," James complimented J. R. "The contribution that we got from him, the scoring, was all predicated on what he did defensively."

The Warriors closed the quarter with a 10-3 run, including eight straight from Klay Thompson. He had a pair of three-point plays—one in transition, the other of the old-fashioned variety, when he slashed through two Cavaliers for the and-one. His effort pulled the Warriors to within eight, 51-43, at the half.

The Warriors shot better than the Cavs (50 percent to 44 percent), thanks to a blistering 12-of-18 second quarter, but only 2-of-14 from three and 3-of-8 from the charity stripe. Cleveland controlled the boards 26-18 and had 21 points off 10 Warrior turnovers while committing seven for six Golden State points. They cooled down severely from that white-hot first quarter (6-of-27, 22 percent).

Lue's big defensive adjustment had been to stop switching off the ball, solving a Game 2 mess of Lewinsky proportions. Now players were expected to follow their man around picks without surrendering responsibility to someone else. By necessity they stuck closer, absent the lifeline of, "Dude, where's *your man*? No way, that's *my man*."

"We wanted to play hard but we made a few mental errors in Games 1 and 2," said Thompson. "So we simplified our coverages."

Offensively they stopped running so many pick-and-roll actions on the wing, tending to operate in the middle of the floor, abetting better side-to-side movement and increased off-ball action.

"We worked on that the last couple days, just moving, trying to create some confusion," Lue said. "If they're going to switch it or not, and if it would give our guys a chance to drive the basketball at the same time."

Operating in the middle of the floor negated some of Golden State's ability to help defensively, and overload the ball side of the court. When the defenses collapsed on Cavs drives, the Warriors' weakside defense remained wary of the pass. Using the elbow and mid-floor areas left less time to cut off the drive, and made it harder to overplay one side.

Cleveland came out with better aggression to start the third. Not only were the Cavs up on their man and engaged, but they were attacking close-outs, not settling for the first open three, continuing to press their advantages and force the Warriors to adjust.

"We talked about it at halftime. We were down eight and they played their best half," said Draymond Green. "We were going to have to come out swinging first in the third quarter, and we didn't. I don't think really they had any adjustments that they made X - and O-wise. They outplayed us."

The Cavaliers scored the first seven points of the half while pushing the pace. Irving took Barnes baseline and hung him out to dry like hand washables with an 18-foot step-back jumper. Thompson finished strong in the middle of the lane over both Green and Bogut on an Irving pick-and-roll feed. Tristan's score was sandwiched between Bogut turnovers, the first a moving screen, the second a fumbled finish in which LeBron grifted him using the swipe-down move.

Over the first seven minutes of the third, the Cavs made 7-of-9 while holding the Warrior to 2-of-10, outscoring them 19-5. A Harrison Barnes three momentarily stopped the bleeding, cutting the lead to 58-46. Smith answered by taking Curry one-on-one off the dribble, spinning toward the elbow, then stepping back for the 16-foot fallaway, after Jefferson saved the possession with a long offensive board.

With the game almost in hand, James took over for several possessions. First he took a 21-foot transition pull-up jumper, inarguably the worst shot on the floor (since a foot further back is worth three) and dropped it directly in Draymond's face. Green received the ball on the right wing and spun baseline past James, but when he went to the front of the rim James slapped it away. Next James took Iguodala one-on-one, sinking a 20-foot step-back (heat-check!) jumper that hardly disturbed the strings.

Iggy posted Irving and scored at the rim. Kyrie fought him valiantly but his size was too much. In Golden State's small, so-called "death lineup" this proved one of their best matchups, which says a lot about how well the Cavaliers defended it. Smith made an escape dribble to dodge the closing Klay, then cashed his third triple of the night.

James followed with a straightaway transition pull-up three for his 20th point and the Cavaliers' largest lead of the night, 70-48. Curry and Livingston keyed a 10-point burst over the final two minutes of the half, but the Cavaliers kept up the offensive pressure with a Tristan layup, two James freebies, and Jefferson's tip-in and baseline slam.

The Warriors got no closer than 23, but Lue didn't trust his reserves, so James and Irving didn't sit until almost the four minute mark in the fourth. James played 40 minutes, Smith 38, and Irving 36 in a game they led by 17+ the final 18 minutes. It may not seem important, but Game 4 was the only one in the series preceded by but one off-day.

The Cavs won 120-90, shooting 43 percent and holding the Warriors to 34 percent in the second half (42 percent for the game). Cleveland was 12-of-25 (48 percent) from three while the Warriors were 9-of-33 (27 percent). The

Cavaliers dominated the boards (52-32), second-chance points (23-3), and points in the paint (54-32). The Cavs also had 21 deflections to just nine for the Warriors, a sign of their greater defensive aggression.

"We weren't tough enough. We weren't strong enough with the ball. We were soft," explained Kerr. "When you're soft, you get beat on the glass and you turn the ball over. Those are the telltale signs."

James finished with 32 points and six assists, while Irving had 30 and eight assists. Smith chipped in 20, while Jefferson added nine points and eight boards in 33 minutes replacing KLove. Meanwhile, Steph and Klay combined for just 29 points (10-of-26 shooting), as both failed to crack 20 for the third game in a row.

"[Jefferson] gave us speed. He gave us the physicality on Harrison Barnes, and that we were able to slide LeBron over to Draymond Green, which helped us out a lot," Lue said. "We were able to switch pick-and-rolls and things like that."

The scribes were shocked. How is it possible for one team to win by 33 and then the other to win by 30? Part of this was how Game 2 played into the media's confirmation bias about the Warriors' dominance. The other was a lack of historical grounding.

The '84 Lakers had beaten the Celtics in the Finals by 33, then lost the next two games and eventually the series. The next year the '85 Celtics opened the series with a 148-114 pasting of the Lakers (aka the Memorial Day Massacre), then lost four of the next five.

"This is how it is," said Kerr. "Most of the teams in the league are pretty equal in talent."

Coach Lue saw the biggest change being his team's willingness to compete hard to the end of every possession. "They're a tough team," he said. "They work the basketball so you've got to defend for 24 seconds. They'll burn you with the last two seconds on the shot clock, so you've got to be prepared and always being aware. I thought our physicality and our attention to detail was really great tonight."

The 63-point turnaround had the media's head spinning like Linda Blair in *The Exorcist*, and it bled over to the next day. Kerr shrugged off the overheated narratives.

"So 14 hours ago? Sixteen hours ago? Everything was great. We were doing great. And 'Boy, what are the Cavs going to do? Are they going to get swept?'" the 50-year-old Golden State coach observed. "They're a great team. They win a game, now it's our lineup changes, and, 'Oh, my God, Steph Curry can't play well, and what's Klay going to do?' When you go through the playoffs, you understand this is all part of it."

Kerr would go on to suggest that while strategies remain in place, tactics start to change around Games 3 and 4. Lue moving LeBron onto Green after his 28-point Game 2 outburst was the first. Now it was Kerr's turn to adjust.

"You make an adjustment before Game 1, the team's kind of looking at you like, 'What are we doing? We're pretty good,'" said Kerr. "So usually both teams, I would say in my experience, kind of wait at least a couple of games before they make any dramatic move. Then it sort of goes back and forth from there."

NBA Finals, Game 4. Friday, June 10, 2016, Cleveland. (2-1 GSW)

Though both coaches continued to cite energy and aggression—almost *de rigueur* given both wanted to push the pace and attack early in the clock—the Warriors also made a more concerted effort to get their backcourt tandem going.

Golden State set 20.4 ball screens per game for Steph Curry in the first three rounds of the playoffs but only 15.7 during the first three games of the Finals, according to SportVU. They scored just 0.67 ppp on those screens. They set 32 in Game 4 and Curry doubled his efficiency.

Yet it wasn't just more screens, but the type of screens. In the first three games most of Curry's screens came from Warriors bigs, hoping to beat James, Love, or primarily Thompson, which proved ineffective. For Game 4, Curry received a lot more screens by "smalls." After receiving 38 of his 47 screens by bigs, he was screened 19 of 32 times by guards or wings in Game 4.

Still, it's unclear whether greater Warrior focus or Cleveland's chronic ADD was responsible for Klay and Steph's better Game 4 play. "There were a couple of possessions, actually a lot of possessions, where we made mental errors," said Thompson the next day. "That's on us. Going back to the film, we see that and those things that we can get better at."

The game got off to a furious start. Each team scored on its first five possessions. Eight of the Warriors' points came from Barnes, who twice sank right-corner threes. When the Cavaliers trapped Curry on the left wing several feet beyond the arc, he skip-passed it to Barnes, then Bogut found him after collapsing the lane with a roll to the basket.

"They're so good at back cutting, getting back screens and different guys open," said Love, who passed the concussion protocol and volunteered to come off the bench.

The Cavaliers answered with threes from Irving and Smith, followed by a Thompson putback and then layup off an Irving pick-and-roll. It was tied at 10 with nine and a half to go.

Bogut mugged Jefferson directly in front of Jason Phillips, one of several calls that should've attracted the attention of Amnesty International as the referees let both teams get very physical.

Midway through the quarter the Warriors went to their small (aka "death") lineup, their most successful combo through the first four games. Lineups featuring Barnes, Thompson, Iguodala, Green, and either Livingston or Curry were +14 per 100 possessions (pCp). Their starting lineup featuring Bogut was -20 pCp.

Kyrie immediately ran a give-and-go with James off the left wing inbound, stepping in bounds and breaking baseline ahead of Klay Thompson. He took the pass, dribbled twice, and hesitated (so Klay bumped him from behind) before lofting it over Green's avenging swat for the and-one. That was the second foul on Thompson, forcing him to sit. A moment later Love had a nice putback on a missed Smith three, where he was hit hard by Curry (no call) but still converted.

The Warriors made 5-of-9 from three in the first quarter, three of those by Klay or Steph, an ominous sign for Cleveland's defense. On offense, Tristan Thompson had become their failsafe with five offensive boards and three putback hoops for eight points. Barnes and Curry both had eight for Golden State, which led 29-28 after one.

The Cavaliers struggled to begin the second quarter as James ran the second team but never got much going. He missed a straightaway transition three and made two turnovers as both teams treaded water the first five minutes of the second. With seven and a half left the Cavaliers had a fastbreak opportunity but ref Jason Phillips cut in front of Shumpert, tripping him in the left corner, causing him to stumble and James' pass to go out of bounds.

James was fouled with 6:41 in the second, putting the Warriors in the bonus. The Cavaliers would get just one more foul call the rest of the way, on which Thompson missed both free throws. As the starters replaced the reserves on the court in the second, ball and people movement slumped as James and Irving drove.

At first it was spectacular. From deep in the post with the clock running down, James hit Smith with a crosscourt pass for three. Then a moment after being posted up by Green, Irving pushed the made basket and got to the rim, laying it high off the backboard over Barnes.

On the other end when Curry got the switch and drove on Tristan, Kyrie leaked over from the weakside to block Steph's shot out of bounds. The Warriors inbounded to Green, but James intercepted his subsequent pass and raced upcourt for a layup. Then James rebounded a last-gasp J. R. prayer and passed to Kevin Love for a right-corner three and a 47-42 lead.

The Warriors answered with an Iggy three and a Thompson three-point play off a Curry steal, James' third turnover of the quarter. LeBron came back with a post-up reverse pivot to the middle of the lane, leaving Barnes waiting to deplane behind James' finger roll. Next he anticipated a Green dish off a drive and threw a bomb to the streaking J. R. Smith, who caught it on the bounce a couple steps ahead of Klay and slammed it home, making it 51-48. The Cavaliers took a 55-50 lead into halftime.

Steph and Klay had their best first half of the series, combining for 25 points and four baskets apiece. Barnes and Green contributed eight apiece. Irving led the Cavs with 17 while Smith and Thompson each added 10. Love gave the bench a nice boost as well with seven points and three boards.

James had only seven points with five assists and all of Cleveland's turnovers (four), which Golden State had turned into eight points. The Cavaliers were doing a good job of getting into the lane (11-of-20, 22 paint points) and controlling the boards (10 offensive rebounds), but were getting hurt by Golden State's threes (8-of-15, 53 percent) while coming up short on their own (5-of-16, 31 percent).

One of the reasons the Warriors loved Bogut was for his screening, which frequently meant grabbing opponents as they went by. Whether hip-checking Irving's baseline drive or grabbing Thompson by the bicep during an inbounds play, the 7-foot Aussie's play suggested a lineage that included Dick Dastardly and Ric Flair.

On Curry's first three of the second, Bogut pulled J. R. Smith's jersey so hard it looked like he was wearing clown suspenders, directly in front of

Danny Crawford on the left baseline. It gave Curry an extra second to sink his fourth three over Smith's contest.

The pace quickened and the Cavaliers got sloppy. James threw away an interior bounce pass to Tristan, then redeemed himself with a right wing pull-up three, when Green went under a Kyrie screen. (They continued to dare him to take threes, which would eventually come to haunt them.) That made it 61-53 with nine and a half left. Over the next five and a half minutes the Warriors would go on a 19-8 run, ignited by their 5-of-7 shooting from three.

On the next possession Bogut plainly grabbed Kyrie's arm going over the pick directly in front of Crawford again, opening up a second consecutive "illicit" three by Curry. Kyrie was so pissed that he had to say something to Crawford. Back the other way Bogut cleanly blocked Thompson's dunk attempt from the right while Green hammered Tristan's left arm in Jason Phillips' sightline without a call.

An unfortunate one-sided grouping of bad calls in a closely matched game can easily swing the tide. While Tristan laid face-first on the floor wondering if someone got the license plate, Draymond raced up the floor with his ill-gotten gains, feeding Klay on the left wing for another three.

"They're a team that if you don't take the opportunities that have been given, they'll make you pay for them, and that's what they did," said Jefferson. "We were up by eight. They hit two quick threes and it brought the game a little bit closer, and we didn't answer it the way we should."

The Cavs scored on their next three possessions, including a Jefferson driving score into Green's body, followed by James and Irving pull-up midrange jumpers. But Cleveland made mental mistakes, yielding Klay Thompson a wide-open wing three out of a Curry trap. Then Smith and Irving followed Klay off a screen, leaving Curry as open as a 7-Eleven.

"We just didn't communicate on certain parts of our defense," said Smith. "Kyrie and I got mixed up on two switches and allowed Klay to hit a three; I think Steph missed his."

After Irving's pull-up jumper, the Cavaliers forced a 24-second violation, giving them the ball with a 69-64 lead. James dribbled for 19 seconds, never advanced beyond the three-line, and finally took a pull-up three from just below the left break, bricking it.

Golden State scored on six of its next seven possessions, four off offensive boards. Several came after Lue pulled Thompson for Love, letting the Wild Thing roam free on the offensive boards. Varejao had three and the Warriors totaled five in this stretch, outrebounding the Cavs 9-2 to take a 79-73 lead with a minute left.

"They got some second-chance points that hurt us. Steph got to the ball, Dray got to the ball, Iguodala got to a couple and they converted. That's what got them over the hump," said Love.

Cleveland scored the last four points of the third and the first four of the fourth to retake the lead at 81-79 with 11 minutes to go in the game. However, Lue made a dangerous call trying to beat the Warriors' fresh second squad with his starters. Kyrie, LeBron, and J. R. played the entire third and Lue decided to push it.

"Going into the fourth quarter, being down 2-1, we're down two points. They brought their bench in, so I thought if we could keep our starters in for a few minutes, we could kind of make a run and then get guys out slowly," Lue explained. "But they were able to go on the run. So it hurt us. I went with my best players in the fourth quarter, but it didn't work."

The trio played the entire second half and seemed to lose steam as the fourth went on. Love scored on a turnaround in the lane and James followed by taking James McAdoo (cousin of onetime NBA scoring champ Bob McAdoo) to the rim off the bounce from the left wing. After a Livingston hook in the lane, Irving came down and beat Klay with help from a Love screen, taking the open lane to the hole. He missed the lay-in, but James cleaned his mess with a dunk, making it 83-81 with a minute and a half gone.

"It starts with, I believe, Harrison Barnes' three at the top of the key. That was a big shot to kind of get their rhythm going," James said. "Then they got some offensive rebounds, some second-chance points, and then defensively they got stops."

James hardly contested Barnes' three. Shumpert rebounded a missed James triple try, but the Warriors intercepted his pass and got an Iguodala jumper in transition. Tristan missed two free throws followed by a Livingston midrange jumper. The Warriors scored twice more on offensive rebounds, capped by a Barnes three off an Iggy board making it 93-84 with six minutes left. The Cavs simply didn't have enough left to get closer than seven the rest of the way.

With the Warriors ahead by 10 and just under three minutes to go, James tossed aside a Green screen for Curry and then straddle-stepped over his prone body. Draymond apparently saw this as disrespect and a provocation (as it was probably intended) and responded as expected, attempting to sock James in the nuts as he went by. Though it had no impact on Game 4, it would have huge repercussions for the series.

The Cavaliers shot 47 percent, but relied too heavily on one-on-one play in the second half, totaling just five assists and seven turnovers. They also missed 11 free throws (15-of-26, 58 percent) with Tristan the futility leader (0-of-5). Meanwhile, the Warriors went 9-of-20 from three in the second half and finished the game with an NBA Finals record 17 threes. The Warriors also beat the Cavs on the boards in the second half, 25-19.

Curry finished with 38 points on 7-of-13 three-point shooting, six assists, two steals, and three big offensive boards. Klay Thompson had 25 points, four threes, a steal, and a block. Barnes added 14, and Iggy chipped in 10.

"This is the first game where they really got going tonight, and it was hard to stop them," said Lue. "It was a combination of both. Letting Steph and Klay get out in transition, getting some early threes, some missed coverages… we made some defensive mistakes that cost us. And every time we made a mistake, they made us pay."

Irving led Cleveland with 34 points, three steals, and four assists. James had 25, 13 boards (four offensive), nine assists, and seven turnovers for the second time in the Finals. The pair took 33 of the team's 38 second-half shots, and accounted for 54 percent of the Cavaliers' touches compared to Steph and Klay with 44 percent of their team's touches.

The stagnant attack produced more dribble-heavy possessions that ended in sketchy last-second shots. Through four games, Cleveland had taken 34 shots in the final four seconds or less of the clock, approximately 10 percent. In the Game 3 win they took just five; in Game 4 they took 15 (and made four)—almost 20 percent of their shots.

The Cavaliers had remained true to their nature by refusing to make it easy on themselves. They chose the hardest adventure—indeed, one no one had successfully negotiated in NBA history. Say what you will about the Cavaliers, but you can't say they didn't love a challenge.

"We feel like the chips have been stacked up against us all year anyway," James said.

CAVALIERS HAVE 'EM RIGHT
WHERE THEY WANT 'EM

I N THE ANNALS of action films and pulp fiction, there's no cliché older or hoarier than the hero's swagger on the brink of oblivion. We all have our favorites, such as the lone fellow telling the enveloping horde he'll give them one last chance to surrender, or the bound bad-ass who spits a tooth and tells the steroidal Venice Beach refugee his grandmother hits harder.

It's a thin line between courageous and foolhardy, between "backed into a corner" and "forgot to fill up the getaway car." It's all in how you spin the story. One version finds the valiant *300*, heels edging the abyss, meeting eyes, digging in, and pushing back with one final furious flurry. Another might feature someone troubled by Munchausen by proxy creating circumstances that allow them to arrive at the last moment to save the day. But what the can you say, everyone loves a grand entrance.

Like stereotypical thrill-seekers, the Cavs had demonstrated an almost sadistic tendency to ramp up the difficulty level to keep themselves engaged. Down 3-1 to the owner of the best regular season record in basketball history, playing two of those three games on the road, you'd have to call that mission accomplished. Only two of the 32 Finals teams to go down 3-1 had even forced a Game 7; none had won. (Was there a moment where Evel Knievel whispered to his stunt coordinator, "*How wide* did you say Snake River Canyon was again?"?)

"When we're really galvanized is when we're told we can't win," GM

David Griffin noted in January when he dismissed David Blatt. "We respond really well to a measure of chaos, and I think, to a huge degree, our circumstances always created that."

Going down to the Warriors 3-1 was when the Cavaliers "hit bottom" in recovery parlance. Any excuses from that point forward were meaningless; there's no *close* in professional sports, just the black and white of winning and losing. The Cavaliers felt all season that *they* weren't given the credit they deserved, their conference diminished and overlooked. Now was their chance to prove people wrong, winning's sweetest side dish.

"We didn't have appropriate fear most of the year, and what I saw when we were down 3-1 was guys understood, okay, I get what it takes now," Griffin told Adrian Wojnarowski after the season. "We aren't going to be able to give less than our best and get away with it. Guys rallied around Ty in way guys probably don't if it happens another way…. They were not fearful. What they were was very disappointed they had put themselves in that position."

The NBA informed the Warriors that Draymond Green would be suspended for Game 6 after being assessed a Flagrant One for twice swinging in the direction of LeBron James' groin late in Game 4.

Former player and analyst Charles Barkley said Green was right to behave that way. "When a guy steps over you, you have a moral obligation to punch him in the balls," he said. "Because that's really disrespectful to step over a guy."

NBA Executive VP of Basketball Operations Kiki Vandeweghe found Green guilty of "unnecessary contact with a retaliatory swipe of his hand to the groin," earning a Flagrant One and his fourth total point, mandating a suspension. "While Draymond Green's actions in Game 4 do not merit a suspension as a standalone act," he said, "the number of flagrant points he has earned triggers a suspension."

This wasn't Green's first offense. Or second. Or really even third. Perhaps emboldened by the deference refs offered Golden State during their run, Green graduated from thug to menace. "He plays physical, chippy," confessed teammate Andrew Bogut. "And he's a talker."

It went beyond his big mouth and overly physical screens. In the last seconds of their April 1 loss to the Celtics, Green not only straddled his way over fallen Celtic Evan Turner, preventing him from getting back into the play, but then took Marcus Smart on his shoulder and threw him down, like a halfback picking up the blitz. No call.

At the end of Game 3's first round loss to the Rockets, Green attempted to throw Michael Beasley to the ground over his leg in a quasi-suplex takedown. Nothing was called until afterward when Green picked up a flagrant foul, earning his first point.

Early in Game 2 against the Thunder, Green kneed Steve Adams in the junk without sanction, leaving Adams (who had bragged in the past about his personal endowment) bent over, grimacing in pain. Green reoffended later, leaping in the air and flailing his foot into Adams' groin, a *noticeable* awkward second after losing the ball, making it harder to dismiss bad intent. Not the second time of the game.

Little-used Cleveland reserve Dahntay Jones popped Bismack Biyombo's package during garbage time and received a Flagrant One *and* a one-game suspension. While Adams' last kick earned a Flagrant Two, the league didn't suspend Green. Perhaps it was sensitive to the television ratings for a Finals rematch involving the league's most marketable team versus a series taking place in Oklahoma.

Green's suspension seemed inevitable after he had received the league's benefit of a doubt twice over—especially given how the retributive shot at James established a malevolent pattern (as if Internet sleuths never created lengthy YouTube collages of Green smashing jewels with questionable intent).

It didn't hurt that Lue made enough of a big deal about James not getting calls in his Game 4 postgame comments to receive a $25,000 fine from the league. As noted earlier, this was a chronic James problem that had reappeared during the Finals. In four games he'd earned 17 free throws compared to 56 through five games the year before.

The NBA didn't hold LeBron harmless. He was retroactively assessed a technical foul for a "physical taunt," amusing given the escalating nature of the series' ensuing off-the-court storm of nonphysical taunts.

James didn't seem entirely aware of Green's swat at his balls in postgame comments but took mighty exception to the words exchanged a moment later. According to ESPN, Green called James "a bitch," prompting LeBron to explain he was a husband and father of three, earning the Green rejoinder, "You're still a bitch." (Barkley said James had a right to sock Green in the mouth for that. Is Chuck on promoter Don King's retainer?)

Beefing about trash talk is one of the lowest forms of pregame media grandstanding, but it quickly escalated to a fevered pitch. Klay Thompson felt LeBron doth protest too much. "I guess his feelings just got hurt," he teased, half chuckling. "I'm just kind of shocked some guys take it so personal. It's like, it's a man's league."

"If it's a man's game, shut up about the [Mozgov] screen," Jefferson told Yahoo Sports' The Vertical. "Or don't say anything about LeBron. Klay, he's like my little brother., but we can't contradict ourselves."

Golden State's Marreese Speights, whose ass lacquered the pine nearly all series, got into the action the only way he could—with his mouth. "I had a lot of respect for LeBron over his career, since he was in high school. But do things like that to get a guy suspended? That's kind of disrespectful," said Speights, who tweeted an emoji of a baby bottle. "It's messed up to suspend a man over nothing. If somebody put their balls on your head, what are you supposed to do?"

James didn't rise to their innuendo, taking "the high road." He knew how to deliver a message they couldn't mistake. It amused him that playing for history with his legacy on the line, reporters believed he could need extra motivation, were he even plugged into social media to hear their disrespect.

"You guys make me laugh. I swear you guys do," said James after the game. "My only motivation is how can I be there for my teammates and my coaching staff. That's it. I mean, at the end of the day, nothing else matters."

Though the odds gave a Cavaliers comeback less than a four percent chance, there was one statistical anomaly always in Cleveland's favor. Six of the last seven times the NBA Finals has featured a rematch, the prior year's loser got their vengeance. (The Bulls are the exception, beating the Jazz in 1997 and 1998.) Sometimes knowing the pain of failure is all the motivation you need.

NBA Finals, Game 5. Monday, June 13, 2016, Oakland. (3-1 GSW)

From the opening tip you could read it in James' *Terminator* visage—steely, stern, stoic, and undeterred. As emotional as James is, it's when he internalizes rather than broadcasts it that he's most dangerous. For Game 5 his emotion was as dense and hot as a neutron star, and similarly, its radiation was the sole visible measure.

Certainly after five championships, Steve Kerr knew what to expect even if he couldn't perhaps convey the proper urgency to his team.

"Game 5 will be the hardest game of the series. Every closeout game is difficult, but when you're at home, for a strange reason it's even more difficult," said Kerr. "We have to understand that this series is not over. We came in and did what we wanted to do, getting the split, but Game 5 will be extremely difficult."

Iguodala started with Green out, offering Love a perfect situation to step back into the starting lineup against a smaller, less physical player.

If the Cavs intended to win this series, they didn't start like it. On the first possession of the game James posted Iguodala, who poked the ball out of LeBron's left hand and raced upcourt for a layup. A James drive-and-dish found Irving standing at the boundary as wide open as Kansas for three.

When Curry hit an answering three in transition, Irving pushed the pace off the made basket but lost it off his knee while finishing in traffic. Smith followed with an offensive foul and Bogut blocked consecutive layup attempts by Love and James. The latter produced an Iguodala layup the other way thanks to a Klay Thompson drop-off feed. With three and a half gone, the Warriors led 9-3 and Lue called a timeout.

The two teams traded 7-2 runs as several themes emerged. On one end, Iguodala received the ball just above the break and James remained several feet away goading him into an airball three. A moment later Irving put Bogut in the pick-and-roll, drawing him away from the basket and then beating him baseline for a picturesque reverse layup.

James followed the next possession by hitting a "dare three" when Iggy likewise hung back several feet. During the first four games Golden State's challenge had been a good strategy as LeBron shot 5-of-16 from the arc. Now with the cup on the line, James was about to give them some long nights of regret.

J. R. Smith faked a dribble hand-off to James, catching the Warriors overplaying and finishing hard, drawing the and-one on Bogut. The Warriors' overplays were giving Smith more opportunities at the rim, and he decided to start taking them.

"I just try to be aggressive. Not only at the three-point line, but when they close out, they close out hard and fast. I've just got to make the best adjustment, whether it's shooting the three or driving in and getting a layup or kicking it to somebody else," said Smith. "RJ's been talking to me a lot at practices and stuff and telling me how they guard me. So I just took heed of it."

Curry used an escape dribble to befuddle Smith and get open for a three, then Iguodala sank a couple free throws and a putback dunk for his eighth point. It pushed the Warriors' lead to 19-13 with under six to go. The Cavs marched right back. J. R. paired a transition finish into traffic with a catch-and-shoot corner three off Kyrie's baseline penetration.

James followed Iguodala's third missed three of the quarter with a straightaway pull-up three when Iggy went under Tristan's screen. That evened things at 22 with four minutes remaining. Both teams closed the quarter sloppy. The Cavaliers committed four more turnovers, giving them eight in the quarter, while Golden State made a couple turnovers and Varejao missed two free throws, earned with a flop, as the Warriors took a 32-29 lead into the second.

"There wasn't much contact, but Andy, he's a smart veteran, he got them extra possessions and that's part of why he's so valuable," said Matthew Dellavedova. "You love it when he's on your team and you hate it when you're going against him, but he plays hard 100 percent of the time."

The Cavs hit their first four shots of the quarter, going on a 9-2 run to take a 38-34 lead. Jefferson dunked a nice Smith drop-off feed on yet another drive, and then Jefferson made a pretty spin at the hole to get to the left side of the rim for the layup. Irving took the scoring yoke with James on the bench, sinking a transition three and a pull-up 20-foot jumper from the left wing over Livingston.

Klay Thompson did his best to answer Irving, scoring 13 of Golden State's next 15 points as both teams went to extremely small lineups featuring five wings with Iggy and James as the putative centers. The Warriors had Klay screen for Livingston, who took advantage of a miscommunication to get all the way to the rack for the flush, as the Cavaliers reprised their Game 4 issues with "small" screens.

Thompson got a three off the same such screen, where two players pass in opposite directions like football crossing patterns. The Cavs doubled Curry, who found Klay before James could get there on the help rotation for his third three-pointer of the night. A moment later he hit one from several feet beyond the line when Irving didn't stay close enough. Ninety seconds later Klay received a screen from Festus Ezeli just over halfcourt, putting Thompson on Thompson. It wasn't much of a contest as Klay sank the heat-check three from maybe three feet in front of the emblem, his fifth three and 23rd point of the half.

"Klay hit some amazing shots in that first half. Steph got going a little bit, too. It's tough to gameplan when a guy has the ability to catch and shoot from 30 feet out," said Jefferson. "I've played with both the guys. They're two of probably the top three shooters in the history of the game."

No sooner had Klay sank that ridiculous three than Shumpert took a Tristan Thompson pick-and-roll to the rack, trimming the Warriors' lead to 49-48 with under five and a half minutes to go. Cleveland matched Klay's sunburst with their own isolation heavy (one assist on seven buckets) combo of hard finishes and Irving's midrange game. Kyrie had made 7-of-9 so far, all but two of them jumpers. Cleveland pounded that small Warriors lineup on the boards, grabbing five offensive to Golden State's four defensive rebounds.

"You've got to be the first one to the 50-50 balls if you're going to play small," said Smith. "We did a better job of that.... But it's got to be a focus for us. Offensive rebounds, limiting second-chance points."

With less than three to go, Iguodala grabbed a missed Speights tip and kicked it out to the right arc where Thompson stuck the wing three, his sixth of the half for 26 points. Barnes and Curry followed with threes of their own.

Like *Walking Tall*'s Buford T. Pusser, James answered with force. Speights gave James too much room so he hit a left-wing jumper. Then James caught Iguodala going under Tristan's screen and beat him to the right of the rim for two. On the next possession LeBron beat Speights to the left of the rim for the stuff and-one, tying the score at 61, which was how the half ended.

"The first quarter they came out aggressive and they hit shots. We allowed them to get where they wanted to and we gave them clean looks. We can't give those guys clean looks," said James Jones. "In the second quarter we still had some mistakes, but later on in the third and fourth quarter we were a little more diligent with our focus on those two things."

While everyone hammered the Cavaliers' one-on-one game, it's hard to argue with results. The Cavs were 25-of-46 (54 percent) from the field and a respectable 5-of-14 (36 percent) from three. They'd committed 11 turnovers, but so had the Warriors. Cleveland's big issue—outside of Klay

Thompson—was the Warriors' overall three-point shooting (11-of-21, 52 percent).

LeBron nearly matched Klay in the first half with 25 points on very efficient 10-of-18 shooting, and also contributed four offensive boards. Irving had 18 points and four of the team's almost embarrassing six assists. But as Lue explained all series, when the other team switches everything, it's often easier and more effective to beat the mismatches, particularly if your team possesses two of the league's best penetrators.

The second half got off to a quick start with a trio of three-point plays. The Cavs put Bogut back in the high pick-and-roll with Irving, who caught it out above the free throw line and went around him like a turnstile to finish the and-one. Curry came off two baseline screens to sink the three despite Irving's contest; then James hit his third three, after Irving cleared a failed penetration to LeBron at the top of the arc, making it 67-64.

On the Cavaliers' next possession Smith drove again to the hole but Bogut blocked his shot, his third of the game. When Smith came down he fell into the 7-footer's left leg, causing a knee injury that while not serious enough to need surgery would force Bogut to miss the rest of the playoffs.

In his absence Kerr tried a super-small lineup featuring Livingston, Thompson, Curry, Iggy, and either Barnes or McAdoo at center. They got to the line nine times, making seven, but shot only 2-of-12 from the field (0-of-5 from three) over the next six minutes as the Cavs went on an 18-11 run. The Warriors were still getting open shots, but weren't knocking them down like in the first half.

"We tried to open things up and play a little different lineup," Kerr told ABC's Doris Burke between quarters. "[We] missed some shots that would've helped us big-time, but our defense just hasn't been very good tonight."

The Cavs made 7-of-11 from the field including 4-of-5 at the rim, absent shot-blocking. First Love found James going backdoor for the baseline slam followed by a wide-open Irving transition three. Golden State strung together a Klay Thompson backdoor layup on Kyrie with a couple beneficial calls, including a mystery out of bounds call and questionable late whistle on a Klay missed three, J. R.'s fourth foul.

James floated a perfect alley-oop to Tristan over two Warrior defenders. Though he couldn't convert the shot, Thompson split the free throws, giving the Cavs a 75-71 lead. James pushed a missed Klay Thompson three, taking it coast to coast. James pushed it again, this time after a Livingston 15-foot, left-baseline pull-up, allowing Irving to sink his second transition three of the quarter as the unchecked trailer, making it 80-73 with less than six remaining in the third.

"Our defensive communication was lacking. We had some plays where we didn't pick up in transition, and we had some cross-matches that we didn't identify and they got free, especially Kyrie, and made a lot of shots in transition where we just weren't there," Kerr said.

After two Curry free throws, James fed Tristan rolling down the center of the lane on the pick-and-roll, where he caught the oop, head-faked, and finished for his first bucket of the game. Curry made a bad entry pass into the lane, which Jefferson grabbed and fed James again for another transition opportunity. He drew a second foul on Klay and split the freebies.

On the other end, Shumpert blocked Iguodala's drive and James pushed it, ultimately finding Jefferson, who beat Livingston off the bounce and finished amidst a lot of uncalled contact that made it 85-75, Cleveland's first double-digit margin with four and a quarter remaining, and they'd take a 93-84 lead into the fourth.

"We tried to adjust on the fly with the different matchups, but we just didn't execute as well," Curry said. "There were a couple switches that we were very lazy on, and when guys get hot like that, if you don't kind of shore up your defense, especially in pivotal moments where you have momentum and can get one or two stops away from either taking the lead or finishing quarters out strong."

After Klay made six first half threes, the Cavaliers worked harder to run him off the arc. Thompson missed his only three long-range attempts in the third and wouldn't take another. After 26 points in the first half, Klay attempted just eight shots and finished with 11 second half points.

"We don't call a ton of plays or sets; we want to play out of motion and get the ball moving," explained Kerr. "And they were doing a good job denying him."

Curry couldn't fill the void, going just 1-of-5, all from three, in the third and making his only three of the fourth in the opening seconds after Shumpert lost his balance coming around a Varejao pick. That left Love dry roasting on Curry Island when Steph stuck a left-wing three. That was Golden State's only three of the quarter against nine misses.

"We had some that were rushed," Kerr said. "I thought there might have been a couple times in the game where Steph got into a little bit of a hurry. But for the most part, lot of good looks. Sometimes they don't go down and that's the way it goes. You've got to make up for it in other areas, with defense and rebounding."

James began the quarter on the bench, and got an extra break when Smith fouled Wild Thing on a drive. The ensuing flop made it look worse than it was (not to mention Varejao writhing on the floor), eliciting a flagrant foul review, affording James another extra couple minutes of rest.

LeBron immediately made a free throw line jumper in front of a retreating Varejao on the pick-and-roll. It was one of two shots he'd hit in the quarter, as he shot 2-of-7 and scored five points. Coming into the quarter James was 14-of-23 for 36 points.

As LeBron slowed down in the fourth, Kyrie stepped it up a notch. He was already 12-of-15 with 29 points and five assists before adding another 12 points on 5-of-9 shooting in the last frame. Up seven, Kyrie drove baseline where Harrison and Thompson tried to trap him, but Curry was ball-watching while Shumpert dove to the rim, receiving Irving's bounce pass for the slam.

Curry answered, leaving both Irving and Love next to Varejao on a high pick-and-roll and quickly accelerating down the lane, where James blocked his shot (third of the night). However, LeBron's momentum carried him out of bounds. Steph grabbed the loose ball and put it off the glass, cutting the deficit to 99-92. The Warriors had a chance to cut it to five with Iggy pushing in transition, but Livingston mishandled his pass out of bounds with seven and a half remaining.

Kyrie would score 10 points in the next two minutes, nearly matching the Warrior scoring total for the quarter (13). He took Klay to the left baseline and spun back to the middle for a short fallaway bank shot and-one. Klay and Steph would answer with short jumpers to pull within 102-96, but Irving was simply too much.

Kyrie put Curry in ISO and beat him from the left arc, elevating at the left block for the driving bank shot. Klay was next in line for dry cleaning. Kyrie took him from the top of the key to toward the left block before spinning right, back toward the elbow, where he rattled home the 14-foot fallaway. Curry missed a step-back and Irving ran it back, stopping on the right wing for a transition three, making it 109-93. The Cavs prevailed 112-97.

James assumed the point guard role much of the evening, running the offense in the middle of the court (complicating attempts to take the ball out of his hands). Irving played more off the ball, attacking the basket from the wing. James responded with seven assists and just two turnovers to go with his 41 points, 16 rebounds, three blocks, and three steals. He hit eight shots outside the paint included four three-pointers, a number he reached or exceeded just six times in the regular season and playoffs. James had saved his best for last.

"Coach Lue said he wanted the ball in my hands a little bit more. I finally did a great job of not turning the ball over and got to my spots, got my teammates involved. Just tried to put us in position to be successful," James said. "That's something I'm very comfortable with, and I've been comfortable with before in the past. Coach wanted to make that adjustment, and I was able to take advantage of it when I had the ball in my hands."

Kyrie also had 41 points and six assists, making them the first teammates to score 40 points in the same Finals game. Irving shot 17-of-24, joining Wilt Chamberlain as the only players in NBA history to score 40+ and shoot over 70 percent. He also became the first James teammate to score 30 in three consecutive games. Irving did so as an attacker, something the media had criticized, noting that Irving was 13-of-39 on possessions where he didn't pass; in Game 5 he was 10-of-15.

"Our spacing was pretty good tonight in terms of where guys were positioning and our weakside action, which I've been talking about almost this whole series waiting for it to happen, and it happened," Irving said, casually ignoring the role of Green's absence. "Guys were in the spots, and it opened and allowed myself and LeBron to see a lot of driving lanes. But also, if we saw guys coming over to help, we were ready to spread out to our teammates."

Lue had no problem acknowledging the (absent) elephant in the room. "[Draymond] is their best defender. I've said it all along that he is the best guy in the NBA as far as reading when to help, triple switches, and kicking guys [!!] out of mismatches, knowing when to go, when not to go. He's an underrated shot-blocker, and he can guard 1 through 5, so that definitely help hurt their defense," Lue said. "But I'm just proud of the way our guys played tonight and competed."

Like Lue after Game 4, Kerr was muted and succinct. "We weren't very good defensively. We obviously knew we were without Draymond, so there's no point in harping on that. We had to play better, and we didn't. [James and Irving] played terrific games."

He noted that they had missed a lot of shots they might normally hit. Indeed, they were 16-of-43 on uncontested shots (21 percent) and 4-of-19 on wide-open threes. Still, Kerr had a positive outlook in the end.

"We made so many mistakes. We were poor in so many areas, and yet with five minutes left it's a six-point game," said Kerr. "We're in the same place we were last year, up 3-2 heading back to Cleveland. If you told me this before the series, I would have taken it.... We're disappointed we didn't win tonight but like I said, they outplayed us."

The Cavaliers had done the improbable, beating the Warriors at home, where during the season and playoffs they were 50-3. They set the NBA record during the regular season for the longest home winning streak (54). They just needed to do it one more time. No sweat.

In winning, the Cavs shifted the pressure onto the shoulders of the Warriors, who would be equally hard-pressed to eliminate the Cavaliers on their home court for the second year in a row. But the Cavs clearly understood they still had work ahead of them.

"We can't change anything. We have to continue to play with desperation to exhaustion," said Smith. "We can't get too ahead of ourselves. We have to be humble, play our game, and see what happens."

19

A KING DEMANDS HIS DUE

STEVE KERR IMPLIED there was déjà vu in Golden State's return to Cleveland for Game 6 up 3-2. Yet other than those superficial similarities, it was a very different series. Dramatically so for the Warriors. Now Cleveland had momentum after a convincing 112-97 Game 5 victory in Golden State.

They'd gone home riding high, having avenged a 30-point blowout with a Game 4 victory in Cleveland, feeling the crown was all but theirs. That sentiment wavered when Draymond Green's suspension was announced, but the Warriors were still confident. After watching Irving and James go through their defense like a neutrino in Game 5, the Warriors finally had "appropriate fear." Like in a horror film, this knowledge came too late, and left Golden State feeling blindsided and victimized.

"In my mind the series was over coming home 3-1. We feel good about ourselves, we have momentum. But then the league goes [and suspends Green]," said Warriors assistant coach Ron Adams. "Now you're back to square one a little bit. It's this truncation of something you felt good about. So then it starts going again."

Adams implied that the press pressured the league into acting on Green. He lamented that itinerate circus barkers could have so much influence on what happens between the lines.

"The narratives are driven by the press and the league this series. The league can screw you over and the press can get the narrative going in a wrong way that affects your team negatively," Adams said. "LeBron gets away with murder in the league. He's an instigator. He's a fantastic player—don't get me wrong—but to let this happen? Probably reasons for it, but to me it's mindboggling."

Obviously Green's absence made a dramatic difference in Golden State's defense. This is no surprise. He had the team's best on/off-court numbers during the season. He led the Warriors throughout the regular season and playoffs in rebounds (9.5 per game) and assists (7.4) while being the team's third-leading scorer.

However, after Green's 28-point outburst in Game 2 the Cavaliers had put James on him, dramatically diminishing his offensive impact. In Games 3 and 4 he was a combined 4-of-17 from the field and 0-of-8 on the threes they were daring him to take.

Draymond didn't have any physical advantage on James, and because putting James on Curry or Thompson didn't provide an advantage, they stopped using Green in the screens. It was part of why they started screening with "smalls," combined with the fact that Draymond couldn't even take advantage of Kyrie on the switch.

"I think by putting [LeBron] on Draymond, it's really ignited him as far as defensively," Lue said. "Offensively he's just been taking his shots in rhythm and taking what the defense gives him. He's been playing at a very high level, but I don't know what got him started with that."

The Love injury also played a role, showing the Cavaliers how much smaller and quicker they could be using Jefferson on the floor without sacrificing rebounding or size. He was able to get his own shot off the bounce, which was important given how few scoring options the Cavaliers had outside Kyrie and LeBron. He also could switch any pick-and-roll and hold his own thanks to his length. Love just wasn't quick enough afoot to handle backcourt players, which is why opponents continually put him in their pick-and-rolls.

Cleveland's ability to switch screens with Jefferson and their success trapping Curry in the high pick-and-roll put the Warriors into more one-on-one situations. None of their players were as good creating for themselves as for each other. The Cavs realized the best way to stop Strength in Numbers was by dividing the fibers.

The long time between games might've worked against the Warriors' complex schemes in a way it didn't against the Cavaliers' simpler, talent-driven, meat-and-potato, pick-and-roll-centric Kyrie/LeBron attack.

"We just have to kill so much time," explained Kerr. "Two days between every game. So you watch a lot of film."

So much so that you know your opponent's game inside out. The Cavaliers heavily overplayed Curry's right hand, practically forcing him left whenever behind the arc. A stray J. R. Smith comment made clear why (and how much film they must have watched).

"We know he likes to do the left-to-right crossover [to set up] for three-point shots, so we try to key on that," said Smith. "Then when we've got our bigs on, just crowd the three-point line and try to make him finish over them."

Naturally a mad genius like LeBron takes advantage: "I start to learn from my mistakes and break into the film and seeing the ways that they're defending me, the ways they're defending our team, ways I can be a little more efficient," James said, explaining his more efficient play. "Just digging in a little bit more and more into the film and also just being a little bit more conscious about how I can be successful for our team."

Yet at the same time, it's possible the media gives too much weight and focus to these in-game adjustments since they provide prime post-facto fodder for their columns. Both teams clearly adjusted to what each other was doing, but their ability to stop it was dependent on effort. While everyone talked about following the gameplan, the vigor and attentiveness with which they did it varied from team to team and game to game.

"I don't think this series has had a whole lot of adjustments one way or another. It's about doing what you set out to do, well. So, the team that has been the most aggressive has basically come out on top each game," offered Adams. "I think when we've gotten in trouble we've let down in some of the areas of aggression and, well, they probably feel the same…. Our offense has been very erratic and it's partly about their aggressiveness. Give them credit."

Beyond Draymond's return, there was the matter of Bogut's replacement. While the onetime first overall pick wasn't anything close to a defining player for the Warriors, he did a number of things they would have difficulty replacing in one player. Though he was only playing 12-14 minutes a game, those were important minutes.

He was the Warriors' best screener and a terrific passer for a 7-footer. Most of all he was rim protection. In the first five games of the series Bogut averaged two blocks a game despite averaging just 12 minutes. Though

Festus Ezeli could provide the length and physicality, he had nowhere close to the offensive guile or ability. Bogut was mostly rest for the Warriors' small lineups. Those lineups were +14 pCp while the Bogut-led starting lineup was -20 pCp. But part of their success was as a curveball. If a pitcher gets by on a steady diet of curveballs, eventually batters will start thwacking them out of the park.

"When we do go smaller, we generally do it in short bursts to change the pace up and change the look, and that can vary from game to game, from series to series," Kerr said. "But, yeah, it's not easy to play small for huge chunks of the game."

But with Bogut out, it seemed like Kerr had no choice. Lue at least had choices about what to do with Kevin Love. He'd volunteered to come off the bench in Game 4, and presumably would understand moving back. Speaking on the off-day, he acknowledged that the way the Warriors played often limited him to the role of decoy and spacer on offense.

"The Warriors are one of the only teams, if not the only team, that kind of plays like that, and when Bogut went down, I think our primary option was for those guys to play downhill and attack the paint and the rim," Love said. "So for me, yeah, it was just kind of—I know it's funny to say, but run in the corner, let those guys do their thing, and on the defensive end try to apply myself as much as I could."

Love was better in Game 5, though his contributions weren't the type to show up in the boxscore. In 32 minutes he was 1-of-5 for two points, with three boards, one assist, and two turnovers. But he did a nice job challenging Curry on the couple occasions he switched onto him and in general competed hard, especially on defense. Indeed, he had the second highest +/- on the team (+18) behind Irving (+20).

While a lot of comments were made in the media about the Cavaliers' lack of ball movement and passing through the regular season and postseason—some of it valid—the situation in Golden State was sort of unique, as Love noted. Their manner of play—particularly the switching—left teams no better choice.

"Golden State is one of the best teams out there—they'll eliminate the trigger and force you to be static," said James Jones, explaining that Golden State would stalemate the read-react offense, forcing individual, ISO actions. "We did a better job of moving and in transition [to counter].

We got movement, guys were catching and attacking. J. R. was attacking. Shump was cutting and got hit for a dunk. Kyrie was triggering on the baseline swinging the ball."

NBA Finals, Game 6. Thursday, June 16, 2016, Cleveland. (3-2 GSW)

One Game 5 theme that carried over to Game 6 was LeBron putting Curry in the pick-and-roll, posting him up and generally making him work. Not that this was unusual.

"Oh, sure, sure…that's something that most teams try to do," Kerr said. "It makes perfect sense. The guy's that good of a shooter and that good of a player. Yeah, you make him work hard at the other end to try to wear him down."

A sports meme that began in January continued through the first couple games of the series noting that James was 0-of-11 when guarded one-on-one by Steph Curry. ESPN writer Ethan Strauss tweeted before Game 6: "Bizarre subplot of LeBron struggling when guarded by Curry has extended into these Finals. I keep expecting it to stop."

He wouldn't have to wait; it was Cleveland's gameplan. "We don't want him to just sit there and rest on the defensive end while he gets his legs coming down on the offensive end," said Smith. "We're trying to make him work on both sides as much as possible."

Jefferson alluded to the injured knee as another reason to make Curry work as hard as possible on the other end.

"I don't think it's any secret, Steph's a little banged up," he said. "Steph will take the challenge defensively, but there are things that are very, very difficult. You look at the last series, he guarded [Andre] Roberson a ton, and it put Roberson in a position where he had to make some plays. But against our team, there's no one who's just going to be standing in the corner not doing anything."

The Warriors did not get off to a strong start in Game 6, going over five minutes before their first score. They missed their first seven shots and made two turnovers. Irving got the first Cleveland bucket when he isolated Curry on the right wing, turned the baseline corner on him, and sank the 13-foot pull-up. Love went to the bench with two fouls 90 seconds in, bringing on Jefferson.

A minute later James knocked away Klay's dribble and started upcourt while RJ grabbed the ball and threw it to LeBron, ahead of the pack, for the two-hand slam. That made it 6-0 with nine remaining and prompted a Warriors timeout. A couple possessions later James isolated Curry on the right wing. As LeBron drove, Tristan grabbed Iguodala's arm, preventing him from providing help while James laid it in.

"We had some good shots early that didn't go in, and it was like 6-0 after about four minutes. Our defense was pretty good. They had a couple run-outs where they got layups, but our halfcourt defense was good," Kerr said. "We just could not get a shot to fall, and then they just blitzed us."

Green split Tristan and LeBron after a physical screen from Curry, opening a four-lane highway through the lane for the Warriors' first points. Irving answered from long distance when (after going 5-of-7 from three in the last game) Klay inexplicably went under J. R.'s screen and Curry followed Smith. Barnes tried to post up Kyrie on defense, but Irving knocked away the ball and turned it into a fastbreak. As he came down the middle of the lane the transition defenders collapsed, leaving LeBron uncovered cutting baseline for the jam and the 13-2 lead as the crowd erupted.

Curry hit a catch-and-shoot three, and on the other end Smith brought Curry to James via a left-wing screen. As LeBron brushed against Steph on his way baseline, Curry flopped and caught the blocking foul, his second of the quarter. In came Livingston and Ezeli, putting the small lineup on the shelf midway through the first. The Warriors doubled James on the right block, but he found Smith unattended on the left wing for the Cavs' second three of the quarter.

"He knows where everybody is on the floor. I was supposed to be in the corner, and he let me know that looking at the film. But he found me," said Smith. "He's probably the best passer I've ever played with as far as vision. Being that big, strong, and fast, and to be able to see the court the way he does, it's remarkable."

It just kept coming. Jefferson had his foot on the line in the left corner for a transition two after a wayward Iggy three. Irving took a crossover 17-foot elbow pull-up, grabbed his own miss, stepped behind a Tristan screen, and sank the 18-foot baseline jumper. That made it 20-7 with four minutes left.

"We got off to a terrible start—not getting stops—and we started the game with way too many jump shots. We put no pressure on their defense," said Green. "When you dig yourself in a hole like that, especially on the road, it's tough to come back against a good team."

Tristan Thompson had already grabbed seven rebounds at that point, all but one defensive, but on offense Golden State wasn't covering him above the free throw line extended. So when Irving went baseline and the Warriors doubled, Tristan cut through the lane, caught the pass, and was met by Ezeli for the foul.

After going 4-of-15 from the line the past two games, Tristan redeemed both freebies. Then after rebounding an errant Steph three, James rewarded Double-T for beating Ezeli down the floor, feeding him for a slam. Then LeBron plied a Tristan screen to beat Green through the lane and to the rim for the left-handed layup and a 26-9 lead.

"Double-T's energy and activity, his level, his rebounding, obviously giving us extra possessions, but his defensive rebounding from the beginning was at an all-time high level for himself," James said. "Even as great as he is, he was spectacular tonight."

By quarter's end the Cavaliers led 31-11, even bettering the fourth quarter of Game 5 when Cleveland held the Warriors to 13 points. It was the Warriors' lowest-scoring quarter of the season. "Everything needs to change," Kerr told ESPN/TNT sideline reporter Craig Sager. "We struggled at both ends, and obviously this crowd is hyped up."

Mo Williams made an appearance in the first and hit a floater, playing ahead of Dellavedova whose ankle was still hurting, or else he just didn't have it in the series (5-of-19 field goal, 1-of-6 from three). Meanwhile, Iguodala did a disappearing act after the first, retreating to the locker room after tweaking his back battling Tristan's (sometimes illegal) screens.

"Thompson's been the key guy in this series," said a frustrated Adams. "They've allowed him to foul on almost every screen. Break the screen down, and they've allowed him on any Steph Curry drive when he's on him, to do this [makes arm bar]. He was pushing from behind in the last game. I'm watching this saying how can this be? If Draymond Green did that? Automatic fouls."

Shumpert allowed a pair of Curry threes by trying to sell contact on screens rather than fighting through them, and Love picked up his third foul on a ticky-tack call on a Draymond drive. But Irving kept the Cavs going while James sat, scoring seven points during the first three minutes of the second. Meanwhile, the Warriors feasted at the charity stripe, with five free throws accounting for all their scoring outside the Curry threes.

With seven minutes left James came back in and hit his first jump shot of the night, taking a rhythm dribble before sticking a three over Iguodala, who on the prior possession hit *his* first three of the night. Over the next couple minutes the Warriors made a 9-0 run, all three of the buckets in transition as the Cavaliers missed four shots in a row and had two offensive fouls. A Green layup cut the lead to 46-38 with four and a half to go, leading Lue to call a timeout.

"They're going to make some runs. That's just who they are. They've always been that way. But it's our job to try to minimize those runs," Lue said. "The guys did a great job coming out of the timeout. Just being focused, regaining our focus, and then coming out and increasing the lead again to 16, 17 points. So, the guys hung with it. They didn't drop their heads. We know they're going to make runs and we were able to sustain it tonight."

The Cavs answered with an 8-0 run featuring four Kyrie free throws (including Curry's third foul), a Tristan transition alley-oop on a James pass from beyond the arc, and a LeBron transition layup after leaving Iggy behind like an unmatched glove with a free throw line crossover dribble. That made it 54-38 with two and a half remaining.

When Jefferson was called for his third foul, Lue came back with Dahntay Jones, a 13-year veteran wing who had signed on the last day of the season for the prorated veteran's minimum, roughly $8,800. (He was obviously eligible for a playoff share.) The several early-round playoff blowouts afforded him over 40 minutes of time in 14 games. Yet until then his most consequential play was the nutshot on Bismack Biyombo that came with a one-game suspension.

Dahntay was immediately memorable in his couple Game 6 minutes, blocking a Klay Thompson shot. Then after the Warriors had pulled to 54-43 on more free throws and Klay's transition 11-foot pull-up, Dahntay staged his own 5-0 run.

Green stayed beneath the basket as Jones ran along baseline to the weakside, then cut to the middle of the lane unguarded, caught James' pass, and finished the and-one over Green. On the other end, Jones boxed out Green on a missed Curry three, but Draymond came over his back for his third foul. Dahntay cashed the freebies, giving Cleveland a 59-43 halftime lead.

"A lot of guys had gotten in foul trouble. RJ had three, Kevin had three, Shump had three. So our next big body that can bring a physicality to the game and a defensive presence was Dahntay. That's a long-time friend of mine and it just felt good to see him get in in such a crucial part of the game," Lue said. "To come in and contribute the way he did, scoring five points in two minutes and just being aggressive defensively, rebounding the basketball, boxing Draymond out, I thought it was fantastic."

The Cavaliers held Golden State below 30 percent shooting and just 5-of-21 (24 percent) from three. Cleveland shot 56 percent with 13 assists on their 20 baskets, and had an advantage at the line (15-of-19 vs. 12-of-13). Curry had 18 points, and none of his teammates had more than seven. Barnes and Livingston were a combined 0-of-11.

Irving led the Cavs with 20 points while James added 14 points and six assists, and Tristan Thompson put up a first half double-double with 11 points and 10 boards. They also built a 13-5 edge on fastbreak points to go with a 22-14 advantage in points in the paint.

The Cavaliers got off to a ragged start offensively, but beat the Warriors on the boards for six straight second-chance points. Tristan grabbed the carom from an Irving step-back. When Klay ball-watched a moment, James cut to the middle of the lane, took a short pitch from Double-T, and elevated for a ferocious flush to the roar of the crowd.

LeBron threw a long outlet off a Harrison Barnes missed three, but Irving missed the driving shot due to a physical contest from Green. Love slid into the scrum for the offensive board and drew a foul on his attempted tap-in, Curry's fourth foul. Barnes missed another three, but blocked Love's ensuing transition layup. LeBron scooped up the loose ball on the wing going right and threw back across his body and the court with one arm to just above the left break, where J. R. dropped the three. It was James' seventh assist and a terrific example of his casual brilliance.

After playing just three minutes in the first half, Love got to the line for a pair. Iguodala took a hard foul from Tristan Thompson on a drive to the basket, wincing noticeably, and missed both free throws. On the following possession Kyrie worked a high pick-and-roll with Tristan, who caught his pass in the middle of the lane. Rather than go up, he swung it to the corner where Love hit the three with under two seconds on the shot clock. That gave Cleveland its largest lead of the game, 70-46, with eight minutes remaining.

"[Kevin] got two early fouls and could never get in a rhythm," Lue said. "He made a big three for us, some good switches and some post-ups that he was aggressive on, got fouled. But he could never quite find his rhythm after he got those two early fouls."

The Warriors weren't going to go out quietly. They put together 9-0 and 10-0 runs to close the gap to 80-71 at the end of the third. The only thing staving off heart-choking oblivion was LeBron James. He scored eight of the Cavaliers points during Golden State's 25-10 run the last eight minutes of the fourth as they made 10 of 12 shots. Klay Thompson had 15 of points on 6-of-7 shooting.

"I thought we slowed down, stopped pushing the basketball, and they made some big shots," Lue told Sager between quarters. "Klay hit some shots. We were up in him but we have to get even closer."

When Draymond failed to get the steal on an inbounds pass to LeBron, it put him out of position, and James drove into the lane where Leandro Barbosa took him. LeBron turned and shot over the 6-foot-3 Brazilian guard. That made it 84-71 Cavaliers and was their first bucket in almost five minutes. During that stretch the Cavs missed six shots, five of them threes.

"With our season on the line at the end of the third quarter he said, 'I'm not coming out.' I didn't have any intention of taking him out," Lue reported. "I don't care what y'all say. We're going to ride him."

James stole a Varejao pass under Cleveland's basket and took it coast to coast, but his layup was too hard and went back the other way for a Barbosa fastbreak layup. Then with 10 minutes left Curry fouled Irving on what appeared to be a clean strip. It was the first time all season Curry had received a fifth foul. Kerr stuck with Steph, just as he had when he picked up his fourth foul in the third quarter. Steph repaid that faith, making a right-wing three to cut the deficit to 84-76. It was his 28th three, a new Finals record.

Draymond Green appeared to foul Irving on a drive to the rim—what would've been his fifth foul—or at least knock the ball out of bounds, but the refs called it off Kyrie. With a chance to cut deeper into the deficit, Curry drove the lane but his finish rolled off the lip of the rim, and on the ensuing possession James put back an Irving three. Barbosa answered with a corner three to cut the lead to seven. Again with Barbosa on him after a switch, James sank the free throw line fallaway jumper.

"That fourth quarter was unbelievable. When he's playing in between like that midrange, and outside, and driving to the rim, and also creating opportunities for all of us, it makes the game a lot easier," said Irving. "Then we're getting out in transition, I mean, it's just unbelievable to be a part of."

On the next possession Curry took a three as Jefferson brushed beside him on his contest. (On many contests, defenders will continue upcourt hoping to create a fastbreak opportunity.) Steph's frustration flared as he barked at officials while play continued upcourt.

Green stripped Irving's drive and threw a long outlet to Barbosa, but didn't see J. R. Smith playing safety. Smith picked it off, and three passes later Irving found James with a drop-off pass and bucket for his 34th point. James had scored the Cavs' last 18 points, making it 90-79 with seven to go. (The Warriors scored only 22 during this stretch.)

"He told us one point in time late in the fourth, 'Get stops and I'll take care of the other end,'" said Jefferson.

Steph impetuously tried to double the entry pass to James in the high post by the right elbow. He threw right back to Curry's man, J. R. Smith, now unguarded, who sank his easiest three of the night. Barbosa answered with another three, his 13th point. James came back and posted Iggy on that elbow again, then took him into the lane and hit the nine-foot fallaway. Iguodala's back was bothering him so bad he just swiped at the ball and didn't bother to contest.

"When [James] is at the elbow, he's able to make one dribble and get to the basket. He's also a great passer from there," said Lue. "He's able to scan and read the floor, and it's harder to double-team from that position."

After a missed Klay three, James ran down the clock and drove the lane. As Green came over to contest, Tristan slid up the baseline, catching James' driving alley-oop loft for the slam. After a Curry layup, Tristan Thompson posted Barnes on the weakside block and James fed him another oop. Tristan had made all six of his shots. That made it 99-86 with fewer than five minutes left in the game.

"They do a great job of protecting the elbows and boxes and loading up. So the last two or three days we really have focused in on Tristan being in the right spots because he's very important to what we're trying to do," Lue said. "Tonight he really got to his spots and really was in the right position every time, and LeBron and those guys could find him when he was open."

Curry beat James down the lane but hesitated, pump-faking before James spiked his shot out of bounds. J. R. stripped Klay on a drive but drew the foul, his fifth. Thompson hit the first free throw but missed the second. James grabbed it and Curry foolishly tried to slap the ball out of his hands, catching arm and then jumping in James' path as he recaptured the ball. It wasn't the wisest behavior with five fouls, earning Curry his sixth.

Steph went ballistic, throwing his mouthpiece like an adolescent sent to bed without dinner. It wasn't a good look for the new face of the NBA and the unanimous MVP. The disgusting mouthpiece that's always dangling from his mouth hit the son of a Cavaliers minority owner. (Curry apologized.)

Then Steph let ref Jason Philips have it, earning a tech and getting thrown out of the game on top of the ejection. Cleveland fans serenaded Steph with Gary Glitter as he walked left: "Na-na-na-na…hey-hey-hey… good-bye." Meanwhile in the Twitter-verse, Curry's wife, Ayesha, suggested the NBA "is absolutely rigged for money…or ratings," complaining like vacationing Vegas gamblers when the slots don't surrender their riches.

Kerr asserted that Curry wasn't getting the star treatment he deserved. (James could've told Kerr and Curry to take a number.)

"He had every right to be upset. He's the MVP of the league. He gets six fouls called on him. Three of them were absolutely ridiculous," Kerr said. "He steals the ball from Kyrie clean at one point. LeBron flops on the last one. Jason Phillips falls for that, for a flop. This is the MVP of the league we're talking about."

Irving converted the technical free throw, and Smith hit a left-corner three despite Klay's good contest making it 103-87 with under four minutes to go, and that sealed the game. The lead grew to 22 in the next 90 seconds, and the reserves sealed the 115-101 victory, forcing Game 7.

It wasn't one thing that beat the Warriors, unless you want to count that early first quarter lead. The Cavs shot better (52 to 40 percent), beat them on the boards (45-35), had more assists (24-19) and two fewer turnovers (12), and won in the paint (42-30) and on fastbreak points (19-10). It wasn't any one thing; it was just an overall better game by the Cavaliers.

"It was too difficult to come back from 20 down," said Curry. "We made a good push in the second half, but that first quarter was a good punch from them."

The Warriors did much better offensively in the second half, shooting 53 percent including 56 percent (10-of-18) from three, but also missed eight free throws. Even so, they only outscored the Cavs by two, 58-56. Indeed, while Kyrie had but three second half points, Love, Tristan, and J. R. Smith (11 in the second half) combined for 21 to fill the gap, and LeBron carried the Cavs the rest of the way.

"We stuck with our game plan, being aggressive and physical defensively, and I thought being aggressive offensively and attacking. I thought in the second quarter we got away from it. We kind of slowed the ball down in the second quarter, which made us stagnant and made us get some shot clock violations," Lue said. "But for the most part I thought we did a great job, just continued to attack in transition in the halfcourt and make them guard us."

James finished with 41 points, 11 assists, and eight boards. Irving added 23 and Smith had 14 and three steals. James became the fifth player in Finals history to post consecutive 40-plus-point games, company that includes Michael Jordan, Rick Barry, Jerry West, and Shaquille O'Neal. However, the real unsung hero was Tristan Thompson who had 15 points and 16 boards and set innumerable screens to free players for better looks.

"He hasn't been having the series he wanted to. Tonight, the last two games actually, was huge," said Smith. "The way he's been playing, hustling down, getting loose balls, rebounds, knocking down his free throws when they try and foul him to slow the game down. He's been doing a hell of a job."

They'd done the seemingly impossible. It had been 50 years since anyone had forced a Game 7 after going down 3-1, let alone win one, not to mention on the road.

20

THE KING AND KY: A ROOM WITH A LUE

I F KYRIE IRVING doesn't get injured in Game 1 of the 2015 NBA Finals, do the Cavs win the title? And if they won, would David Blatt now be contemplating a championship legacy rather than returning to Europe, unable to find a 2016-17 NBA head coaching job? Certainly the 2016 Finals put 2015 in a different perspective.

Yet it's difficult for anyone who spent time around the team to discount Tyronn Lue's impact. His cool demeanor helped toughen the skin of a team prone to frustration-based loss of focus. They needed that poise in the face of Golden State's three-driven blitzkrieg runs. The needed the discipline to keep pushing the ball, even when they were tired, to be aggressive even when the tide turned against them.

For much of the season they were a terrific bunch of individual talents still learning how to collectively bring their best. "One of the things that I think is really difficult when you coach our team is that we tend to believe we're better than we really are sometimes," Griffin told Adrian Wojnarowski.

That was one of the virtues in firing Blatt. It made a strong impression on the players, which may have greased the team's attitude and demeanor change.

"Anytime there is a change like that there's a shock. It's a bit of a rude awakening," said Matthew Dellavedova. "A good man lost his job because we weren't performing up to expectations. Anytime that happens everyone is going to be on their toes, and I think everyone reevaluates what they're doing and how they should be doing it."

While much of Lue's people skills are undoubtedly wrapped up in his personality, something must be be said for his breadth of experience.

"Ty was an overachiever as a player. He was gritty. He took pride in his defense. He was all about winning," said Griffin in announcing Lue's ascension to head coach. "He was on great teams, was a first-round pick, struggled through injuries, was on some very bad teams and played for some incredible coaches. Most importantly, through all of this, he was the type of person that was humble enough to learn from those coaches."

That humility and inner confidence undoubtedly traveled south from his mother, who is a minister. In a similar manner, Lue's firsthand understanding and self-knowledge allowed him to connect his experiences to others. He knew how to find the right frequency.

"I just think the guys take a liking to me because I can relate to them. I've been in every situation you can possibly be in. I've been a starter. I've been off the bench. I've not played. I've been injured for a whole season. I've been in the Finals. I've been on the worst team in the NBA," Lue said. "So I can relate to these guys when guys are not playing or they're struggling with their shot, or when a guy gets injured. So, I mean, it's the same relationship I've had with all the guys in the locker room. Nothing's different."

LeBron suggested the same thing, and having the King's ear is never a bad thing.

"We connect—that's something that's bigger than basketball—our upbringing. Being from a single-parent household, being from an inner-city community, being a statistic that you weren't supposed to make it out and there's no way you're going to make it out," James said. "You're going to be another one of those African-American kids, and we both made it out from tough situations growing up, and people just saying there's no way you can do it. So before we even met each other, you have a sense of that type of feeling."

Being able to relate helped bring them together and help them to understand the sacrifices necessary to get on the same page. Accommodations had already been made, something Griffin alluded to when he dismissed Blatt.

"We've put an awful lot in the playbook to take care of an awful lot of people," Griffin said at the time. "Now I think it's about identifying which of those things we can believe in and go to with some kind of regularity."

In the end the players took accountability, and believed in Lue's gameplan enough to follow it even when times were tough. During the season, they continued to backslide into bad habits and lose the thread on the court, but during the 2016 Finals they became a disciplined team capable of following the plan, or willing to die trying. They weren't flawless in their execution, but their effort was unimpeachable during the last three games.

Griffin told Wojnarowski that by the Finals the Cavs "had a really cool calm confidence about ourselves." A lot of that comes from Lue by way of the Zen Master, Phil Jackson, Lue's coach his first three years in the league.

"The poise [came] from my first three seasons of being in L.A. with Phil Jackson and just saw how he was in practice: He's teaching, he's coaching, he's on the floor. But when the game started, he was always poised and he let the guys figure it out," Lue said. "That meant a lot to me just seeing that because as players, if you're sitting on the bench and you hear coaches talking about certain players on the floor or getting mad or getting upset. You realize they say the same thing about you when you go in the game.

"Guys are going to make mistakes," he continued. "It's part of the game. But the effort, that can always be there; the unselfishness, that can always be there. So I just attribute the calmness to Phil Jackson and just seeing as a player what works and what doesn't."

NBA Finals, Game 7. Sunday, June 19, 2016, Oakland. (Even)

Before Game 5 Lue quoted Mark Twain, telling the team, "The two most important days in your life are when you were born and when you discovered the reason you were born. I think we were born to be champions." Now their implausible odyssey had reached its pinnacle, and it was time to make that thought reality.

The Cavaliers drew first blood, with Irving driving baseline and under the basket, finding Double-T in the middle of the lane for the pump-fake and layup. On the defensive end, Golden State swung the ball around, culminating in a Draymond Green drive and high drop-off feed to Festus Ezeli, who was making his first postseason start with Iguodala moving to the bench. Tristan snuffed Ezeli's dunk attempt, and James scooped up the loose ball, taking it all the way to the rack for the transition layup over Barnes.

The Warriors came right back, showcasing good ball movement. Draymond Green screened for Klay Thompson off the ball, then rolled down the lane. Ezeli, posted on the left block, hit him with a bounce pass for the uncontested slam off miscommunication between Tristan and James. Barnes ended Golden State's next possession with a three, which brought a roar from the crowd, given his struggles the previous two games (2-of-22, missed last 14 shots). Barnes passed on an open straightaway three next time down, swinging it to his left where Green sank the uncontested triple.

A moment later Tristan Thompson blocked Ezeli's driving layup. Back the other way, the Warriors left Love unguarded on the baseline. Ezeli recovered and altered Love's driving shot. Kevin got it back, missed the follow, lost the rebound to Ezeli, and then just ripped the rock from Festus' hands like a selfish two-year-old and put it in for the Cavaliers' third bucket. While a small thing, it set a tone and spoke to Love's aggression and intensity all night.

After an Irving jumper tied it at 8, Kerr called timeout and brought in Iguodala, going to the smaller lineup. "We're just in a little bit of a rush," he told them. "[It's] Game 7, we're all pumped up and everything, that's okay. But get the ball moving. The first few possessions, we kept it moving, we got great stuff."

Kerr had spoken of the importance of finding not just open shots, but rhythm shots. He suggested his team's low shooting percentage on open shots was related to this.

"You can get open shots that aren't rhythm shots. Normally we have a lot of rhythm to our offense, the ball is moving, it's changing sides of the floor. I think the last couple games we haven't had as much rhythm. I don't think the ball has moved as much," Kerr said. "For whatever reason, karma, the basketball gods, whatever you want to call it, you run a great offensive set and the ball swings side to side and everybody touches it and, boom, it hits somebody's hands in rhythm, the ball tends to go in."

Out of the timeout Curry came off a couple baseline screens, took the pass, and stepped inside Kyrie's pursuit for a left-wing three with under three seconds on the shot clock.

J. R. Smith triggered the offense next time down, another of Lue's little wrinkles. It gave LeBron and Kyrie an opportunity to play off the ball and create opportunities for themselves as cutters and screeners. "It's different. It's not traditional," Smith affirmed. "[But] I don't mind doing it."

It worked with J. R.'s increasing tendency to attack the rim in response to

Golden State's overplay at the arc. Sure enough, when Draymond switched onto Smith after the inbounds, he isolated Green at the arc, and took him off the dribble, beating him to the left side of the rim for the finger roll. That cut the Warriors' lead to 11-10 with six minutes to go.

LeBron worked the ball deep in the left post, but—as some have lamented over the years—James did not own a trustworthy hook shot. When he turned to shoot, Iguodala and Green (who helped on James at the rim all series) went for the ball. Green pulled it away and passed upcourt, where Klay Thompson quickly isolated Kyrie on the left block. Jefferson, just in for Love, came with the double but Klay turned baseline for the short turnaround.

All series the Cavaliers had trouble scoring outside transition, doubling the Warriors' fastbreak points the last five games (86-43). Curry lost his behind-the-back dribble in the deep frontcourt, and Jefferson grabbed it to start a three-on-two break, which he finished over Green. Curry tried the little step-in three move on the left side and missed this time, while J. R. released upcourt. James rebounded it and threw a rope to Smith, who took one step and finished at the rim ahead of Green, for a 14-13 lead.

Klay Thompson got an unmolested three, when the Warriors ran that frontcourt slip screen action they had used so successfully in Game 4. This time Draymond was the playmaker, not Curry. This put LeBron in the action. He failed to follow Klay, who slipped the screen on Green while J. R. made the switch, leaving Klay wide open on the right wing for a 16-14 lead.

James quickly tied it, putting J. R. in the pick-and-roll to switch Curry onto him. Smith got the ball on the left wing as James rolled baseline. Curry tried to intercept the pass, but it went through his hands. James grabbed it, took one dribble, and dunked.

Golden State took the lead right back. Curry ran left to right across a couple baseline screens, with Kyrie tagging along behind like a kid brother. Steph received the ball on the right wing and ran a give-and-go with Varejao on the right block. Curry made for the right corner; Andy tossed it back to him and hopped over to screen Kyrie so he couldn't contest as Curry hit the Warriors' fifth bomb of the quarter.

The Cavaliers ran their own clever action with Irving screening for James on the left wing. Kyrie received the ball and a Love screen at the top of the arc, forcing Varejao to switch onto Kyrie. He drove right, stopped as Anderson went by, and hit a pull-up 16-foot bank shot. Draymond answered, taking Jefferson one-on-one, spinning right toward the elbow, then crossing over to his left for the finish as RJ flailed from behind. That gave the Warriors a 21-18 lead, and they finished the quarter with a 23-22 edge.

"We need to be a little more clean on our switches," Lue told ESPN's Doris Burke between quarters. "What we're doing defensively, I don't think we're executing on a high-enough level."

Both teams' defensive intensity climbed a notch in the second, as scoring grew harder to come by. Cleveland had but two buckets over almost five minutes—a slithering James finish with his left around Speights and Mo Williams' layup, the perverse reward for not getting back on defense after James stole Green's driving transition dish.

The Warriors had but three buckets in that stretch, a couple Livingston hoops and a Draymond Green three over Tristan Thompson, who'd been taking Green while LeBron dealt with Speights. It was Green's second three of the night, coming after a string of 12 consecutive missed threes going back to his white-hot Game 2.

With just over seven left, James drove the lane from the right wing. Love was on the right block causing Livingston to sag into the lane as Draymond rotated over to meet LeBron. James hit Shump just below the weakside break. Livingston scrambled back to his man and hit Shumpert on the arm as he let go, sinking the three and converting the and-one. It was the Cavs' first three after seven misses, and their only one of the quarter.

On the other end, Shumpert came off a Barnes screen too high and wound up beside Curry when Steph received the ball from Green. Not only did Curry get to the hole, but Iman compounded the error by fouling him for the and-one, giving the Warriors a 32-31 lead.

They battled toe to toe, like two heavyweights trading haymakers. James lost the ball in the lane, not even striking rim amidst heavy contact. Green emerged with the ball and outleted to Klay, who threw upcourt to Livingston. But Shaun lost the ball off his leg, near Love, who threw it to James fastbreaking the other way. He beat Green off the dribble and Curry's contest to give the Cavs back the lead.

Curry had a breakaway off the long rebound from an errant Irving triple, but James blocked his layup out of bounds. Green sank a straightaway three with six minutes remaining and drained another two minutes later, after

Irving had tied it at 35 with a floater in the lane. Irving drove again, pushing the made basket, and tossed in a drive-by layup while falling out of bounds, drawing the and-one foul on Klay Thompson.

That tied it at 38 and Kerr called a timeout. Each team emptied their bag of tricks this game, as the Warriors ran a horns set, gave Iggy the ball on the right elbow, and ran a revolving door of screens above the right wing that finally spit out Green like a slots jackpot for a wide-open straightaway three, his fourth of the night. James went at Iggy next possession, getting to the rack for the and-one, which he failed to convert.

The Warriors closed the half with a burst. Green spun baseline from the right post on J. R. Smith, getting the reverse layup and-one. Then James bounced a pass to Shumpert, expecting him to cut, only he didn't and Iguodala stole the ball. Iggy passed to Klay Thompson flashing into the lane, who got it to Barbosa for a right-corner three and a 47-40 lead with just over two minutes left. The Warriors took a 49-42 lead into the half.

Golden State shot 40 percent from the field but 10-of-21 (48 percent) from the arc. Consistent with that preoccupation, the Warriors were just 3-of-4 from the line. The Cavs were shooting 38 percent and were 1-of-14 from beyond the arc, but held a 27-22 edge on the boards and were 9-of-11 from the line.

Green led the Warriors with 22 points, six boards, and five assists, but Steph and Klay were just 5-of-17 and just 3-of-12 from three. James led the Cavs with 12 points, seven boards, and five assists, and Irving had nine, as Cleveland's Big Two accounted for only half of their 42 points.

"I just told the guys at halftime I didn't think we were giving it our all in the first half. We made a lot of mistakes. We didn't give the maximum effort for a Game 7," Lue said. "I just told them that in Game 6 in Toronto, that was maximum effort. I thought we really played as hard as we could possibly play. In that first half, I didn't think we did that."

The second half began much like the first—with Tristan Thompson defending an Ezeli shot attempt. Love grabbed the board and threw upcourt, where Smith sank a fallaway jumper over Ezeli. Then with LeBron on the left wing, J. R. cut for the corner and Ezeli took a couple steps in that direction, leaving Tristan uncovered on the left elbow. LeBron found Double-T for a six-foot, left-handed floater, cutting the Warriors' lead to 49-46.

Klay Thompson hit a three after coming around a stacked screen on the left wing. Next time down Thompson used an Ezeli transition screen to get downhill on Love on the switch. When he reached the right block he stopped and popped an eight-foot fallaway, pushing the lead back to 54-46, their largest lead of the night, with ten and a half remaining.

The Cavaliers, being regular tubthumpers, got up again. J. R. screened for James and flared to the left wing, catching the pass and sticking the three ahead of Draymond's recover contest. Then James posted on the right elbow and found Smith on the left wing for a second three, thanks to a crafty backscreen on Green by Kyrie.

On the other end Smith deflected Klay Thompson's pass and the ball went to Irving with Festus Ezeli on him in isolation. No help arrived before Kyrie drove the right baseline and finished at the bucket, tying it at 54, just 100 seconds after Golden State established their largest lead of the night.

"In the second half we came out, we really had a defensive mindset. J. R. came out and made eight straight points for us, which was big for us and that kind of got us going," said Lue.

But Smith tried to get too fancy, leaving an alley-oop feed for the trailing James on the fastbreak, and Curry knocked it away and created a layup for himself the other way. Curry followed by catching an Iguodala pass curling around a Green screen near the boundary, with Irving trailing, and knocked it down with his famed hair-trigger release.

The Cavaliers called a timeout while trailing by five with seven and a half minutes remaining. Coming out of that timeout they went on an 11-0 run, as Golden State missed its next four shots and Curry made two turnovers.

First James found a cutting Love near the front of the rim for an alley-oop lay-in with the shot clock running down. Irving poked the ball away from Varejao, who appeared destined for a layup on a very nice cut, which turned into a pair of James freebies after a foul in transition. Love picked off Curry's bounce pass to a rolling Varejao and fed Kyrie in transition, who beat Draymond's contest with a layup high off the backboard. That gave Cleveland a 60-59 lead, with just under six and a half to go in the third.

That began a 10-point Irving run, featuring a pair of free throws and Irving going end to end after stealing a bad Curry feed behind Varejao. He again beat Green, this time to the left side of the rim with a soft left-handed flip off the backboard, converting the and-one. Barnes got a layup on a nice play out of a Kerr timeout, but Kyrie answered with an open three (his first of the night), thanks to Tristan's screen and Draymond's failure to contest. That made it 68-61 with four minutes remaining.

"It was a mixture of some execution, some tough shots," Green said. "Those tough shots led to transition buckets for them, which is where they thrive."

The Cavs were up 71-66 when Livingston got loose on a nice cut into the lane. When Cleveland collapsed, he casually flipped it behind his back to Draymond for his sixth (and final) three, his 28th point of the game.

A lot of James dribbling resulted in a surprising decent nine-foot runner in the lane, but when he missed Golden State beat the Cavs upcourt for a Livingston fastbreak slam, tying the game at 71 as Oracle went loco. Two minutes after the Cavs took a seven-point lead, the Warriors had erased it. Touché.

James backed down Livingston, then hit the left baseline fallaway ahead of Draymond's help. On the other end Barnes hit his second three of the night after Green got into the lane and threw to Harrison in the left corner. With eight seconds left on the shot clock James passed to Tristan, who faced up Barnes in the right post, drove to the middle of the lane, and made a fallaway left-handed jump hook for the one-point lead. Iguodala took back the lead with a short hook in the lane after a nice penetration bounce pass from Livingston with four ticks on the shot clock.

"[We need to] trust each other. We got a little away from that in the third quarter," Kerr told Burke between quarters. "Keep moving the ball and good stuff happens. I think we got a little careless."

James received the ball at the left with six seconds on the shot clock and thought about three, but drove on Livingston and hit a six-foot jumper in the lane to give the Cavs a one-point lead. Love pushed it to three by posting Klay Thompson and taking him into the lane for the right-handed half-hook, making it 79-76.

Golden State started doubling Love in the post, picking off one of his passes and shutting off that option. So after another failed attempt with the clock running down, Kyrie took Draymond to the middle of the lane and tried a pull-up floater in front of the rim. It was short, but he grabbed the rebound and went back up off the backboard. Green responded by beating James to the hole from the left boundary on two dribbles, to cut the Cavs' lead to 81-80 with under nine minutes to go.

The fevered intensity was wearing on the players. Guys started front-rimming shots. Iguodala drew the foul on a fastbreak drive, but missed both free throws. Lue gave Irving a blow, going with Love, Jefferson, James, Smith, and Shumpert. LeBron drove down the left edge of the lane with four seconds on the clock, after getting Barnes in a switch, and finished over Green for an 83-80 lead.

"Both teams played exceptional defense in the fourth quarter. Shots were hard to come by. The few that we did have that were open we weren't able to knock down," Kerr said. "But this is kind of how it goes in Game 7. It's not going to be a 36-31 quarter. It's going to be hand-to-hand combat."

Curry answered by crossing over Thompson in the frontcourt and hitting the straightaway three from several feet beyond the line, tying the game at 83 with seven remaining. It was their only three-pointer of the quarter (1-of-10). Smith airballed a wide-open wing three, and Klay Thompson got a good look the other way, hitting the corner foot-on-the-line two over Shumpert, who went for the swipe instead of the contest. Kerr called a timeout with six to go and a two-point lead, inserting Ezeli.

"My thought there was that they were not making threes, and LeBron in particular had not made a three, and I really felt like we needed rim protection," Kerr said. "They had gone big. They had Love and they had, obviously, LeBron and they had Tristan. I felt like we needed to have rim protection. And Festus obviously gives us our best option there."

Jefferson completely took away Curry's left hand, forcing him right. Steph missed the layup, but Green put back his 11th rebound (and first offensive) for an 87-83 lead.

"We got good shots," Green said. "We got a little bit of a flow going, especially throughout the game. There at the end they just made more plays."

LeBron had Tristan set a screen to get Ezeli switched on him, then pump-faked Festus into the air to draw the foul on a three-pointer. On the other end Curry got too fancy tossing a behind-the-back pass intended for Klay Thompson by the right break. It went out of bounds for his fourth turnover (three in the second half).

Tristan screened twice for—because Green recovered the first time—but James finally got Ezeli isolated on the left wing again. This time LeBron knocked down the three—his only success in five attempts—and at the right time, giving the Cavs an 89-87 lead. Klay responded by pump-faking Smith at the boundary, going by him to the left, and finishing off the glass over Tristan, with four and a half to go.

Over the next three and a half minutes each team missed six shots. Curry missed an open left-wing three. Iggy blocked a James layup. Green missed an open three. Irving missed a Euro-step drive around Curry, with Iguodala grabbing the rebound. Iggy drove the center with J. R. backpedalling and Steph on his left. He fed Curry, who bounce passed it right back, Smith jumped, as Iggy used his body to shield the ball finishing at the right of the rim.

But James had shadowed the play and somehow made it from the left side of the court to the rim in six steps, leaping like a building-bounding Superman to block the ball a moment after it left Iggy's hand and a split second before it hit the backboard (which would have triggered a goaltending call). It was LeBron's third block of the game, and arguably the biggest block in NBA Finals history.

James dribbled into the lane for a short jump hook over Iggy that he left short. Curry grabbed the rebound and attempted to hit a step-back three over Irving (again, with no passing or ball movement) that only hit the backboard. The Cavaliers rebounded and Tyronn Lue called timeout with 70 seconds left, the score still tied at 89.

"I couldn't believe that," LeBron told *Sports Illustrated* writer Lee Jenkins. "I made a great move, spin, and left it short."

Coming out of the timeout, Lue sat Thompson in favor of the smaller lineup with Jefferson on the floor and Love at center. J. R. screened for Kyrie, putting Curry on him at the right wing. He crossed the ball between his legs twice before getting back to his right, taking one dribble while stepping to his right, and launching a three that rattled home, giving the Cavs a 92-89 lead with 53 second remaining.

"We tried to get Kyrie with the basketball with Steph Curry guarding him and let them go one-on-one," Lue said. "Like I said before, they're a good defensive team. They switch 1 through 5 on pin-downs, on pick-and-rolls, so it's hard to get two on the ball. Because when you're playing basketball, you always try to get two on the ball so someone's going to be open. But the way they play defense, that's not going to happen. So we just try to get the matchup that we wanted. I wasn't sure if it was going to be a three or not. But Kyrie, the player he is, he's not scared of the big moment, and he made a big shot for us."

The Warriors didn't take a timeout, advancing the ball and putting Love into a screen to switch him onto Curry at the top of the arc with 14 seconds on the shot clock. Curry went behind his back, getting Love on his left hip. He reached the right wing arc and hesitated, forsaking the drive, as Love recovered in front of him. Steph crossed back to his left through his legs, but Love stayed in front of him, knees bent, hands and arms up and out, in textbook defensive position.

Curry cleared the ball to Green and got it back with seven seconds on the clock. He faked the three and took a side dribble to his left. Love over-pursued as Curry went back to his right and took the shot with three seconds on the shot clock. It hit the right side of the rim and James rebounded.

"I was searching for a three and rushed and didn't take what was there, which was probably better to go around him and try to get into the paint," said Curry. "That's basically it."

LeBron passed to Irving, who drove and appeared to be fouled by Iguodala before losing the ball on the baseline. Kyrie grabbed it and, while almost falling out of bounds, lobbed it back to Love. He passed to James, who Golden State fouled. They had a foul to give, but it added four more seconds to the shot clock, now set to 14, while the game clock said 18.7.

Inbounding to Irving in the backcourt, Kyrie drove into the frontcourt against pressure from Klay Thompson, almost to the rim before throwing the ball back to James, who was cutting down the center of the lane behind him. LeBron elevated for the slam and was fouled by Green.

James came down hard on his right wrist and lay for a moment on the floor, pounding the hardwood in apparent pain with 10.6 seconds remaining. Cavaliers fans gulped and held their breath, before James finally rose and stepped to the line. He back-rimmed the first free throw but made the second to make it 93-89.

The Warriors inbounded and Thompson looked for a shot, but James was up tight. He passed to Draymond, who was fouled, as the Cavs had a foul to give. Golden State inbounded with six seconds left, down four. Curry missed a three as Shumpert was careful not to foul him. Speights rebounded it and headed to the corner for another (missed) three as the buzzer sounded, ending Northeast Ohio's half-century-old curse.

The Cavaliers had one more basket than the Warriors on one less shot (33-of-82 vs. 32-of-83), and had 11 more free throws (21-10) to go with large advantages in the paint (42-30), fastbreak points (19-10), and points off turnovers (16-10).

Golden State's deadly backcourt proved rather pedestrian in the biggest moment. Steph and Klay went 12-of-36 from the field and 6-of-24 from three, with just one free throw—a combined 31 points and four assists between them. However, Draymond was a monster, scoring 32 points and coming one assist short of a triple-double, though only 10 of his points came after halftime.

"We don't run a lot of plays for Draymond to get shots. He shoots when he's open," Kerr said. "They might have tightened up on him a little bit in the second half. But Draymond does everything. You look at the line: 15 boards, nine assists, 32 points. He did everything for us out there."

Kyrie had 26 points, 17 of them in the second half. Smith had 12 points, including eight crucial points early in the third when the Cavaliers were struggling. Tristan had nine points but just three rebounds, limited by all the time he spent on the perimeter chasing Golden State's guards.

Love turned in an underappreciated gem. He had nine points and 14 rebounds, including a game-high four offensive boards. Kevin also tallied two steals and three assists, and when it counted he defended Curry better than even Perry Mason could have. After being unfairly maligned, Kevin came up big, manifested in his team-best +19, almost doubling his next best teammate (Irving, +10).

"I knew that tonight I just had to have one great game. I was going to go out and be aggressive on both sides of the ball as far as rebounding the basketball," Love said. "I was just told to rise above it, especially by my teammates. We knew what all of us were capable of."

LeBron was as magnificent as the prior two games, even if the scoring total wasn't as gaudy. He finished with a triple double—27 points (9-of-24 shooting), 11 rebounds, and 11 assists—as well as three blocks and two steals. He was only the third player to ever get a triple-double in Game 7, joining Jerry West (1969) and James Worthy (1988).

"He's such a force physically, so powerful," Kerr said. "He brought more force to the last three games than he did the first four. But he's one of the great players of all time and obviously was the key to the turnaround."

"It's LeBron being LeBron," Lue said. "He's one of the greatest of all time. Our back was against the wall and he took it upon himself the last couple of games—himself and Kyrie [Irving]—to really put this team on their backs."

James was the unanimous Finals MVP, and became only the second player in pro basketball history to lead both teams in scoring (29.7), rebounds (11.3), assists (8.9), steals (2.6), and blocked shots (2.3) in one playoff series. (Julius Erving did it in the 1976 ABA Finals.) It was even more impressive than his performance the year before, both for the efficiency and the outcome. James did it by channeling a remorseless killing machine those last three games.

"I was calm," James said. "Like Jay-Z said, 'you've got to stay low and keep firing' [actually from The Notorious B.I.G.'s "Kick in the Door"], and that's exactly what I did."

21

WHO LOVES A PARADE ?

IN SOME SENSE all sports championship celebrations are similar. They're an expression of the courage, unity, and resilience it takes to survive a grueling season and finish atop the mountain. Rarely is that secured without buckets of blood, sweat, and tears. But perhaps the outpouring is somehow commensurate with the number of times a region choked back frustration with a rueful "wait until next year."

Northeast Ohio swallowed hard for 52 years, and through 146 hopeful but ultimately fruitless seasons in the NBA, NFL, MLB, and NHL. In that span, 56 different franchises in those four largest sports leagues won titles. But after enduring a queue the likes of which no major American city (or its DMV) had ever seen, Cleveland was finally a winner again.

When that dam burst, everyone got wet. Tyronn Lue remained on the bench, his head bowed, crying. The initial postgame rugby scrum surrounding LeBron—including Thompson, Love, and Mozgov—finally broke up, allowing James to bow to the ground, sobbing, letting the spigots loose of years of hope and weight.

Said Richard Jefferson: "I've never seen a man in my life tell an entire state, 'Get on my back and I got you. Get on my back and I'm going to carry you and I don't care if we fail, I'm going to wake up the next morning, start preparing for the next year. I don't care what people say, I don't care anything about it.' He didn't have to come back here. He could've stayed in Miami or gone other places. He said, 'You know what, I'm going to come back home because I promised them that I would be able to do something.' And he carried us the whole way."

In his article for The Players' Tribune, Jefferson had related a moment in the plane on their way back from Toronto. It was an emotional moment for Jefferson. For him, it had been a record-tying length of time between Finals, and indeed, Jefferson had been denied that winner's cup again and again, much like Cleveland.

"I lost the national championship game to Duke, then I lost two straight NBA Finals, then my third year we lost to Detroit after being up 3-2 and they won the championship," he related at the postgame presser. "Then I lost to Miami and they won the championship. Then to top it off I went to the Olympics and we were the worst team of all time. My whole career has been so, so close.

"I was staring off into space and shaking my head. I didn't notice he was watching me. Bron got up from his seat and sat down next to me," wrote Jefferson in the *Tribune*. "'Richard, I know.' I was still shaking my head. 'Richard, I know.' Head shaking. I didn't know what to say. I was a little emotional. 'Four more, come on,' he said."

It took a singular focus to overcome a region's heartbreak. A singular focus for James to take that weight upon his shoulders and not make it about the past, not make it about those ghosts, but make it about him and what he intended to do.

"Just knowing what our city has been through, Northeast Ohio has been through, as far as our sports and everything for the last 50-plus years," LeBron said. "You could look back to the Earnest Byner fumble, Elway going 99 yards, to Jose Mesa not being able to close out in the bottom of the ninth to the Cavs went to the Finals—I was on that team—in 2007, us getting swept, and then last year us losing 4-2. And so many more stories. Our fans, they ride or die, no matter what's been going on, no matter the Browns, the Indians, the Cavs, and so on, and all other sports teams. They continue to support us. And for us to be able to end this, end this drought, our fans deserve it. They deserve it. And it was for them."

Jefferson, who's played all over this great nation, from the Big Apple to Dallas, Golden State, Utah, and San Antonio, felt a special affinity for this place. He did the region a favor sharing those Snapchats and bringing everyone another step closer—really closer than any fans had ever been to an NBA team—to make the triumph that much more special. Apparently the feeling was mutual.

"To be in Cleveland, to be around them and see, even when we were down 3-1, it was eerie how optimistic they were. It really was. It was the messages and 'We believe in you guys, keep going; regardless of what's happened, we're just so proud of you.' You're just like, 'Where are those pissed-off fans from New Jersey that I grew up watching, those pissed-off New Yorker fans?" Jefferson laughed. "I will tell you, they have the best fans I've ever seen. I swear they were louder more when we were down 3-1 because they wanted things to be more difficult. They never lost faith, and I have to give them all the credit."

Tears streamed down the cheeks of J. R. Smith, the most misunderstood Cavalier. Long the villain, the troublemaker, or the knucklehead in the eyes of the press, it wasn't a mantle he wore easily. But he fought through it, and redeemed a poor 2015 Finals shooting performance with a terrific 2016 Finals on both ends of the court.

"Today is so special to me. It's on Father's Day. My dad put the ball in my crib," Smith said. "I mean, my parents, my family, that's the biggest inspiration in my life. I've been in a lot of dark spots in my life, and if it wasn't for them, I wouldn't be able to get out of it. But they are who they are. They fought with me. They yelled at me, they screamed at me, they loved me, they hugged me, they cried with me, and they always stuck by my side no matter right or wrong."

In some sense Smith was speaking for a lot of men there in talking about his father's influence, and even on some level the region's faith and support of the Cavs as well.

"My dad is easily one of my biggest inspirations to play this game. To hear people talk bad about me, it hurts me because I know it hurts him, and that's not who I am. And I know he raised better, and I know I want to do better. Just everything I do is for my parents and my family," he said. "I mean, I don't really—the cars are nice, the houses are nice, but none of this matters without them. If it wasn't for them, I wouldn't be here. I don't know where I would be, honestly. If it wasn't for them, if it wasn't for the structure and the backbone that I have, I wouldn't be able to mess up and keep coming back and being able to sit in front of you as a world champion."

Ty Lue, the boy from a town of 11,000 who made good, thought about how he could fit his town in Oracle Arena twice over. "So it's just an unbelievable feeling. And I'm just happy that small-town boy could do something positive and show the younger kids that there is hope. There is time to grow as a person and to do the right thing," he said.

James had done everything he promised, and to do so, he'd taken the Cavaliers where no team had gone before. He led them with three consecutive performances that were among the greatest the Finals had ever seen. Three times he went to that well and each time proved there was no one like him.

"I gave everything I had. I put my heart, my blood, my sweat, my tears into this game and against all odds, against all odds. I don't know why we want to take the hardest road," James told Doris Burke afterward, briefly breaking into a smile. "I don't know why the man above give me the hardest road, but it's nothing. The man above don't put you in situations you can't handle. And I just kept that positive attitude, and instead of saying, 'Why me?' I said this is what he wants me to do. And Cleveland! This is for you!"

To do so they had beaten a team fresh off the greatest regular season in the history of the game. They beat the NBA's first unanimous MVP, Stephen Curry, who had broken the NBA record (his own) for threes by well over a hundred with 402. Poor Curry discovered that next to James even a great player's efforts are easily overshadowed.

Lue revisited the defensive plan that had been so successful that first three games of the 2015 Finals, before the Cavaliers' depth proved too shallow to compete with the Warriors small ball lineup. This year they not only were able to trap the Warriors backcourt out of the game, but doubled their fastbreak points the last five games.

Indeed, Lue used several things Golden State had done well against them. Not only did the Cavs get into transition more frequently, but they largely prevented the Warriors from dong the same by minimizing their turnovers the last three games. Jefferson's agility and positional flexibility allowed Cavs lineups to switch on defense just like the Warriors, eliciting the same kind of offensive stagnation Golden State imposed on others.

Finally, by taking away Steph and Klay, Cleveland tested the Warriors' "Strength in Numbers," and demonstrated there's a reason great players are great players and role players are role players. Over the last three games, Warriors' players outside their primary trio (Steph, Klay, Draymond) shot

35-of-113 (31 percent), coming up just as small as the Cavaliers' role players the last three games of the 2015 Finals.

Curry was nearly as pedestrian as the role players. He shot 22-of-60 (37 percent) from the field and 15-of-42 (36 percent) from three, while nearly making twice as many turnovers as assists (12-7). Cleveland dared free agent-to-be Harrison Barnes to shoot, and he blew off half of Golden State's foot, taking the third-most attempts on the team and going 5-of-32 (16 percent).

If the series was bad news for the Warriors' legacy, it was great news for the networks. First, the Thunder-Warriors Western Conference Finals Game 7 was the most-watched cable sports broadcast of all time, and the best-rated show ever on TNT. Then the Cavaliers-Warriors Finals was the most-watched NBA Finals since Jordan beat the Utah Jazz in their 1998 rematch. Game 7 earned an 18.9 rating, the best ABC had ever drawn, beating the 18.2 for 2010's Lakers-Celtics finale.

In the Cleveland locker room, bubbly showered the room, forming sloshing lakes in the green garbage bags on the floor (to protect the carpeting), an armada of corks bobbing in them like buoys. There was enough cigar smoke to trigger a smog alert in the crammed room, which felt like janitors had push-broomed the celebration off the Oracle court and right into the Cavaliers' locker room, making it denser, hotter. Family and friends of the players passed the Larry O'Brien Trophy about the room, taking selfies with it—the ultimate tchotchkes. It was Time Square on New Year's Eve at midnight, only more jubilant.

The party didn't end there. The players flew to Vegas, where the celebration continued in the VIP area of the XS nightclub. They ate a trophy-shaped cake catered by waitresses in LeBron James jerseys, while the players continued to make it rain champagne. Finally arriving home around noon on Monday, the team was greeted by hundreds of fans at the airport, where James came off the airplane trolling Golden State in a throwback wrestling jersey for The Ultimate Warrior.

While it had been 52 years since the Browns won the NFL championship, they hadn't even had a parade that year. They'd grown used to championships, winning seven from 1955 to 1964. The despair grew such that Cleveland had a parade for the Indians after they lost to the Braves in the World Series (Atlanta's only baseball title) in 1995, a second-place parade.

While the Cavaliers were making their playoff run, sympathetic vibrations reverberated through the area. First on May 14, Croatian-born, Euclid, Ohio-based UFC fighter Stipe Miočić won the heavyweight title over Alistair Overeem. Then on June 11, Cleveland's minor league hockey team, the Lake Erie Monsters, won their league championship, the Calder Cup. Meanwhile, the Indians were enjoying their best season since their '90s glory days. From June 16—the day after Game 6 of the Finals—through July 1, the Tribe won 14 games in a row.

From Red Right 88 thru The Drive, The Fumble, The Shot, The Move, and The Decision, the Cavaliers had given names to their torments, in the tradition of "Little Boy" and "Fat Man." Then a brilliant ballplayer from Akron came along to play the Max von Sydow role in Cleveland's production of *The Exorcist*, and the curse was lifted.

On Wednesday, June 22, more than a million people came to Cleveland to toast their hometown heroes. Fans spilled off the sidewalks and overflowed into the streets. The police, many on horseback, had to push the crowd back to make room for the parade cars. Even highway traffic was backed up bad enough to delay some outgoing flights because crews couldn't make it to their planes.

There were plenty of other VIPs in attendance beyond the Cavaliers, including Miočić, the Lake Erie Monsters, Ohio State football coach Urban Meyer, Browns Hall of Fame fullback Jim Brown, former Browns quarterback Bernie Kosar, and former Browns running back Earnest Byner, best known for The Fumble, and now fully absolved. J. R. Smith was naturally topless, as he had been—seemingly—since the end of the game. In his phone call to Coach Lue, President Barack Obama told Lue to get a shirt on Smith. James posed on a Rolls, arms outstretched, echoing his pose in the 10-story banner hanging from the Sherwin-Williams building across from the Q.

When Cavaliers General Manager David Griffin spoke, he noted the ill-fated history and proposed that "The Shot, The Drive, The Fumble all must now be replaced by The Block, The Three, and The D," noting the contributions of each of the Big Three. He also thanked fortune for sending an opponent as good as the Warriors.

"I think it took a team that good to force us to the brink, to force us to ignore the noise and lean on one another, to sacrifice for one another and to find what Steve Kerr, whom I once worked with, called 'appropriate fear,'" said Griffin, who knew about appropriate fear after having beaten the odds and testicular cancer. Twice.

When he made the stage, James singled out each player, much as he had at a dinner at his house before the first round began, which Jefferson mentioned in his article.

"In the middle of the meal, he stood up and addressed each guy in the room. He pointed out something that each player brought to the team, and explained how it was going to be vital if we wanted to win a championship," Jefferson wrote. "I think it just struck us all in that moment how special a position we were in. Bron was saying to us, 'We can only do this if we do it together. That's all that matters.'"

This time it wasn't motivation. It was approbation. They'd done it.

LeBron noted that Smith "was a throw-in," Mozgov was a "big motherfucker," swore if Delly met a bear, "he would tear that damn bear up," and that Shumpert loved his flattop fade too much to go head first, "but he would go face first!" He called Dahntay Jones "the luckiest man in the world. We picked his ass up like two months ago." And he again asserted Kyrie's greatness: "He thought I was blowing smoke up his ass when I said he can be the best point guard in the league."

James probably felt like a lot of fans in barely believing it had happened, that it might just be a dream he might wake from.

"It still hasn't hit me. For some crazy-ass reason I believe I'm going to wake up and it's Game 4," James laughed. "I'm like, 'Shit, we're down 2-1 still.'"

Now it's something Ohioans can laugh about. "Woe are we" had in an instant changed to "Remember when…?" It was more than a half century in the making, long enough for Northeast Ohio to grow sick of lemonade. Now it's a badge of Believeland honor.

"Every day is not a bed of roses," James said after Game 7. "You have to be able to figure out how to get away from the thorns and the prickers of the rose and things of that nature to make the sunshine."

Or put another way, "Nothing is given, everything is earned," all of which makes it that much sweeter in the end.

ACKNOWLEDGMENTS

FIRST BOOKS ARE precious as a first child. As such it would be impossible to name everyone that helped along the way. However a few stand out.

My wife Michele and parents were incredibly supportive. My best friend Pete Kotz was a constant inspiration as were the very ardent fans of realcavsfans.com, whose support included editing and proofreading. David Henry Sterry and Arielle Eckstut helped with the book proposal during LeBron James' first year back. David Aretha was one of several editors that worked on it, and his feel, encouragement and our shared *Michigan Daily* history, led me back when the book became a reality.

The *Cleveland Scene* was a great partner, and I can't say enough for editor Vince Grzegorek and managing editor Eric Sandy. Cavaliers PR was huge, particularly Senior VP of Communications Tad Carper, who extended me several courtesies, not the least of which was ensuring I had credentials for the 2015 Finals after originally being passed over.

Among my media colleagues, Chris Haynes, Terry Pluto, Aaron Coleman, Matthew Medley merit mention for their class, intelligence and friendliness. *USA Today's* Jeff Zilgitt and Cleveland 19's Tony Zarrella are great guys and fun hangs. Photographers Emanuel Christian Wallace and Bryon Miller were a tremendous help. Ditto art designer Ron Kretsch and editor John Schacht.

Big ups also to Michael James Pultz, how had me on the Defend Cleveland radio show on WRUW-91.1 every Monday for two years, WAKR's Brad Russell of the Average Sports Show, and Tim Smith and St. Edward/U.S. Junior National coach Eric Flannery, who had me on their Worthy of the Jersey podcast on several occasions, including the day I predicted the Cavs' seven-game Finals victory.

ABOUT THE AUTHOR

CHRIS PARKER HAS written about music, arts, culture, science, policy and corruption for two decades, interviewing artists ranging from the Black Keys to the Black Eyed Peas to Jack Black for publications such as *Billboard*, *Hollywood Reporter*, NPR and AVClub. He's spoken to Mavis Staples, Ray Davies, Elvis Costello, Lindsay Buckingham, and Doc Watson, among others, and one crazy evening spent time with David Bowie, Liv Tyler, and Kate Moss.

He's penned longform articles on the hacker collective Anonymous, online poker's Black Friday shutdown, larcenous for-profit colleges, tax-evading corporations, Medicare fraud, our healthcare system, the real estate bubble, the fracking oil crash, the microbiome and other subjects for numerous weeklies including the *Village Voice*, *LA Weekly*, *City Pages*, *SF Weekly*, *Dallas Observer*, *San Antonio Current*, *Miami New Times*, *Phoenix New Times*, and *Orlando Weekly*.

When LeBron James returned to Cleveland he decided to jump into sports journalism as beat reporter for *Cleveland Scene*. He subsequently also covered basketball for *The Guardian* and *The Jerusalem Post*. He never lost faith in the Cavaliers' ability to win the championship and publicly predicted Cleveland in seven before the finals began.

He lives in Ohio with his eclectic interests and wife Michele. He's found on Twitter @CRS_1ne. You may read many of his articles at chrisparker. contently.com or at muckrack.com/chris-parker.